1992

THE

100

BEST

MUTUAL

FUNDS

You Can Buy

Includes Money Market Funds

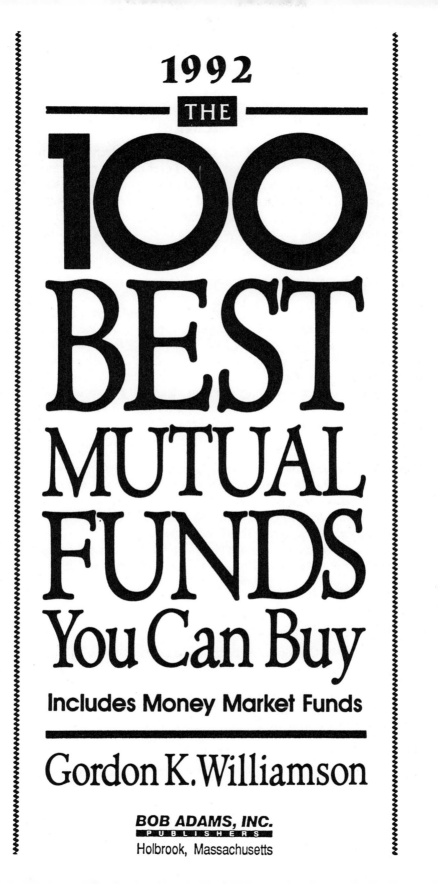

1992

THE

100 BEST MUTUAL FUNDS

You Can Buy

Includes Money Market Funds

Gordon K. Williamson

BOB ADAMS, INC.
PUBLISHERS
Holbrook, Massachusetts

Dedication

This book is dedicated to my family for all they have given me. To my father, Murray D. Williamson, the smartest person I ever met. To my mother, Ann G. Williamson, for the patience, affection, and understanding she passed on to me. To my sister, Viki Greene, for the love and generosity she shows toward everyone. And finally to my brother, Joel S. Williamson, an educator who has been a tremendous success in the hardest profession of all: father of three children and husband to a wonderful woman.

Special thanks go to Nathan Baty, the research assistant for this book. Nathan always went the extra mile, never leaving a stone unturned.

While due care has been taken to ensure accurate and current data, the ideas, principles, conclusions, and general suggestions contained in this volume are subject to the laws and regulations of local, state, and federal authorities, as well as to court cases and any revisions of court cases. Due to the magnitude of the database and the complexity of the subject matter, occasional errors are possible; the publisher assumes no liability direct or incidental for any actions or investments made by readers of this book, and strongly suggests that readers seek consultation with legal, financial, or accounting professionals before making any investment.

This publication is designed to provide accurate and authoritative information with regard to the subject matter covered. It is sold with the understanding that the publisher is not engaged in rendering legal, accounting, or other professional advice. If legal advice or other expert assistance is required, the services of a competent professional person should be sought.

—From a Declaration of Principles *jointly adopted by a Committee of the American Bar Association and a Committee of Publishers and Associations.*

Published by Bob Adams, Inc.
260 Center Street
Holbrook, Massachusetts 02343

Cover design: Joyce C. Weston

Manufactured in the United States of America.

ISBN: 1-55850-045-6

A B C D E F G H I J

Contents

I.
About This Book

Mutual funds are the best investment vehicle of the twentieth century. When properly chosen, these vehicles combine professional management, ease of purchase and redemption, simple record keeping, risk reduction, and superb performance, all in one. There are dozens of other kinds of investments, but none match the overall versatility of mutual funds.

A mutual fund is simply one kind of investment. When you invest in a fund, your money is pooled with thousands of other investors' monies. This large pool of money is overseen by the fund's management. These managers invest this pool of money in one or more kinds of investments. The universe of investments includes common stocks, preferred stocks, corporate bonds, tax-free municipal bonds, U.S. government obligations, zero coupon bonds, convertible securities, gold, silver, and even real estate. The amount of money invested in one or more of these categories depends on the fund's objectives and restrictions and on management's perception of the economy.

The beauty of mutual funds is that once the investor decides on the *type* of investment desired, there are several funds that fulfill that criteria. The track record of these funds can easily be obtained, unlike those of stockbrokers, who are not ranked at all. A few mutual fund sources even look at a fund's *risk-adjusted* return, a standard of measurement that has not been emphasized enough in the past.

This book was written to fill a void. There are already several mutual fund books and directories, but none deal exclusively with the very best funds. There are over 3,000 mutual funds. In fact, there are now more mutual funds than there are stocks listed on the New York Stock Exchange!

Existing sources give almost endless numbers and performance statistics for hundreds and hundreds of mutual funds, leaving readers to draw their own conclusions as to what are the best funds. This book will save you a great deal of time, because it has taken the 3,000 existing funds and narrowed them down to the best 100, ranked by specific category.

Investors and financial advisors are not concerned with mediocre or poor performers; they simply want the best fund, given certain parameters. Personal investment considerations should include your time horizon, existing portfolio, tax bracket, financial goals, and risk tolerance. Parameters within a given fund category include performance, risk, and consistency.

Current books and periodicals that cover funds focus on how a fund has performed in the past. Since there is little correlation between the past and the future when it comes to market returns, this book concentrates on consistency in management and the amount of risk being taken.

The model used to rank the 100 best is fully described in a later chapter. It is a logical approach that cuts through the statistical jargon; it is also easy to understand. As my dad used to say, "There is nothing as uncommon as common sense."

II.
What Is a Mutual Fund?

A mutual fund is an investment company: an entity that makes investments on behalf of individuals and institutions sharing common financial goals. The fund pools the money of many people, each with a different amount to invest.

Professional money managers then use the pool of money to buy a variety of stocks, bonds, or money market instruments that, in their judgment, will help the fund's shareholders achieve their financial objectives.

Each fund has an investment objective, described in the fund's prospectus, which is important to both the manager and the potential investor. The fund manager uses it as a guide when choosing investments for the fund's portfolio. Prospective investors use it to determine which funds are suitable for their own needs. Mutual funds' investment objectives cover a wide range; some follow aggressive investment policies, involving a greater risk in search of higher returns; others seek current income from more conservative vehicles.

When the fund earns money, it distributes the earnings to its shareholders. Earnings come from stock dividends, interest paid by bonds or money market instruments, and gains from the sale of securities in the fund's portfolio. Dividends and capital gains are paid out in proportion to the number of fund shares owned. Thus, shareholders who invest a few hundred dollars get the same return per dollar as those who invest hundreds of thousands.

III.
How to Invest in a Mutual Fund

Investing in a mutual fund means buying shares of the fund. An investor becomes an owner of shares in the fund just as he or she might own shares of stock in a large corporation. The difference is that a fund's only business is investing in securities, and the price of its shares is directly related to the value of the securities held by the fund.

Mutual funds continually issue new shares for purchase by the public. A fund's share price can change from day to day, depending on the daily value of the securities held by the fund. The share price is called the net asset value (NAV) and is calculated as follows: the total value of the fund's investments at the end of the day, after expenses, is divided by the number of shares outstanding. The resulting number is the value of one share of the fund.

Newspapers report mutual fund activity every day. An example is shown below.

Everett Funds:			
Evrt r	12.38	NL	-.01
MaxRtn	18.39	NL	+.06
ValTr	12.33	NL	-.01
LtdSl	17.71	NL	-.14
ExtrMid	2.82	2.95	-.02
ExJY p	7.24	7.60	+.01
FBK Gth t	11.06	11.06	....
FJA Funds:			
Capit f	14.67	15.69	-.02
NwHrz	9.65	10.10	....
Permt	12.91	13.81	....
Perrin	20.96	22.42	-.02

The first column in the table presented is the fund's abbreviated name. Several funds under a single heading indicate a "family of funds."

The second column is the Net Asset Value (NAV) per share as of the close of the business day. In some newspapers, the NAV is identified as the sell or the bid price — the amount per share you would receive if you sold your shares. Each mutual fund determines its net asset value every business day by dividing the market value of its total assets, less liabilities, by the number of shares outstanding. On any given day you can determine the value of your holdings by multiplying the NAV by the number of shares you own.

The third column is the offering price or, in some papers, the "buy" or the "asked" price — the price you would pay if you purchased shares. The buy price is the NAV plus any sales charge. If there is no sales charge, an NL for "no-load" appears in this column and the buy price is the same as the NAV.

The fourth column shows the change, if any, in the net asset value from the preceding quotation — in other words, the change over the most recent one-day trading period.

A "p" following the abbreviated name of the fund denotes a fund that charges a fee for marketing and distribution costs, also known as a 12b-1 plan (named after the federal government rule that permits them).

If the fund name is followed by an "r", the fund has a contingent deferred sales load (CDSL) or a redemption fee. A CDSL is a charge if shares are sold within a certain period; a redemption charge is a fee applied whenever shares are sold.

A footnote "f" indicates a fund that habitually enters the previous day's prices, instead of the current day's.

A "t" designates a fund that has a CDSL or redemption fee *and* a 12b-1 plan.

IV.
How a Mutual Fund Operates

A mutual fund is owned by all of its shareholders, the people who currently own shares of the fund. The day-to-day operation of a fund is usually delegated to a management company.

The management company, often the organization that created the fund, may offer other mutual funds, financial products, and services. The management company usually serves as the fund's investment advisor.

The investment advisor manages the fund's portfolio of securities. The advisor is paid for its services in the form of a fee based on the total value of the fund's assets; fees average one-half of one percent. The advisor employs professional portfolio managers who invest the fund's money by purchasing a number of stocks or bonds or money market instruments, depending on what kind of fund it is.

These fund professionals decide where to invest the fund's assets. The money managers make their investment decisions based on extensive, ongoing research into the financial performance of individual companies, taking into account general economic and market trends. In addition, they are backed up by economic and statistical resources.

On the basis of their research, money managers decide what and when to buy, sell, or hold for the fund's portfolio, in light of the fund's specific investment objective.

In addition to the investment advisor, the fund may also contract with an underwriter who arranges for the distribution of the fund's shares to the investing public. The underwriter may act as a wholesaler, selling fund shares to security dealers, or it may retail directly to the public.

V.
Different Categories of Mutual Funds

Aggressive Growth. The investment objective of aggressive growth funds is maximum capital gains. Such funds invest in common stocks and tend to stay fully invested over the market cycle. Sometimes, these funds will use leverage, and some may engage in trading stock options or index futures.

Aggressive growth funds typically provide low income distributions. This is because they tend to be fully invested in common stocks that pay low or no cash dividends.

Many aggressive growth funds concentrate their assets in just a few industries or segments of the market; their degree of diversification may not be as great as other types of funds. These investment strategies result in increased risk. Thus, they tend to perform better than the overall market during bull markets but fare worse during bear markets.

In general, long-term investors who need not be concerned with monthly or yearly variation in investment return will find this investment rewarding. Because of the extreme volatility of return, however, risk-averse investors with short-term investment horizons may wish to allocate a greater portion of their total assets to a relatively risk-free investment, such as a money market fund. During prolonged market declines, aggressive growth funds can sustain severe declines in net asset value.

Balanced. The balanced fund category has become less distinct in recent years, and a significant overlap in fund objectives exists between growth and income funds and balanced funds. In general, the portfolios of balanced funds consist of investments in common stocks, bonds, and convertibles. The proportion of stocks and bonds that will be held is usually stated in the investment objective, but it may vary over time. Balanced funds are generally less volatile than aggressive growth, growth, and income funds.

As with growth and income funds, balanced funds provide a high dividend yield. Similarly, high tax bracket investors who want to invest in these funds should consider using tax-sheltered money.

Corporate Bonds. These funds invest in debt instruments issued by corporations. Bond funds have a wide range of average maturities. The name of the fund will often indicate whether it is made up of short-term or medium-term obligations. If the name of the fund does not include the words "short-term" or "intermediate," then the fund most likely invests in bonds that have average maturities over fifteen years. The greater the maturity, the more the fund's share value can change; there is an inverse relationship between interest rates and the value of a bond. When one moves up, the other goes down.

Government Bonds. Government bond funds include mortgage-backed securities, such as GNMAs and FNMAs, as well as U.S. Treasury obligations. Such funds are attractive to bond investors because they provide diversification and liquidity, which are not as readily available in direct bond investments.

Bond funds have portfolios with a wide range of maturities. Many funds use their names to characterize their maturity structure. Generally, "short-term" means that the portfolio has a weighted average maturity of less than five years. "Intermediate" implies an average maturity of five to fifteen years, and "long term" is over fifteen years. The longer the maturity, the greater the change in fund value when interest rates change. Longer-term bond funds are riskier than short-term funds but tend to offer higher current yields.

Since bond funds provide diversification, investors should invest in large funds. Large bond funds hold many more bond issues than do smaller funds and, as a result of economies of scale, tend to operate more efficiently.

Growth. The investment objective of growth funds is to obtain long-term growth of invested capital. They generally do not engage in speculative tactics, such as using financial leverage.

Growth funds are typically more stable than aggressive growth funds. Generally they invest in growth-oriented firms that are older and larger and that pay cash dividends. You are likely to find companies such as IBM, Pepsico, and McDonald's in the portfolios of growth funds. The degree of concentration of assets is not as severe as with aggressive growth funds. Additionally, these funds tend to move from fully invested to partially invested positions over the market cycle. They build up cash positions during uncertain market environments.

In general, growth fund performance tends to mirror the market. Some growth funds were able to perform relatively well during recent bear markets because their managers were able to change portfolio composition by a much greater degree or by maintaining much higher cash positions than aggressive growth fund managers. However, higher cash positions can cause the funds to underperform aggressive growth funds during bull markets.

Growth funds can sustain severe declines during prolonged bear markets. Since some portfolio managers of growth funds attempt to time the market over the longer market cycle, using these funds to move in and out of the market may be counterproductive.

Growth and Income. Such funds generally invest in the common stocks and convertible securities of seasoned, well-established, dividend-paying companies. The funds attempt to provide shareholders with income along with long-term growth. They generally attempt to avoid excessive fluctuations in returns. One tends to find a high concentration of public utility common stocks and sometimes corporate convertible bonds in the portfolios of growth and income funds. The funds also provide higher income distributions, less variability in return, and greater diversification than growth and aggressive growth funds. Names such as equity-income, income, and total return have been attached to funds that have charac-· teristics of growth and income funds.

Because of the high current income offered by these kinds of funds, potential investors should keep the tax consequences in mind. Remember that, although capital gains are now taxed at the same rate as income, it is always an effective tax strategy to defer paying taxes whenever possible. The distributions from these funds are fully taxable in the year paid. High-tax-bracket individuals should consider investing in these kinds of funds by using IRAs, 401(k)s, and other retirement plans.

High-Yield. These funds generally invest in lower-rated debt instruments. Bonds are either characterized as "bank quality" (also known as "investment grade") or "junk". Investment grade bonds are those bonds that are rated AAA, AA, A, or BAA. Junk bonds are those instruments rated less than BAA (ratings such as BB, B, CCC, CC, C and D). High-yield bonds, also referred to as "junk," offer investors higher yields because of the additional risk of default. High-yield bonds are subject to less *interest rate* risk than regular corporate or government bonds. However, when the economy slows or people panic, these bonds can quickly drop in value.

International Bonds. International bond funds invest in foreign fixed-income securities. These fixed-income obligations are denominated in various currencies, including U.S. dollars. Of course, fixed-income markets do involve some risk, which can be reduced through global diversification.

As countries move in different economic cycles, so do the capital gain prospects of the bonds issued in those countries. At any one time, a certain country may offer the best bond price increases; then, as global economic cycles turn, a different country may hold out the best opportunities. International bond portfolios allow for this diversification for the individual investor.

International Equities. International, also known as foreign, funds invest in securities of firms outside the United States. Some funds specialize in regions, such as the Pacific Basin or Europe, and others invest worldwide. In addition, some funds, termed "global," invest in both foreign and American stocks.

International funds provide investors with added diversification. The most important factor, when diversifying a portfolio, is selecting assets that do not behave the same under similar economic scenarios. Within the United States, investors can diversify by selecting securities of firms in different industries. In the international realm, investors take the diversification process one step further by holding securities of firms in different countries. The more independently these foreign markets move in relation to the American market, the greater will be the diversification potential for the American investor – and ultimately, the lower the risk.

In addition, international funds overcome some of the difficulties investors would face in making foreign investments directly. For instancce, individuals would have to thoroughly understand the foreign brokerage process and foreign taxes, be familiar with the various marketplaces and their economies, be aware of currency fluctuation trends, and have access to reliable financial information. This can be a monumental task for the individual investor.

Metals. Precious metals funds specialize in investments in foreign and domestic companies that mine gold and other precious metals. Some funds also hold gold directly through investments in gold coins or bullion. Gold options are another method used to invest in the industry.

Gold and precious metals mutual funds offer advantages similar to bond funds; they allow investors interested in this area to invest in a more liquid and diversified vehicle than would be available through a direct purchase.

The appeal of gold and precious metals is that they have performed well during extreme inflationary periods. Over the short term, the price of gold moves in response to a variety of political, economic, and psychological forces. As world tension and anxiety rise, so does the price of gold. In periods of peace and stability, the price of gold declines. Because gold tends to perform in an *inverse* relationship to stocks, bonds, and cash, it can be used as a stabilizing component in one's portfolio. Silver and platinum react in a fashion similar to gold. Precious metals funds, like the metals themselves, are very volatile, often shooting from the bottom to the top and back to the bottom in fund rankings over the years. Investors should understand, however, that because most gold funds invest in the stock of gold mining companies, they are still subject to some stock market risk.

Money Market. These funds invest in short-term money market instruments. By maintaining a short average maturity, usually less than sixty days, and investing in high-quality instruments, money market funds are able to maintain a stable price of $1 pershare. As money market funds offer yields higher than insured bank money market deposit accounts, they are a very attractive haven for savings or temporary investment dollars. Like bond funds, money market funds come in both taxable and tax-free versions. Reflecting their tax-free status, municipal money market funds pay lower *before-tax* yields than taxable money market funds.

Municipal Bonds. Also known as tax-free, these funds feature tax-free debt instruments issued by states, countries, districts, or political subdivisions. Interest from municipal bonds is normally exempt from federal income tax. In almost all states, interest is also exempt from state and local income taxes if the portfolio is made up of issues from the investor's state of residence, a United States territory (Puerto Rico, the Virgin Islands, etc.), or the District of Columbia.

Until the early 1980s, municipal bonds were almost as sensitive to interest rate changes as corporate and government bonds. During the last few years, however, tax-free bonds have taken on a new personality. Now, when interest rates change, municipal bonds exhibit only one-half to one-third the price change that occurs with similar funds comprised of corporate or government issues. This decreased volatility is due to a smaller supply of municipal bonds and the elimination of almost all tax shelters, which have increased the popularity of tax-free bonds.

VI.
Which Fund Is Best for You?

When asked what they are looking for, investors typically say, "I want the best." This could mean that they are looking for the safest or highest total return. Unfortunately, there is no single "best" fund. The top performing fund may have incredible volatility, causing shareholders to redeem their shares at the first sign of trouble. The "safest" fund may be devastated by risks not previously thought of: inflation and taxes.

As you read through the book, you will see that there are several different categories of mutual funds, ranging from tax-free money market accounts to precious metals. At one period or another, each of these categories has dominated a periodical's *ten best funds* list. These impressive scores may only last a quarter, six months, or a year. The fact is that no one knows what will be the *next* best performing category.

For some fund groups, such as international stocks, growth, growth and income, and aggressive growth, their reign at the top may last for several years. For other categories, such as money market, government bond, and precious metals, the glory may only last a year or less. Trying to guess, chart, or follow a guru in order to determine the next trend is foolish: the notion that anyone has special insights into the marketplace is sheer nonsense. Countless *neutral* and lengthy studies attest to this fact. If this is the case, what should we do?

Step 1:
Categories That Have Historically Done Well

First, look at those *generic* categories of investments that have historically done well over long periods of time. A time frame of 20 years or more is recommended. True, your investment horizon may be a fraction of this, but keep in mind two points: 20 years includes good as well as bad times, and bad results cannot be hidden when studying the long term. Even the investor looking at a one- or two-year holding period should ask, "Do I want something that does phenomenally once in every five years or do I want something that has a very good return in eight or nine out of every ten years?" Unless you are a gambler, the answer is obvious.

All investments can be categorized as either debt or equity instruments. *Debt* instruments in this book include corporate bonds, governments bonds, high yield bonds, international bonds, money market accounts, and municipal bonds. *Equity* instruments include aggressive growth, growth, growth and income, international equities, and metals funds. Three other categories are hybrid instruments: income, balanced, and convertible funds. In this book, these three categories are combined under the heading of "balanced."

Throughout history, *equity has outperformed debt.* The longer the time frame reviewed, the better equity vehicles look. The very *best* fifteen years in a row for bonds is still not as good as the very *worst* fifteen years in a row for stocks. In fact, stocks have outperformed bonds in every decade. Put another way, would you have rather lent Henry Ford or Stephen Jobs the money to start their companies, or would you rather have given them money in return for a piece of the action?

Step 2:
Review Your Objectives

Decide what you are trying to do with your portfolio. Everyone wants one of the following: growth, current income, or a combination of growth and income. The fact that you are looking for current income does not mean that your money should go into a bond or money market fund. There is a way for you to set up an equity fund so that it will give you a high monthly income. This is known as a "systematic withdrawal program" and is discussed in appendix D. Conversely, the growth-oriented investor should consider certain types of debt instruments or hybrid securities.

Goals and objective are certainly important, but so is the element of time. The shorter the time frame and the greater the need for assurances, the more likely it is that debt instruments should be used. A growth investor who is looking at a time frame of one year and who wants a degree of safety is probably better off in a series of bond and/or money market market accounts. On the other hand, the longer the commitment, the better equities look.

A retired couple in their sixties should realize that one or both of them could live at least fifteen more years. Since this is the case, and since we know that equities have outperformed bonds over the past fifty years, our emphasis should be in stocks when looking at a horizon of ten or more years.

The conservative investor may say that stocks are too risky. True, the day-to-day or year-to-year volatility of equities can be quite disturbing. However, it is also true that the medium and long-term effects of inflation and the resulting diminished purchasing power is even more devastating. At least with an equity there is a better than fifty-fifty chance that it will go up. In the case of inflation, what do you think are the chances that the cost of goods and services will go *down* during the next one, three, five, or ten years? The answer is "not likely."

Remember, over the past fifty years, stocks have gone up 76 percent of the time on an annual basis. Looking at a three- or five-year time frame, stocks have shown a postive return 96 percent of the time. The figure goes up to 100 percent when any ten-year period is used.

Step 3:
Ascertain Your Risk Level

No investment is worthwhile if you stay awake at night worrying about it. If you do not already know or are uncertain about your risk level, contact your financial advisor. These professionals usually have some kind of questionnaire that, once completed, will give you a good indication of which investments are proper for you and which should be avoided. If you do not deal with a financial advisor, try the test below. Your score, and what it means, is shown at the end of the questionnaire.

Test for Determining Your Risk Level

One. "I invest for the long term, five to ten years or more. The final result is more important than daily, monthly, or annual fluctuations in value."

(10) Totally disagree; (20) Willing to accept some volatility, but not loss of principal; (30) Could accept a moderate amount of yearly fluctuation in return for a good *total* return; (40) Would accept an *occasional* negative year if the final results were good; (50) Agree.

Two. Rank the importance of current income.

(10) Critical: the exact amount must be known; (20) Important, but I am willing to have the amount vary each period; (30) Fairly important, but other aspects of investing are also of concern; (40) Only a moderate amount of income is needed; (50) Current income is unimportant.

Three. Rank the amount of loss you could tolerate in a single *quarter*.

(10) None; (20) A little, but over a year's time, the total value of the investment should not decline; (30) Consistency of total return is more important than trying to get big gains; (40) One or two quarters of negative returns is the price you must pay when looking at the total picture; (50) Unimportant.

Four. Rank the importance of beating inflation.

(10) Factors such as preservation of principal and current income are much more important; (20) I am willing to have only a little variance in my returns, *on a quarterly basis only,* in order to have at least a partial hedge against inflation; (30) Could accept some annual volatility in order to offset inflation; (40) I consider inflation to be important, but have mixed feelings about how much volatility I

could accept from one year to the next; (50) The long-term effects of inflation are devastating and should not be ignored by anyone.

Five. Rank the importance of beating the stock market over any given two to three year period.

(10) Irrelevant; (20) A small concern; (30) Fairly important; (40) Very important; (50) Absolutely critical.

Add up your score from questions A-E. Your risk, as defined by your total point score is as follows: 0-50 = extremely conservative; 50-100 points = somewhat conservative; 100-150 points = moderate; 150-200 points = somewhat aggressive; 200-250 points = very aggressive.

Step 4:
Review Your Current Holdings

Everyone has heard the expression, "Don't put all your eggs in one basket;" this advice applies to investing. No matter how much we like investment X, if a third of our net worth is already in X, we should probably not add any more to this vehicle. After all, there is more than one good investment.

Since no single investment category is the top performer every year, it makes sense to diversify into several *fundamentally* good categories. By using *proper* diversification, we have an excellent chance to be number one with a portion of our portfolio every year. Babe Ruth may have hit more home runs than anyone of his day, but he also struck out more. As investors, we should be content consistently hitting doubles and triples.

Trying to hit a homer every time may result in financial ruin. Bear in mind that losses always have a greater impact than gains. An investment that goes up 50 percent the first year and falls 50 percent the next year still has a net loss of 25 percent. This type of philosophy is emphasized throughout the book.

Step 5:
Implementation

There is no such thing as the perfect time to invest. No matter how much you or some "expert" individual or publication thinks the market is going to go up or down, no one actually knows.

Once you have properly educated yourself is the right time to invest. If you are afraid to make the big plunge, consider some form of dollar-cost averaging. This is a disciplined approach to investment; it also reduces one's risk exposure significantly.

Reading investment books and attending classes is encouraged, but some people remain on the sidelines indefinitely. For them, there is no "perfect" time to invest. If the stock market drops 200 points, they are waiting for the next 100 point drop. If stocks or bonds are up 15 percent, they are certain that things are peaking, and they will invest as soon as it drops by 10 percent. If the stock or bond market does drop that magical figure, these same investors are now certain that it will drop another 10 percent.

The "strategy" suggested above is frustrating. More importantly, it is wrong. One can look back in history and find lots of reasons not to have invested. But the fact is that all of the investments in this book have gone up almost every year. The "wait and see" approach is foolish; the reasons for not investing will exist in the present and throughout the future.

Remember, your money is doing something right now. It is invested somewhere. If it is under the mattress, it is being eaten away by inflation. If it is in a "risk-free" investment, such as an insured savings account, bank CD, or U.S. Treasury Bill, it is being subjected to taxation and the cumulative effects of reduced purchasing power. Do not think you can hide by having your money in some "safe haven." Once you understand that there can be things worse than market swings, you will become an educated investor who knows there is no such thing as a truly risk-free place or investment.

If you are still not convinced, consider the story of Louie the Loser. There is only one thing you can say about Louie's timing: It is *always* awful. So it is no surprise that when he decided to invest $10,000 a year in AMCAP, a fund featured in this book, he managed to pick the *worst* possible times. *Every year*, for the past 20 years, he has invested on the very day that the stock market *peaked*. How has he done? He now has over $554,000, which means his money has grown at an average rate of 15.2 percent a year.

What happened? Louie chose a fund managed by an organization with a consistently outstanding record. And he found that, while there are good times and bad times, over the long haul any day is a good day to invest.

If, perchance, Louie had managed to pick the best day each year to make his investments, the day the market bottomed each year, his account would have been worth $732,000 by the beginning of 1990. But even by picking the *worst* possible days, Louie still came out way ahead of the $241,000 he would have had if he had put his money in a savings institution each year.

So even though his timing was terrible, he stilled fared much better than if he had done what many people are doing today: waiting for the "perfect" time to invest.

After asking you a series of questions, your investment advisor can give you a framework within which to work. Investors who do not have good advisors may wish to look at the different sample portfolios below. These general recommendations will provide you with a sense of direction.

THE CONSERVATIVE INVESTOR

20%	balanced/convertibles
15%	government bonds
15%	growth & income
10%	international bond
10%	international equities
10%	money market
20%	municipal bonds
	(depending on your tax bracket)

THE MODERATE INVESTOR

10%	aggressive growth
10%	balanced/convertibles
10%	growth
10%	growth & income
10%	high yield
10%	international bond
25%	international equities
5%	metals
10%	municipal bonds
	(depending upon your tax bracket)

THE AGGRESSIVE INVESTOR

30%	aggressive growth
10%	growth
10%	growth & income
10%	international bond
30%	international equities
10%	metals

Step 6:
Review

After implementation, it is important that you keep track of how you are doing. One of the beauties of mutual funds is that if you choose a fund with good management, they will do their job and you can spend your time on something else. Nevertheless, review your situation at least quarterly. Once you feel comfortable with your portfolio, only semi-annual or annual reviews are recommended.

Daily or weekly tracking is pointless. If a particular investment goes up or down 5 percent, it does not mean that you should rush out and buy more or sell off. That same investment may do just the opposite the following week or month.

By watching your investments too closely, you will be defeating one of the major benefits of mutual funds: professional management. Presumably these fund managers know a lot more about their particular investment than you do. If they do not, then you should either choose another fund or start your own mutual fund.

Step 7:
Relax

If you do your homework by reading this book, you will be in fine shape. There are a few thousand mutual funds. Some funds are just plain bad. Most mutual funds are mediocre. And, like everything else in this world, a small portion is truly excellent. This book has taken those thousands of funds and eliminated all of the bad, mediocre, and fairly good. What remain are all excellent mutual funds.

VII.
Fund Features

Listed below are some of the features of mutual funds — advantages not found in other kinds of investments.

Ease of purchase. Mutual fund shares are easy to buy. For those who prefer to make investment decisions themselves, mutual funds are as close as the telephone or the mailbox. Those who would like help in choosing a fund can draw upon a wide variety of sources.

Many funds sell their shares through stockbrokers, financial planners, or insurance agents. These representatives can help you analyze your financial needs and objectives and can recommend appropriate funds.

For these professional services you may be charged a sales commission, usually referred to as a "load." This charge is expressed as a percent of the total purchase price. In some cases there is no initial sales charge or load, but there may be an annual fee and other charges if shares are redeemed during the first few years of ownership. Information on fees is included in the fund's prospectus.

Other funds distribute their shares directly to the public. They may advertise in magazines and newspapers. Most can be reached through toll-free telephone numbers.

Because there are no sales agents involved, most of these funds, often called "no loads," charge a much lower fee, or no sales commission at all. With these funds it is generally up to you to do your investment homework.

In order to attract new shareholders, some funds have adopted 12b-1 plans (named, as we noted earlier, after a federal government rule). These plans enable the fund to pay its own "distribution costs." Distribution costs are those associated with marketing the fund, either through sales agents or through advertising.

The 12b-1 fee is charged against fund assets and is paid indirectly by existing shareholders. Distribution fees of this type usually range between 1/10 percent and 1.25 percent.

Fees charged by a fund are described in the prospectus. In addition, a fee table listing all transactional fees and all annual fund expenses can be found at the front of this document.

Access to Your Money (marketability). Mutual funds, by law, must stand ready on any business day to redeem any or all of your shares at their current net asset value. Of course, the value may be greater or less than the price you originally paid, depending on the market.

To sell shares back to the fund, all you need to do is give the fund proper notification, as explained in the prospectus. The fund will then send your check promptly. In most instances, the fund will issue a check when it receives the notification; by law it must send you the check within seven business days. You receive the price your shares are worth *on the day* the fund gets proper notice of redemption from you.

If you own a money market fund, you can also redeem shares by writing checks directly against your fund balance.

Exchange Privileges. As the economy or your own personal circumstances change, the kinds of funds you hold may no longer be the kinds you need. Many mutual funds are part of a "family of funds" and will offer an option called an exchange privilege.

Within a family of funds there may be several choices, each with a different investment objective, varying from highly conservative funds to those that are more aggressive and carry a higher degree of risk. An exchange privilege allows you to transfer from one of these funds to another. Exchange policies vary from fund to fund. The fee for an exchange is nominal, five dollars or less. For the specifics about a fund's exchange privilege, check the prospectus.

Automatic Reinvestment. You can elect to have any dividends and capital gains distributions from your mutual fund investment turned back into the fund, automatically buying new shares and expanding your current holdings. Most shareholders opt for the reinvestment privilege. There is usually no cost or fee involved.

Automatic Withdrawal. You can make arrangements with the fund to automatically send you, or anyone you designate, checks from the fund's earnings or principal. This system works well for retirees, families who want to arrange for payments to their children at college, or anyone needing monthly income checks.

Detailed Record Keeping. The fund will handle all the paperwork and record keeping necessary to keep track of your investment transactions. A typical statement will note such items as your most recent investment or withdrawal and any dividends or capital gains paid to you in cash or reinvested in the fund. The fund will also report to you on the federal tax status of your earnings.

Retirement Plans. Many financial experts have long viewed mutual funds as appropriate vehicles for retirement investing. Indeed, they are quite commonly used for this purpose. They are used in Keoghs, IRAs, 401(k) plans, and other employer-sponsored retirement plans. Many funds offer prototype retirement plans and standard IRA agreements. Consult the fund's prospectus for details.

Risk Reduction: Importance of Diversification. If there is one ingredient to successful investing that is universally agreed upon, it is the benefit of diversification. It is also a concept that is backed by a great deal of research and market experience.

The benefit that diversification provides is risk reduction. Risk to investors is frequently defined as volatility of return; in other words, how much an investment's return might vary. Investors prefer returns that are relatively predictable and thus less volatile. On the other hand, they want high returns. Diversification eliminates most of the risk without reducing potential returns.

The fund's portfolio managers will normally invest the fund's pool of money in fifty to a hundred different securities to spread the fund's holdings over a number of investments. This diversification lessens the fund's overall investment risk. Such diversification is beyond the financial capacity of most individual investors. The table below shows the relationship between diversification and investment risk, defined as the variability of annual returns of a stock portfolio.

number of stocks	risk ratio
1	6.6
2	3.8
4	2.4
10	1.6
50	1.1
100	1.0

Note that the variability of return, or risk, associated with holding just one stock is more than six times greater than the risk of a 100-stock portfolio. Yet, the *increased* potential return found in a portfolio comprising a small number of stocks is minimal.

VIII.
Reading a
Mutual Fund Prospectus

The purpose of the fund's prospectus is to provide the reader with full and complete disclosure. The prospectus covers the following key points:

- the fund's investment objective: what the managers are trying to achieve
- the investment methods it uses in trying to achieve these goals
- the name and address of its investment advisor and a brief description of the advisor's experience
- the level of investment risk the fund is willing to assume in pursuit of its investment objective; this will range from maximum to minimum risk, depending on the type of fund
- any investments the fund will *not* make (for example, real estate, options, or commodities)
- tax consequences of the investment for the shareholder
- how to purchase shares of the fund, including the cost of investing
- how to redeem shares
- services provided, such as IRAs, automatic investment of dividends and capital gains distributions, checkwriting, withdrawal plans, and any other features
- a condensed financial statement (in tabular form, covering the last 10 years, or the period the fund has been in existence if less than 10 years) called "Per Share Income and Capital Changes." The fund's performance may be calculated from the information given in this table.
- a tabular statement of any fees charged by the fund and their effect on earnings over time

IX.
Commonly Asked Questions

Q. Are mutual funds a new kind of investment?
No. In fact, they have roots in 18th-century Scotland. The first U.S. mutual fund was organized in Boston in 1924. Some mutual fund companies have been in operation for 60 years or more.

Q. How much money do you need to invest in a mutual fund?
Anywhere from a few dollars to several million. Many funds have no minimum requirements for investing. A few funds are open to large institutional accounts only. The vast majority of funds require a minimum investment of between $250 and $1,000.

Q. Do mutual funds offer a fixed rate of return?
No. Mutual funds invest in securities such as stocks, bonds, and money market accounts, whose yields and values fluctuate with market conditions.

Mutual funds can make money for their shareholders in three ways. They pay their shareholders dividends earned from the fund's investments. If a security held by a fund is sold at a profit, funds pay their shareholders capital gains distributioons. And if the value of the securities held by the fund increases, the value of the securities held by the fund increases, which results in the value of each mutual fund share increasing.

In none of these cases, however, can a return be guaranteed. In fact, it is against the law for a mutual fund to make a claim as to its future performance. Ads quoting returns are based on past performance and should not be interpreted as a "fixed rate" yield. Past performance should not be taken as a predictor of future earnings.

Q. What are the risks of mutual fund investing?
Mutual funds are investments in financial securities with fluctuating values. The value of the securities in a fund's portfolio, for example, will rise and fall according to general economic conditions and the fortunes of the particular companies that issue those securities. Even the most conservative assets, such as U.S. government obligations, will fluctuate in value as interest rates change. There are risks that investors should be aware of when purchasing mutual fund shares.

Q. How can I evaluate a fund's long-term performance?
You can calculate a fund's performance by referring to the section in the prospectus headed, "Per Share Income and Capital Changes." This section will give you the figures needed to compute the annual rates of return earned by the fund each year for the past ten years (or for the life of the fund if less than ten years). There are also several periodicals that track the performance of funds on a regular basis.

Q. What's the difference between *yield* and *total return*?
Yield is the income per share paid to a shareholder, from the dividends and interest, over a specified period of time. Yield is expressed as a percent of the current offering price per share.

The term "total return" is a measure of the per-share change in total value from the beginning to the end of a specified period, usually a year, including distributions paid to shareholders. This measure includes income received from dividends and interest, capital gains distributions, and any unrealized capital gains or losses. Total return provides the best measure of overall fund performance; do not be misled by an enticing yield.

Q. How much does it cost to invest in a mutual fund?
A mutual fund normally contracts with its management company to provide for most of the needs of a normal business. The management company is paid a fee for these services, which usually include managing the fund's investments.

In addition, the fund may pay directly for some of its costs, such as printing, mailing, accounting, and legal services. Typically, these two annual charges average 1.5 percent. In such a fund you would be paying 10-15 dollars a year year on every $1,000 invested.

Some fund directors have adopted plans (with the approval of the fund's shareholders) that allow them to pay certain distribution costs, such as the costs of advertising, directly from fund assets. These costs may range from 1/10 percent to 1.25 percent annually.

There may be other charges involved — for example, in exchanging shares. Some funds may charge a redemption fee when a shareholder redeems his or her shares, usually within five years of original purchase.

All costs and charges assessed by the fund organization are given in its prospectus.

Q. Is the management fee part of the sales charge?
No, the management fee is paid by the fund to its investment advisor for services rendered in managing the fund's portfolio. An average fee ranges from ½ percent to 1 percent of the fund's total assets each year. As described above, the management fee and other business expenses generally total somewhere between one and 1.5 percent. These expenses are paid from the fund's assets and are reflected in the price of the fund shares. In contrast, most sales charges are deducted from your initial investment.

Q. Is my money locked up for a certain period of time in a mutual fund?
Unlike some kinds of financial accounts, mutual funds are liquid investments. That means that any shares an investor owns may be redeemed freely on any day the fund is open for business.

Since a mutual fund stands ready to buy back its shares at their current net asset value, you always have a buyer for your shares at current market values.

Q. How often do I get statements from a mutual fund?
Mutual funds ordinarily send immediate confirmation statements when an investor purchases or redeems (sells) shares. Statements alerting shareholders to reinvested dividends are sent out periodically. At least semiannually, investors also receive statements on the status of the fund's investments. Tax statements, referred to as "Substitute 1099s," are mailed annually.

Q. I've already purchased shares of a mutual fund. How can I tell how well my investment is doing?
There are two steps in judging how well your fund is faring. First, you need to know how many shares you now own. The "now" is emphasized, because if you have asked the fund to plow any dividends and capital gains distributions back into the fund for you, it will do so by issuing you more shares, thereby increasing the value of your investment.

Once you know how many shares you own, look up the fund's net asset value (sometimes called the "sell" or "bid" price) in the financial section of a major metropolitan daily newspaper. Second, multiply the net asset value by the number of shares you own to figure out the value of your investment as of that date. Compare today's value against your beginning value.

You will need to keep the confirmation statements you receive when you first purchase shares and as you make subsequent purchases in order to compare the value "then" versus "now." You will also need these statements for tax purposes.

Q. Do investment experts recommend mutual funds for IRAs?
Most financial experts view many mutual funds as compatible with the long-term objectives of saving for retirement. Indeed, fund shareholders cite this reason for investing more than any other. Many types of funds work best when allowed to ride out the ups and downs of market cycles over long periods of time.

Funds can also offer the IRA owner flexibility. By using the exchange privilege within a family of funds, the investor can shift investments from one type of security to another in response to changes in personal finances or the economic outlook or as retirement approaches.

X.
How the 100 Best Funds Were Determined

With an entry field that numbers over 3,000, it is no easy task to determine the 100 best mutual funds. Magazines and newspapers report on the "best" by relying on performance figures over a specific period, usually one, three, five, or ten years. Readers often rely on these sources and invest accordingly, only to be later disappointed.

Studies from around the world bear out what investors typically experience, namely, *there is no correlation between the performance of a stock or bond from one year to the next*. The same can be said for individual money managers. And sadly, the same can be said for most mutual funds.

The criteria used to determine the 100 best mutual funds is unique and far reaching. In order for a fund to be considered for the book, it must pass several tests. First, all equity funds that have had the same management for less than five years were excluded; in the case of bond funds, a more liberal approach was taken, and only those funds with management in place less than three years were excluded.

The first step eliminated close to half the contenders. The reasoning for this cutoff is simple: a fund is only as good as its manager. An outstanding ten-year track record may end up in a periodical, but how relevant is the performance if the manager who oversaw the fund left a year or two ago? Bond fund selection was liberalized because these categories of funds normally require less expertise. More importantly, there would not be enough excellent bond funds for the book if a five-year management requirement were used.

Second, any fund that ranks in the bottom 20 percent of its *category's* risk level is excluded. No matter how profitable the finish line looks, the number of investors will be sparse if the fund demonstrates too much negative activity. In most cases, a little performance was gladly given up if a great deal of risk was eliminated. This is one of the book's major attributes: looking at returns in relation to the amount of risk that was taken. In most cases, the funds described in the book possess outstanding risk management. In those few instances where risk control has been less than stellar, the fund has shown tremendous performance and its risky nature has been highlighted to warn the reader.

Virtually all sources measure risk by something known as *standard deviation.* Determining an investment's standard deviation is not as difficult as might first be imagined. First you calculate the asset's average annual return. Usually the most recent three years are used, updated each quarter. Once an average annual rate of return is determined, a line is drawn on a graph representing this return.

Next the monthly returns are plotted on a graph. Since a three-year period is a commonly accepted time period for such calculations, a total of thirty-six individual points are plotted — one for each month over the past three years. After all of these points are plotted, the standard deviation can be determined. Quite simply, it measures the variance of returns from the norm.

There is a problem in using standard deviation to determine the risk level of any investment, including a mutual fund. The shortcoming of this method is that standard deviation punishes *good* as well as bad results. An example will help expose the problem.

Suppose there were two different investments, X and Y. Investment X went up almost every month by exactly 1.5 percent, but had a few months each year when it went down 1 percent. Investment Y went up only 1 percent most months but it always went up 6 percent for each of the final months of the year. The standard deviation of Y would be substantially higher than X. It might be so high that we would avoid it because it was classified as being "high risk." The fact is that we would love to own such an investment. No one ever minds *upward* volatility or surprises; it is only negative or downward volatility that is cause for alarm. Accordingly, the standard deviation method is not employed here.

The system for determining risk in this book is not widely used, but is certainly a fairer and more meaningful measurement than some others. The book's method for determining risk is to see how many months over the past three years a fund underperformed what is popularly referred to as a "risk-free" vehicle, something like a bank CD or U.S. Treasury Bill. The more months a fund falls below this safe return, the greater the fund will be punished in its risk ranking.

Third, the fund must have performed well for the last three and five years. A one or two year time horizon could be attributed to luck or nonrecurring events. A ten- or fifteen-year period is certainly better but suffers from the reality that the overwhelming majority of funds are managed today by a different person than they were even eight years ago.

Finally, the fund must either possess an excellent risk-adjusted return or have had superior returns with very low levels of risk. It is assumed that most readers are equally concerned with risk and reward. Thus, the foundation of the text is based on which mutual funds have the best *risk-adjusted* returns.

Some funds were reluctantly eliminated, despite their performance and risk control, because they were less than three years old, had short-term management, or were closed to new investors.

XI.
The 100 Best Funds

This section describes the 100 very best funds. As discussed previously, the method used to narrow down the universe of funds is based on performance, risk, and management.

Every one of these 100 funds is a superlative choice. However, there must still be a means whereby each of these funds is compared and ranked within its peer group.

Each one of the 100 funds is first categorized by its investment objective. The category breakdown is as follows:

aggressive growth	10 funds
balanced	9 funds
corporate bonds	4 funds
government bonds	10 funds
growth	19 funds
growth & income	11 funds
high-yield bonds	4 funds
international bonds	2 funds
international equities	8 funds
metals	2 funds
money market	11 funds
municipal bonds	10 funds
total	**100 funds**

There are five areas to be ranked: total return, risk/volatility, management, current income, and expenses. Of these five classifications, management, risk/volatility, and total return are the most important.

The track record of a fund is only as good as its management. That is why extensive space is given to this section for each fund. The areas of concern are how long the manager or team has overseen this fund, what type of background management has, and what their investment philosophy is.

The risk/volatility of the fund is the second-biggest concern. Investors like to be in things that have somewhat predictable results, as opposed to a fund that is up 60 percent one year and down 25 percent the next. A few such highly volatile funds are included, but the risk associated with such a fund is clearly highlighted, informing the prospective investor.

Total return is the third most important concern. When all is said and done, people like to make lots of money with an acceptable level of risk, or at least get decent returns by taking little, if any, risk. This is also known as the *risk-adjusted* return. So, although the very safest funds within each category were preferred, it had to be in tandem with magnificent returns.

The fourth category, current income, is of lesser importance. Income is important to a lot of people, but often gets in the way of selecting the proper investment; preservation of capital should also be considered. There is a better way to get current income than to rely on monthly dividend or interest checks. This is known as a systematic withdrawal plan (SWP). A fifty-six year example of a SWP is shown in appendix D. Income-oriented investors will be truly amazed when they see how such a system works.

Nevertheless, the current income of each fund has been rated. In most categories, such as aggressive growth, growth, international equities, and metals, the ranking is not very important. Investors go into these investments for growth, and properly so. In fact, many tax-conscious investors want to downplay current income as much as possible. For them, a high current income simply means paying more in taxes. For other categories, such as growth and income and balance, a healthy current income stream often translates into lower risk. And, for still other categories, such as corporate bonds, government bonds, international bonds, money market, and municipal bonds, current income is, and rightfully should be, a major determinant for selection.

The final category, expenses, rates how frugal management is in operating the fund. High-expense ratios for a given category mean either that the advisors are too greedy or that they simply do not know or care about running an efficient operation. The actual expenses incurred by a fund are not directly seen by the client; such costs are deducted from the portfolio's gross returns.

In addition to looking at the expense ratio of a fund, the turnover rate is studied. The turnover rate shows how often the fund buys and sells its securities. There is a real cost when such a transaction occurs. These transaction costs, also known as commissions, are borne by the fund and eat into the gross return figures. Expense ratios do not include transaction costs incurred when management decides to replace or add a security. Thus, expense ratios do not tell the whole story. By scrutinizing the turnover rate, the rankings take into account excessive trading.

Each fund is ranked in each one of these five categories. The rating ranges from zero to five points in each category. The points can be transcribed as follows: zero points = poor, one point = fair, two points = good, three points = very good, four points = superior, and five points = excellent.

All of the rankings for each fund are based on how such a fund fared against its peer group category. Thus, even though a given rating may be only "fair" or even "poor," it is within the context of the category — a category that includes only the very best. There is a strong likelihood that a fund in the book given a low score in one category would still rate as great when compared to the entire universe of funds.

Do not be fooled by a low rating for any fund in any of the five areas. All 100 of these funds are true winners. The purpose of the ratings is to show the best of the best.

Aggressive Growth Funds

These funds focus strictly on appreciation, with no concern about generating income. Aggressive growth funds strive for maximum capital growth, making frequent use of such trading strategies as leverage, purchasing restricted securities, and purchasing stocks of "emerging growth" companies. Portfolio composition is almost always exclusively comprised of American stocks.

Aggressive growth funds can go up in value quite rapidly during favorable market conditions. These funds will often outperform other categories of American stocks during bull markets, but suffer greater percentage losses during bear markets.

Over the past fifteen years, small stocks have outperformed common stocks, as measured by the Standard & Poor's 500 Stock Index, by almost 20 percent. From 1976 to 1990, small stocks averaged 18 percent compounded per year, versus 16 percent for common stocks. A $10,000 investment in small stocks grew to $119,200 over the past fifteen years; a similar initial investment in the S & P 500 grew to $97,100.

During the past thirty years, there have been eleven twenty-year periods (1961-1980, 1962-1981, etc.). The Small Stock Index, made up from the smallest 20 percent of companies listed on the NYSE as measured by market capitalization, *outperformed* the S & P 500 in *every one* of those eleven twenty-year periods.

During the past twenty years, there have been eleven ten-year periods. The Small Stock Index *outperformed* the S & P 500 in *nine* of those eleven ten-year periods.

Over the past fifty years there have been forty-one ten-year periods. The Small Stock Index outperformed the S & P 500 in *thirty-one* of those forty-one ten-year periods, including the last such period, 1971-1990.

A dollar invested in small stocks in 1941 grew to more than $1,411 by the beginning of 1991. This translates into an average compound return of 16 percent per year. Over the past fifty years, the worst year for small stocks was 1973, when a loss of 31 percent was suffered. Two years later, these same stocks posted a gain of almost 53 percent in one year. The best year so far has been 1943, when small stocks posted a gain of 88 percent.

In order to obtain the kinds of returns described above, investors would have needed quite a bit of patience and understanding. Small company stocks have had a standard deviation of 35 percent, versus 21 percent for common stocks and 8 percent for long-term government bonds. This means that an investor's return over the past 50 years would have ranged from +51 percent to -19 percent two-thirds of the time.

The p/e ratio for the typical aggressive growth fund is 19, a figure 23 percent higher than the S & P 500. The average beta is 1.06, which means that the group is only 6 percent more volatile than the S & P 500. During the past three years, aggressive growth funds have underperformed the S & P 500 by just over 3 percent per year; the figure climbs to almost 6.5 percent annually for the past five and ten years. Average turnover during the last three years has been 148 percent. There is close to $6 billion in all aggressive growth funds combined. The average aggressive growth fund throws off an income stream of just under 1.5 percent annually. The typical annual expense ratio for this group is 1.94 percent.

Forty-five funds make up the category "aggressive growth." Another category, "small company stock" funds, has been combined with aggressive growth. Thus, for this section there were a total of 108 possible candidates. Total market capitalization of these two categories combined is $15 billion.

Over the past three years, aggressive growth funds have had an average compound return of 11 percent per year. The *annual* return for the past five years has been 8 percent; 9 percent for the past decade. The standard deviation for aggressive growth funds has been 5.4 percent over the past three years. This means that these funds have been more volatile than any other category except metals funds.

Aggressive growth funds are certainly not for the faint of heart. They should probably be avoided by traditional investors, perhaps making up no more than 10 percent of a *diversified*, conservative portfolio.

The sample portfolio shown in a previous chapter recommends a 10 percent commitment to this category for the moderate investor and 30 percent for the aggressive portfolio. As is true with any category of mutual funds, whenever larger dollar amounts are involved, more than one fund per category should be used.

Acorn

Acorn Fund
2 North LaSalle Street
Chicago, IL 60602
1/800-922-6769

total return	★ ★
risk	★ ★ ★
management	★ ★ ★
current income	★ ★ ★
expenses	★ ★ ★ ★ ★
symbol ACRNX	16 points

TOTAL RETURN　★ ★

Over the past five years, the Acorn Fund has taken $10,000 and turned it into $16,900 ($13,700 over three years and $34,000 over ten years). This translates into an average annual return of 11 percent over five years, 11 percent over the past three years, and 13 percent for the decade.

A $10,000 investment in the fund at its 1970 inception was worth over $225,000 at the beginning of 1991. This translates into an average compound rate of 17 percent per year.

RISK/VOLATILITY　★ ★ ★

Over the past five years, Acorn has been riskier than about 60 percent of all mutual funds; however, it has been 90 percent safer than other mutual funds whose investment objective is "aggressive growth" or "small company." During the past five years, the fund has had only one negative year but has underperformed the S & P 500 four of these five years.

MANAGEMENT　★ ★ ★

Portfolio manager Ralph Wanger has spent his entire investment career with Harris Associates, the management company that oversees Acorn; he has been making investment decisions for the fund since its 1970 inception. Wanger has an MS from MIT and is a Chartered Financial Analyst.

His management technique is unique. The fund's performance has benefited from Wanger's willingness to pursue an idea wherever it takes him, a management approach that has proven very successful.

Acorn looks for areas of the economy that it believes will benefit from favorable trends for a number of years. The fund particularly seeks smaller companies not yet widely recognized as growth companies.

There are 225 stocks in this $740 million portfolio. Close to 85 percent of the fund's holdings are in common stocks. The median market capitalization of the portfolio's typical stock is $270 million, a mere 3 percent the size of the average stock in the S & P 500.

CURRENT INCOME ★ ★ ★

Over the past three years, the average small company fund has averaged an annual income stream of 1.3 percent, compared to Acorn's income stream of 1.47 percent. The dividend rate helps to reduce overall volatility slightly. Nevertheless, aggressive growth funds should be purchased for capital appreciation purposes, not current income.

EXPENSES ★ ★ ★ ★ ★

The expense ratio for Acorn has averaged about 0.8 percent for each of the last three years. Acorn's expense level is three-quarters of a point lower than the typical small company fund. And, since expenses are taken off the top of shareholder profits, this significantly lower-than-average expense ratio helps to enhance the bottom line for investors.

Over the past three years, the small company growth fund has had an average turnover rate of 107 percent annually. Acorn has had a significantly lower turnover rate of 31 percent. A low turnover rate means reduced transaction costs for a fund and helps increase performance results.

SUMMARY

Acorn must be commended for its strong performance and unique management style. Although this style is difficult to define, the constant innovation of new ideas has led to strong, consistent performance. Acorn is to be congratulated for its excellent risk control and management. These strengths, coupled with a superior track record, make this a fine choice for the aggressive portion of one's portfolio.

Alliance Quasar A

Alliance Fund Distributors
P.O. Box 1520
Secaucus, NJ 07096
1/800-227-4618

total return	★ ★
risk	
management	★
current income	
expenses	★ ★
symbol QUASX	5 points

TOTAL RETURN ★ ★

Over the past five years, the Alliance Quasar Fund has taken $10,000 and turned it into $13,400 ($13,300 over three years and $34,000 over ten years). This translates into an average annual return of 6 percent over five years, 10 percent over the past three years, and 13 percent for the decade.

The fund began operations at the beginning of 1971. A $10,000 investment in the fund at that time grew to over $176,000 by the beginning of 1991. This translates into a cumulative return of over 1,700 percent and an average compound rate of 15 percent per year.

RISK/VOLATILITY

Over the past five years, Alliance Quasar has been riskier than 95 percent of all mutual funds and 80 percent riskier than other aggressive growth funds. It is given a poor risk rating here because its negative volatility is much higher than most other aggressive growth funds shown in this book.

During the past five years the fund has had two negative years and has underperformed the S & P 500 four of these five years.

MANAGEMENT ★

Portfolio management is in the hands of Jenkel and Burr, both with the fund since 1970. Paul H. Jenkel previously served as a vice president of Tsai Investment Services and as part of an investment management group with Citibank. He has an MBA from NYU and over twenty-eight years of investment experience. Frank W. Burr was part of the investment team at Citibank prior to joining Alliance. He has a master's from Harvard and over thirty years of investment experience.

Management is supported by a team of fifteen internal analysts; multiple outside research firms are also used. This team management technique focuses primarily on industry groups. The fund primarily seeks stocks whose price/earnings ratios are very low or issues whose price is below book value. Jenkel and Burr concentrate on smaller companies with annual sales in the $100-$500 million range. Often they follow an opinion contrary to the prevailing wisdom and buy lesser known or out-of-favor stocks. Their final watchword is patience.

Alliance Quasar seeks growth of capital through the use of investment techniques involving greater than ordinary risks. There are 160 stocks in this $270 million portfolio. Close to 90 percent of the fund's holdings are in common stocks. The median market capitalization of the portfolio's typical stock is $240 million, a mere 2 percent the size of the average stock in the S & P 500.

CURRENT INCOME
Over the past three years, Alliance Quasar has averaged an annual income stream of zero, compared to 1.4 percent for aggressive growth funds as a group. Such a poor level of income is advantageous for the investor concerned with current income taxes.

EXPENSES   ★ ★
The expense ratio for Alliance Quasar has averaged 1.4 percent for the last three years, versus 1.9 percent for the average aggressive growth fund. Alliance's ratio is considered very good when compared to other aggressive funds in this book.

Over the past three years, the average aggressive growth fund has had an average turnover rate of 148 percent annually. Alliance Quasar has had a rate of only 75 percent. This is slightly higher than the average turnover rate of the ten funds that make up the aggressive growth portion of this book.

SUMMARY
Alliance Quasar's strongest suit is its track record. Its management and risk rating mean that the fund should be avoided by everyone except patient investors. This fund would be appropriate for a diversified portfolio, provided the participant looks at portfolio volatility as a whole and not by investment objective alone.

Founders Special

Founders Asset Management
3033 East First Avenue
Denver, CO 80206
1/800-525-2440

total return	★ ★ ★ ★
risk	★ ★
management	★ ★
current income	★ ★ ★
expenses	★ ★ ★
symbol FRSPX	14 points

TOTAL RETURN ★ ★ ★ ★
Over the past five years, Founders Special has taken $10,000 and turned it into $19,300 ($17,300 over three years and $31,100 over the past ten years). This translates into an average annual return of 14 percent over five years, 20 percent over the past three years, and 12 percent for the decade.

RISK/VOLATILITY ★ ★
Over the past five years, Founders has been riskier than 85 percent of all mutual funds, but 65 percent less volatile than other aggressive growth funds. During the past five years, the fund has had only one negative year and has underperformed the S & P 500 twice.

MANAGEMENT ★ ★
Portfolio manager Stuart Roberts has overseen the fund since 1985. He has an MBA from the University of Colorado. His success has come from focusing on stocks whose capitalization is below $500 million. Extremes in volatility and performance can be attributed to co-manager Erik Borgen.

Founders generally invests in common stock of smaller companies that have the potential for strong sales and earnings growth. The fund also invests, to a lesser extent, in stocks of larger companies whose earning power has been depressed but is expected to improve. Finally, the fund incorporates aggressive techniques, including leveraging and short-term trading.

There are forty stocks in this $60 million portfolio. Close to 90 percent of the fund's holdings are in common stocks. The median market capitalization of the portfolio's typical stock is $1 billion, a mere 9 percent of the size of the average stock in the S & P 500.

CURRENT INCOME ★ ★ ★
Over the past three years, the fund has averaged an annual income stream of 1.2 percent, slightly lower than the typical small company fund. The level of income

for Founders over the past couple of years has been in the 1 percent range, making it attractive for high-tax-bracket investors.

As is true with other aggressive growth funds, this one should not be purchased because of its income stream. Aggressive growth and "small company" mutual funds are not noted for distributing high levels of dividends.

EXPENSES   ★ ★ ★
The annual expense ratio for Founders has averaged 1.1 percent for the last three years. This is 40 percent less than comparable small-company funds.

Over the past three years, the small company growth fund has had an average turnover rate of 107 percent annually. Founders has had a turnover rate of 174 percent, giving it the second-highest turnover rate of any aggressive growth fund in this book.

SUMMARY
Founders Special is only for the disciplined investor willing to accept volatility over the short term in favor of long-term results. The fund must be commended for its ability to outperform the stock market the majority of the time. Overall, the fund ranks as "superior" when compared to other aggressive growth funds but only as "good" in this section.

GIT Equity Special Growth Portfolio

GIT Investment Services
1655 North Fort Myer Drive
Arlington, VA 22209
1/800-336-3063

total return	★ ★
risk	★ ★ ★
management	★ ★ ★
current income	★ ★ ★ ★
expenses	★ ★
symbol GTSGX	14 points

TOTAL RETURN   ★ ★
Over the past five years, GIT Equity Special Growth has taken $10,000 and turned it into $15,400 ($13,300 over three years). This translates into an average annual return of 9 percent over five years and 10 percent over the past three years.

RISK/VOLATILITY   ★ ★ ★
Over the past five years, GIT has been riskier than 70 percent of all mutual funds; yet within its category it is safer than 85 percent of its peers. During the past five years, the fund has had two negative years and has underperformed the S & P 500 four of these five years.

GIT's criteria for selecting stocks helps keep risk in check by choosing only quality holdings. This is done by focusing on companies with low debt levels and strong earnings. At other times, relatively large cash holdings also serve to keep risk levels very low.

MANAGEMENT   ★ ★ ★
Portfolio manager Richard Carney, has been the portfolio manager of GIT since its 1983 inception. His management technique emphasizes selection of high-quality holdings. Carney succeeds at this by selecting companies that have a good established history. He favors balance sheets with low debt and at least a 20 percent return on equity. When such companies are in short supply, Carney does not hesitate to build up sizable cash positions.

Carney is particularly concerned with a company's debt load. He believes that when recessions occur a smaller company can have a tougher time going to the bank than a large firm. According to Carney, "If a firm is debt-free and enjoying a higher return, it can just sail through recessionary periods."

Over long time frames, statistics show that small companies have outperformed larger ones. They do not do it all the time, but history has always favored the smaller-sized group, the kind this fund specializes in.

There are forty stocks in this $35 million portfolio. Close to 80 percent of the fund's holdings are in common stocks; the balance is in cash. The median market capitalization of the portfolio's typical stock is $115 million, a mere 1 percent the size of the average stock in the S & P 500.

CURRENT INCOME   ★ ★ ★ ★
Over the past five years, the small company fund has averaged an annual income stream of 1.3 percent, compared to GIT's income stream of 1.9 percent.

EXPENSES   ★ ★
The expense ratio for GIT has averaged 1.5 percent annually for the past three years. This is an average expense level for its peer group.

Over the past three years, the small company fund has had an average annual turnover rate of 107 percent. GIT has had a significantly lower turnover rate of 24 percent, making it one of the lowest within its category.

SUMMARY
The GIT Equity Special Growth Portfolio should be recognized for its selection of exclusively high-quality small-capitalized issues. A majority of the fund's selections have been with the portfolio for many years. Overall, GIT is a strong aggressive growth fund with a sensible approach to stock selection. It has demonstrated very good risk reduction, coupled with a good track record and very good management.

Janus Venture

Janus Group
100 Filmore Street, Suite 300
Denver, CO 80206
1/800-525-3713

total return	★ ★ ★ ★ ★
risk	★ ★ ★ ★
management	★ ★ ★
current income	★ ★ ★ ★
expenses	★ ★
symbol JAVTX	18 points

TOTAL RETURN ★ ★ ★ ★ ★

Over the past five years, the Janus Venture Fund has taken $10,000 and turned it into $21,900 ($28,200 over three years). This translates into an average annual return of 16 percent over five years and 15 percent over the past three years.

RISK/VOLATILITY ★ ★ ★ ★

Over the past five years, Venture has been more volatile than about half of all mutual funds; however, it has been 95 percent safer than other mutual funds whose investment objective is "aggressive growth" or "small company." During the past five years, the fund has had only one negative year, off less than 1 percent in 1990. It has underperformed the S & P 500 only once.

MANAGEMENT ★ ★ ★

Portfolio manager James P. Craig has managed the fund since its 1985 inception. His management style cannot be easily classified. Often the fund has a high weighting in cash, yet at other times Craig will heavily commit himself to favored trends.

The fund emphasizes investments in stocks of small companies with a market capitalization of less than $250 million. Its portfolio includes domestic as well as foreign equities.

There are seventy stocks in this $250 million portfolio. Close to 65 percent of the fund's holdings are in cash; only 35 percent is in common stocks. The median market capitalization of the portfolio's typical stock is $370 million, a mere 3 percent the size of the average stock in the S & P 500.

CURRENT INCOME ★ ★ ★ ★

Over the past three years, the average small company fund has had an annual income stream of 1.3 percent, compared to Venture's income stream of 2.2 percent. The higher-than-normal dividend rate helps to reduce overall volatility slightly. Nevertheless, aggressive growth funds should be purchased for capital appreciation purposes, not current income.

EXPENSES   ★ ★
The expense ratio for Venture has averaged about 1.4 percent for each of the last
three years. Venture's expense level is similar to the typical small company fund.

Over the past three years, the typical small company fund has had an average
turnover rate of 107 percent annually. Venture has had a significantly higher turnover rate of 256 percent, higher than any other small company or aggressive
growth fund featured in the book. A high turnover rate means increased transactions costs for a fund and can hinder its performance results.

SUMMARY
Janus Venture must be commended for its extremely strong performance and unique management style. This style has led to strong, consistent performance as a
result of management's uncanny ability to move in and out of the market at the
right times. Venture is to be congratulated for its superior risk control and very
good management. These strengths, coupled with an excellent track record, make
this a fine choice for the aggressive portion of one's portfolio.

Nicholas II

Nicholas
700 North Water Street, Suite 1010
Milwaukee, WI 53202
1/800-227-5987

total return	★ ★	
risk	★ ★ ★	
management	★ ★ ★ ★	
current income	★ ★ ★ ★	
expenses	★ ★ ★ ★ ★	
symbol NCTWX	18 points	

TOTAL RETURN ★ ★
Over the past five years, the Nicholas II Fund has taken $10,000 and turned it into $16,900 ($14,100 over three years). This translates into an average annual return of 11 percent over five years and 12 percent over the past three years.

RISK/VOLATILITY ★ ★ ★
Over the past five years, Nicholas II has been safer than only 35 percent of all mutual funds; within its category it is safer than 85 percent of its peers. During the past five years, the fund has had only one negative year and has underperformed the S & P 500 three times.

The fund focuses on small capitalized stocks but does hold a fair amount of medium-sized issues. Risk is reduced by stressing purchases of fairly priced issues and avoiding Wall Street's herd instinct.

MANAGEMENT ★ ★ ★ ★
Portfolio manager Albert O. Nicholas has been with the fund since its 1983 inception. Nicholas has over thirty-four years of investment experience; he is a Chartered Financial Analyst and has an MBA from the University of Wisconsin. Prior to forming the Nicholas Company, he was an investment analyst at Marshall & Illsley Bank for nine years.

Individual stock selection is the focal point of the fund's equity philosophy. The fund seeks well-run companies whose shares are trading at discounts due to temporary troubles. Often this results in the purchase of stocks that are lesser known or "out of favor," usually stocks of smaller companies with sales volumes in the $100-$500 million range. Nicholas is one of the few small stock investors that have been able to post consistent gains since their inception.

There are eighty stocks in this $350 million portfolio. Close to 95 percent of the fund's holdings are in common stocks. The median market capitalization of the portfolio's typical stock is $310 million, a mere 3 percent the size of the average stock in the S & P 500.

CURRENT INCOME   ★ ★ ★ ★
Over the past three years, Nicholas II has averaged an annual income stream of 1.7 percent, compared to the small company average of 1.3 percent. This slightly higher than average dividend stream helps reduce overall risk.

EXPENSES   ★ ★ ★ ★ ★
The expense ratio for Nicholas II has averaged 0.7 percent for the last three years. This is less than half the expense level for all small company funds. The fund has the lowest expense ratio in its group.

Over the past three years, the average small company fund has had an average turnover rate of 107 percent annually. Nicholas has had an incredibly low rate of 15 percent, making it the lowest of all small company and aggressive growth funds reviewed in this book.

SUMMARY
The low level of risk this fund has consistently shown makes it a strong candidate for any portfolio, even a non-diversified set of holdings. "Consistency" is the word to describe this fund. Its performance has been good, but may prove somewhat disappointing for the risk-taker.

Pennsylvania Mutual

Pennsylvania Mutual Fund
1414 Avenue of the Americas
New York, NY 10019
1/800-221-4268

total return	★ ★
risk	★ ★ ★ ★ ★
management	★ ★ ★ ★ ★
current income	★ ★ ★ ★ ★
expenses	★ ★ ★ ★
symbol PENNX	21 points

TOTAL RETURN ★ ★

Over the past five years, Pennsylvania Mutual has taken $10,000 and turned it into $16,100 ($13,700 over three years and $40,500 over ten years). This translates into an average annual return of 10 percent over five years, 11 percent over the past three years, and 15 percent for the decade.

A $10,000 initial investment since the fund's 1962 inception was worth $120,000 by the beginning of 1991. This translates into an average compounded annual return of 9 percent.

RISK/VOLATILITY ★ ★ ★ ★ ★

Over the past five years, Pennsylvania Mutual has shown greater volatility than almost 60 percent of all mutual funds; within its category it is safer than 95 percent of its peers. During the past five years, the fund has had only one negative year, but has underperformed the S & P 500 four times.

The fund attempts to reduce the risks associated with small and medium-sized company ownership. Market risk is lowered by using non-mainstream securities; company risk is lessened by favoring excess cash flow and low-leverage firms. Valuation risk is lowered by using strict pricing standards. Reduced portfolio risk is achieved by wide diversification.

MANAGEMENT ★ ★ ★ ★ ★

Portfolio manager Charles Royce has been with the fund since 1973, co-manager Thomas Ebright came on board in 1978. Royce has an MBA from Columbia University; Ebright received his MBA from Harvard. The management division of the fund is Quest Advisory Corporation. Quest also oversees assets for the State of Oregon, The World Bank, and Xerox.

Quest uses a strict fundamental approach that emphasizes analysis of balance sheets, cash flow, and internal rates of return. The dynamics of cash flow, especially excess cash flow, is considered to be the lead indicator of corporate activity. Royce and Ebright believe they are buying a part of a real business, not just a stock.

Management prefers smaller companies for two reasons. First, this universe has historically generated higher returns. Second, small and medium-sized companies are generally less well known and are therefore less likely to be understood and properly priced by investors.

There are 760 stocks in this $525 million portfolio. Close to 90 percent of the fund's holdings are in common stocks; the balance is in cash. The median market capitalization of the portfolio's typical stock is $160 million, a mere 2 percent the size of the average stock in the S & P 500.

CURRENT INCOME   ★ ★ ★ ★ ★

Over the past three years, Pennsylvania Mutual has averaged an annual income stream of 2.5 percent, making it the number one current income choice of all small company and aggressive growth funds in this book. This income stream, almost twice the amount of the average small company fund, helps to slightly decrease overall portfolio volatility.

EXPENSES   ★ ★ ★ ★

The annual expense ratio for this fund has averaged 1 percent over the last five years. This is about one-third less than the average expense ratio found in other small company funds.

In addition to having a superior expense level, Pennsylvania Mutual has an excellent turnover ratio, averaging only 19 percent annually over the past three years compared to a category average of 107 percent over the same period.

SUMMARY

It is unfortunate that Pennsylvania Mutual has a track record only moderately better than the average aggressive growth fund, because it ranks so high in important categories such as risk and management. This fund would be a good choice for the investor who understands that a high flying track record may be fleeting but excellent risk reduction and fantastic management are not.

Putnam OTC Emerging Growth

Putnam Financial Services
1 Post Office Square
Boston, MA 02109
1/800-225-1581

total return	★ ★ ★
risk	
management	★
current income	
expenses	★ ★
symbol POEGX	6 points

TOTAL RETURN ★ ★ ★

Over the past five years, Putnam OTC Emerging Growth has taken $10,000 and turned it into $17,600 ($14,400 over three years). This translates into an average annual return of 12 percent over five years and 13 percent over the past three years.

A $10,000 investment at the fund's inception in 1982 was worth over $44,000 by the beginning of 1991. This translates into a compound return of 18 percent per year.

RISK/VOLATILITY

Over the past five years, Putnam OTC has ranked in the bottom 10 percent of all mutual funds; within its category this fund has also shown greater-than-average risk. During the past five years, the fund has had only one negative year. It has underperformed the S & P 500 in each of the past five years, usually trailing the index by less than 0.5 percent.

MANAGEMENT ★

Portfolio manager Richard Jodka has been with the fund since 1985; he joined Putnam in 1982 as a research analyst. Prior to Putnam, he held analyst positions with Babson, Loomis Sayles, and Aetna Life. Jodka has an MBA from Boston University and is a Chartered Financial Analyst. He has over twenty-one years of investment experience.

His management technique can be described as forward looking; Jodka is always looking for the emergence of the next big sector. The fund continues to focus on three industries: cellular, cable, and pollution control.

There are 140 stocks in this $150 million portfolio. Close to 95 percent of the fund's holdings are in common stocks. The median market capitalization of the portfolio's typical stock is $400 million, 4 percent the size of the average stock in the S & P 500.

CURRENT INCOME

Over the past five years, Putnam OTC fund has not had a positive income stream. Of all aggressive growth funds described in this book, this fund is dead last.

EXPENSES   ★ ★

The expense ratio for Putnam OTC has averaged 1.6 percent over the last five years. This ratio is slightly better than the typical aggressive growth fund, but at the bottom of the list when compared to other aggressive growth funds in this book.

What has helped give Putnam OTC a "good" expense rating is its better-than-average annual turnover rate of 81 percent.

SUMMARY

Putnam OTC Emerging Growth certainly lives up to its name. So far it has done an excellent job in discovering the next "hot" industry, as demonstrated by its track record. This fund is an excellent choice for the investor who already has a diversified portfolio. It would also be a fine selection for someone who is not concerned with risk and believes in focusing on a small handful of industry groups.

Putnam Voyager

Putnam Financial Services
1 Post Office Square
Boston, MA 02109
1/800-225-1581

total return	★ ★ ★ ★ ★
risk	★ ★
management	★ ★ ★
current income	★
expenses	★ ★
symbol PVOYX	13 points

TOTAL RETURN ★ ★ ★ ★ ★

Over the past five years, Putnam Voyager has taken $10,000 and turned it into $20,100 ($16,400 over three years and $44,100 over the past ten years). This translates into an average annual return of 15 percent over five years, 18 percent over the past three years, and 16 percent for the decade.

A $10,000 investment at the fund's inception in 1969 was worth over $118,000 by the beginning of 1991. This translates into a compound return of 12 percent per year.

RISK/VOLATILITY ★ ★

Over the past five years, Voyager has been in the bottom 20 percent of stability for all mutual funds but safer than 70 percent of its peers. During the past five years, the fund has had only one negative year and has underperformed the S & P 500 only once.

MANAGEMENT ★ ★ ★

Matthew A. Weatherbie has overseen Voyager since 1983. He came to Putnam following ten years with Massachusetts Financial Services, where he was manager of its emerging growth fund. Weatherbie has an MBA from Harvard and is a Chartered Financial Analyst. He has over sixteen years of investment experience.

There are 145 stocks in this $760 million portfolio. Its largest area of concentration is in communication stocks; the fund also has sizable positions in retail and business services. Close to 97 percent of the fund's holdings are in common stocks. The median market capitalization of the portfolio's typical stock is $1.8 billion, 16 percent the size of the average stock in the S & P 500.

CURRENT INCOME ★

Over the past three years, Voyager has averaged an annual income stream of 0.71 percent, approximately half its group average.

EXPENSES   ★ ★

The expense ratio for Putnam Voyager has averaged 1.6 percent over the past three years. This expense ratio is about 20 percent less than the average aggressive growth fund. The turnover rate for Voyager has been 81 percent over the past three years, well below its category average of 148 percent.

SUMMARY

As demonstrated by its track record, Putnam Voyager is a highly favored choice. Its performance, coupled with very good management, makes it hard to beat. Of all aggressive growth and small company stock funds reviewed, this should be an investor's first or second choice by a wide margin.

Royce Value

1414 Avenue of the Americas
New York, NY 10019
1/800-221-4268

total return	★	
risk	★ ★ ★ ★	
management	★ ★ ★	
current income	★ ★ ★	
expenses	★	
symbol RYVFX	12 points	

TOTAL RETURN ★

Over the past five years, the Royce Fund Value Series has taken $10,000 and turned it into $14,700 ($13,000 over three years). This translates into an average annual return of 8 percent over five years and 9 percent over the past three years.

RISK/VOLATILITY ★ ★ ★ ★

Over the past five years, Royce Value has been more volatile than about half of all mutual funds but 90 percent more stable than other mutual funds whose investment objective is "small company." Since the fund's 1982 inception, it has had only one negative year but has underperformed the S & P 500 four of the last five years.

MANAGEMENT ★ ★ ★

Portfolio managers Charles Royce and Thomas Ebright have managed the fund since its inception. Both fund managers are particularly bullish, since small stocks are selling at their 1982 prices.

Despite an industry desire to focus on earnings momentum, Royce believes such a strategy is pointless. According to Royce, companies cannot be properly valued based on their earnings because this fails to account for liquidity or net worth, two key components of value measurement.

There are 610 stocks in this $160 million portfolio. Close to 95 percent of the fund's holdings are in common stocks. The median market capitalization of the portfolio's typical stock is $150 million, 2 percent the size of the average stock in the S & P 500.

CURRENT INCOME ★ ★ ★

Over the past three years, the average small company fund has averaged an annual income stream of 1.3 percent, exactly that of Royce Value's. Small company and aggressive growth funds should be purchased for capital appreciation purposes, not current income.

EXPENSES   ★

The expense ratio for Royce Value has averaged about 1.85 percent for each of the last three years. Royce Value's expense level is close to 20 percent higher than the typical small-company fund.

Over the past three years, the small company growth fund has had an average turnover rate of 107 percent annually. Royce Value has had a significantly lower turnover rate, 22 percent. A low turnover rate means reduced transactions costs for a fund and helps increase performance results.

SUMMARY

Royce Value must be commended for its strong performance and atypical management style, a style that has led to superior risk control and very good management. These two items, coupled with a modest track record, make this a fine choice for the defensive investor.

Balanced Funds

The objective of balanced funds, also referred to as *total return funds*, is to provide both growth and income. Fund management purchases common stocks, bonds, and convertible securities. Portfolio composition is almost always exclusively American stocks. Weighting of stocks versus bonds depends on the portfolio manager's perception of the stock market, interest rates, and risk levels.

Balanced funds offer neither the best nor worst of both worlds. They will often outperform the different categories of bond funds during bull markets but suffer greater percentage losses during stock market declines. Conversely, when interest rates are on the rise, balanced funds will typically decline less than a bond fund. When rates are falling, balanced funds will also outperform bond funds if stocks are also doing well.

Balanced funds are the perfect choice for the investor who cannot decide between stocks and bonds. This hybrid security is a middle-of-the-road approach ideal for someone who wants a fund manager to determine the portfolio's weighting of stocks, bonds, and convertibles.

The p/e ratio for the balanced fund is 14, a figure 3 percent lower than the S & P 500. The average beta is .6, which means that this group only has 60 percent of the volatility of the S & P 500. During the past three years, balanced funds have underperformed the S & P 500 by just under 6 percent per year; the figure drops to 4 percent annually for the past five and falls to less than .4 percent annually for ten years. Average turnover during the last three years has been 101 percent. The average balanced fund throws off an income stream of 5 percent annually. The typical annual expense ratio for this group is 1.2 percent.

There are forty funds that make up the category "balanced"; market capitalization is just under $18 billion. Two other categories, "income" and "convertible" funds, have been combined with balanced. Thus, for this section, there were a total of sixty-nine possible candidates. Total market capitalization of these three categories combined is $27 billion.

Over the past three years, balanced funds have had an average compound return of 10 percent per year. The *annual* return for the past five years has been 10 percent; 13 percent for the past decade. The standard deviation for balanced funds has been 2.7 percent over the past three years. This means that this group has been less volatile than any stock fund.

Conservative investors should have no more than 40 percent of their portfolio committed to this category. Moderate investors could place up to 80 percent of their holdings in balanced funds. These high levels assume that a portfolio's diversification is largely dependent upon using only a few categories of mutual funds.

The sample portfolio shown in chapter VI recommends a 20 percent commitment to this category for the conservative investor and only 10 percent for the moderate portfolio. As is true with any category of mutual funds, whenever larger dollar amounts are involved, more than one fund per category should be used.

American Balanced

American Funds Distributors
333 South Hope Street
Los Angeles, CA 90071
1/800-421-0180

total return	★ ★ ★ ★	
risk	★ ★ ★	
management	★ ★ ★ ★	
current income	★ ★	
expenses	★ ★ ★ ★	
symbol ABALX	17 points	

TOTAL RETURN ★ ★ ★ ★

Over the past five years, American Balanced has taken $10,000 and turned it into $16,100 ($14,100 over three years and $37,100 over the last 10 years). This translates into an average annual return of 10 percent over the last five years, 12 percent over three years, and 14 percent for the decade.

A $10,000 investment in the fund at its mid-1975 inception was worth $65,000 by the beginning of 1991. This translates into an average compound return of 13 percent per year.

RISK/VOLATILITY ★ ★ ★

Over the past five years, American has been less volatile than 65 percent of all mutual funds; within its category it has been safer than 60 percent of its peers. During the past ten years, the fund has had only one negative year. It has underperformed the S & P 500/bond index in two of the past five years.

It is too bad that horizons of ten years or greater are not the norm for most investors. If this were the case, American Balanced would certainly earn an "excellent" rating in this category.

MANAGEMENT ★ ★ ★ ★

The fund has been managed by Capital Research since its inception. Like all funds managed by Capital Research, American Balanced is an example of consistency and safety. There are seven American Funds monitored by CDA Investment Technologies, a mutual fund rating service that tracks over 1,000 equity funds. According to CDA, all seven of these funds rank in the top 10 percent of all accounts more than one-third of the time. All seven funds rank in the top 20 percent more than two-thirds of the time, and all seven rank in the top 30 percent every single time. The time frame for this study is quite meaningful; it contains ten rolling ten-year periods, beginning in 1970.

American Balanced is run by a management team consisting of three to seven managers. Each manager is responsible for a specific sector or series of industries.

Every fund managed by Capital Guardian is divided into smaller, more manageable segments, which are then assigned to individual counselors. Counselors decide how each segment will be diversified: how much in securities and how much in cash, as well as which securities and which industries.

Portfolio counselors get bonuses based on investment results over extended periods of time. The research division of Capital Guardian also manages a certain portion of the fund's assets. Besides giving input to the portfolio counselors, research has an opportunity to make direct investments. Research also operates on a bonus system based on fund performance.

Management is rated as "superior" over the past five years because of the fund's ability to avoid down markets. When viewed over a ten-year period or greater, Balanced's management would rate an "excellent."

The folks at Capital Research are known as value-oriented buyers. They have a tendency to own a security for many years. Some of their equities now throw off dividends that are greater than the original price paid for the stock.

The portfolio's composition of blue-chip stocks with below-market price-earnings ratios, coupled with its fixed-income weighting of United States government agencies and high-quality corporate bonds, helps to reduce risk. Management's decision to have a healthy amount in cash reserves in order to snatch up bargains helps to enhance long-term returns and reduce risk even further.

There are seventy stocks in this $330 million portfolio. Close to 50 percent of the fund's holdings are in common stocks; the balance is in bonds and cash. The median market capitalization of the portfolio's typical stock is $4.8 billion, 44 percent of the size of the average stock in the S & P 500.

CURRENT INCOME ★★
Over the past three years, Balanced has averaged an annual income stream of 5.5 percent, slightly above its group's average of 5 percent.

EXPENSES ★★★★
All funds within the American Funds family are known for their low expense ratios and turnover rates, and Balanced is no exception. Its expense ratio for the last three years has averaged 0.74 percent, close to 40 percent less than the average balanced fund.

Over the past three years, American Balanced has had an average turnover rate of 40 percent, a figure over 60 percent lower than the average balanced fund. This low rate helps keep down costs not reflected in a fund's expense category, but certainly helps to increase the net results enjoyed by its investors.

SUMMARY
The consistency, professionalism, and risk management employed by the management at the American Funds group are common knowledge. American Balanced, a member of the American Group exemplified this success. Its "very good" to "superior" ratings will result in excellence across the board for the investor who is willing to stick with this fund for longer than five years.

Dodge & Cox Balanced

Dodge & Cox
1 Post Street, 35th Floor
San Francisco, CA 94104
1/800-225-1581

total return	★ ★ ★ ★	
risk	★	
management	★ ★ ★	
current income	★	
expenses	★ ★ ★ ★	
symbol DODBX	13 points	

TOTAL RETURN   ★ ★ ★ ★

Over the past five years, Dodge & Cox Balanced has taken $10,000 and turned it into $17,600 ($14,400 over three years and $37,100 over the past 10 years). This translates into an average annual return of 12 percent over five years, 13 percent for the last three years, and 14 percent for the decade.

RISK/VOLATILITY   ★

Over the past five years, Dodge & Cox has been safer than 60 percent of all mutual funds; within its category it has been more volatile than 65 percent of its peers. During the past five years, the fund has had only one negative year and has underperformed the S & P 500/bond index twice.

MANAGEMENT   ★ ★ ★

Portfolio manager Peter Avenali has overseen this fund since 1972. Avenali is the chairman of the board of Dodge & Cox. He has an MBA from Harvard and is a Chartered Financial Analyst and a Chartered Investment Counselor.

Avenali usually maintains a ratio of stocks to bonds in the two-to-one range. The equity portion tends to be in large, well-established companies that throw off above-average dividends. The debt side is made up of high-quality utility, industrial, and transportation bonds.

The fund's equity strategy is to own an array of companies, each of which has fundamental investment value. They look for well-established companies with positive, long-term earnings prospects not reflected in current price. The portfolio tries to maintain representation in major economic sectors with long-term profit potential.

Dodge & Cox's fixed-income philosophy combines fundamental research with a long-term investment horizon, trying to uncover inefficiencies in the marketplace. When this research effort is combined with management's risk control, above-market returns can be earned over three-to-five-year time periods.

There are fifty five stocks in this $65 million portfolio. Close to 60 percent of the fund's holdings are in common stocks; the balance is in bonds and cash. The median market capitalization of the portfolio's typical stock is $6.5 billion, 59 percent the size of the average stock in the S & P 500.

CURRENT INCOME   ★

Over the past five years, Dodge & Cox Balanced has averaged an annual income stream of 5 percent, the same as its industry average. This fund is given only a "fair" rating in this category because of its failure to beat the average balanced fund and because it ranks dead last for the nine funds reviewed in this section.

EXPENSES   ★ ★ ★ ★

The expense ratio for Dodge & Cox has averaged 0.74 percent for the last three years, making it 40 percent less costly to run than its peer group average.

The turnover rate for this fund over the past five years can only be described as amazingly low. A turnover rate of 12 percent, compared to a rate of 101 percent for the average balanced fund, makes this fund quite impressive in this category. Its turnover rate is the lowest of all balanced funds reviewed in this book.

SUMMARY

Dodge & Cox Balanced is to be commended for its high levels of total return. The risk rating of "fair" means that this fund should be held by investors who own other mutual funds containing stocks and bonds. Fortunately, the fund's volatility is almost always in the plus column, leaving shareholders to wonder only about *how much* they will make during any given year.

Franklin Income
Franklin Distributors
777 Mariners Island Boulevard
San Mateo, CA 94404
1/800-342-5236

total return	★
risk	★ ★
management	★ ★ ★ ★
current income	★ ★ ★ ★ ★
expenses	★ ★ ★ ★ ★
symbol FKINX	17 points

TOTAL RETURN ★
Over the past five years, the Franklin Income has taken $10,000 and turned it into $14,700 ($12,300 over three years and $34,000 over the past ten years). This translates into an average annual return of 8 percent over five years, 7 percent over the past three years, and 13 percent for the decade.

An investment in the fund twenty years ago was up over 800 percent by the beginning of 1991, versus a 791 percent increase in the S & P 500 Common Stock Index and a 523 percent increase in the Salomon Brothers High Grade Corporate Bond Index.

RISK/VOLATILITY ★ ★
Over the past five years, Franklin has been more stable than 70 percent of all mutual funds; within its category, it has also done 70 percent better than its competitors. During the past ten years, the fund has had only one negative year and has underperformed the S & P 500/bond index four times.

Over the past twenty years, an investment in Franklin Income has been 30 percent less risky than the S & P 500 and 25 percent safer than the Salomon Brothers High Grade Bond Index.

MANAGEMENT ★ ★ ★ ★
Portfolio manager Charles B. Johnson has been with the fund since 1957; co-manager Avery came on board in 1989. Johnson is a graduate of Yale. Management continues to favor bonds over stocks by a two-to-one ratio. The fund's large cash position and modest exposure to gold mining stocks has helped to balance this portfolio.

There are fifty stocks in this $1.3 billion portfolio. Close to 50 percent of the fund's holdings are in bonds; the balance is in stocks and cash. The median market capitalization of the portfolio's typical stock is $4.5 billion, 41 percent the size of the average stock in the S & P 500.

CURRENT INCOME ★ ★ ★ ★ ★
Over the past three years, Franklin Income has averaged an annual income stream of slightly over 10 percent, compared to 7.2 percent for the typical "income" fund. More than 80 percent of the fund's shareholders reinvest their dividends to help their accounts grow. This fund clearly lives up to its name, emphasizing income rather than a high total return. It has an income stream markedly higher than any of the balanced funds ranked in this book.

EXPENSES ★ ★ ★ ★ ★
The expense ratio for income has averaged 0.6 percent over the past three years, a figure 50 percent less than its peer group. Such a low expense figure makes this the leanest within its category.

Over the past three years, this group's turnover rate has averaged 101 percent annually. Franklin Income's turnover rate has been 13 percent, making it the second-lowest within its category.

SUMMARY
This fund is definitely designed for the investor who is oriented toward current income but still wants to see positive total returns virtually every year. Stressing income over appreciation makes this an excellent choice for low-tax-bracket investors or participants in a tax-sheltered retirement plan.

IDS Mutual

IDS Financial Services
IDS Tower 10
Minneapolis, MN 55440
1/800-328-8300

total return	★ ★ ★
risk	★ ★
management	★ ★
current income	★ ★
expenses	★ ★ ★ ★
symbol INMUX	13 points

TOTAL RETURN ★ ★ ★

Over the past five years, IDS Mutual has taken $10,000 and turned it into $16,100 ($13,300 over three years and $37,100 over the past ten years). This translates into an average annual return of 10 percent over five years, 10 percent over the past three years, and 14 percent for the decade.

RISK/VOLATILITY ★ ★

Over the past five years, IDS Mutual has been safer than 65 percent of all mutual funds; within its category it has done better than only half of its peers. During the past ten years, the fund has had only two negative years. It has underperformed the S & P 500/bond index in only two of the past five years.

MANAGEMENT ★ ★

Thomas W. Medcalf has been with the fund since 1983; co-manager Edward Labenski came on board in 1987. Medcalf is responsible for the equity portion of IDS Mutual, the company's oldest fund. Prior to joining IDS in 1977, Medcalf was employed by Northwestern Life Insurance. He is a graduate of the University of Minnesota and is a Chartered Financial Analyst. Labenski directs the fixed-income portion of the fund. He joined the fixed-income research unit of IDS in 1975. Labenski has been in the investment business since 1961.

Management emphasizes equity instruments; large-capitalized industrial, financial, and utility stocks make up over half the fund's holdings. By placing emphasis on stocks with low price-earnings and high-quality bond issues, Medcalf and Labenski have been able to maintain a very limited risk exposure.

There are sixty stocks in this $1.7 billion portfolio. Close to 60 percent of the fund's holdings are in common stocks; most of the balance is in bonds. The median market capitalization of the portfolio's typical stock is $5.5 billion, 50 percent the size of the average stock in the S & P 500.

CURRENT INCOME   ★ ★
Over the past three years, IDS Mutual has averaged an annual income stream of 6.1 percent, compared to its category average of 5 percent.

EXPENSES   ★ ★ ★ ★
The expense ratio for this fund has been excellent, averaging only 0.64 percent annually for the past three years compared to almost twice that for its group. With an average turnover rate of 53 percent, this fund is just about half its category average of 101 percent.

SUMMARY
IDS Mutual rates as "superior" in all five of the important categories. Its consistency over the past ten years certainly makes it a strong option for the balanced investor.

Income Fund of America
American Funds Distributors
333 South Hope Street
Los Angeles, CA 90071
1/800-421-0180

total return	★ ★ ★	
risk	★ ★ ★	
management	★ ★ ★	
current income	★ ★ ★	
expenses	★ ★ ★ ★ ★	
symbol AMECX	17 points	

TOTAL RETURN ★ ★ ★

Over the past five years, Income Fund of America (IFA) has taken $10,000 and turned it into $16,100 ($14,100 over three years and $40,500 over the past ten years). This translates into an average annual return of 10 percent over five years, 12 percent over the past three years, and 15 percent for the decade.

A $10,000 investment at the late 1973 inception of the fund was worth over $83,000 by the beginning of 1991. This translates into an average compound return of 13 percent per year.

RISK/VOLATILITY ★ ★ ★

Over the past five years, IFA has been safer than 70 percent of all mutual funds; within its category it has done better than over half its competitors. During the past ten years, the fund has had only one negative year. It has underperformed the S & P 500/bond index in two of the past five years.

IFA has achieved superior results in declining markets but has often outpaced the stock market in times of rising prices. Since its inception the fund has done better than all the leading stock and bond market averages.

MANAGEMENT ★ ★ ★

Capital Research has managed this fund since its 1973 inception. Its stock portfolio is almost 50 percent greater than its bond holdings. A healthy cash reserve gives Income Fund of America the ability to buy bargains when they become available. Such a high liquid reserve also helps to reduce risk.

The stock portion of Capital Research's portfolio is largely composed of conservative oil, electric, and finance companies. The majority of the fund's bonds are of very good quality. The overriding theme of management is consistency and value. Over the past decade this fund has trailed the S & P 500 by only a slight amount, yet it has possessed only half the risk of the average stock fund. This is a true tribute to the management expertise of the people at Capital Research.

There are sixty five stocks in this $2 billion portfolio. Close to 80 percent of the fund's holdings are evenly divided between stocks and bonds; the balance is in cash. The median market capitalization of the portfolio's typical stock is $3.7 billion, 34 percent the size of the average stock in the S & P 500.

CURRENT INCOME   ★ ★ ★
Over the past five years, IFA has averaged an annual income stream of 7 percent, just slightly below its "income" fund category average of 7.2 percent. Since inception, dividends to fund shareholders have risen in all but two years.

EXPENSES   ★ ★ ★ ★ ★
The annual expense ratio for this fund has averaged 0.6 percent over the past three years, making it the lowest of all income funds and the second-lowest when compared to balanced funds in this book.

Over the past three years, ICA has had a very low average annual turnover rate of 39 percent. This rate is half that found with the average income fund and is another reason why the fund's returns have been so high.

SUMMARY
The Income Fund of America is a favored choice over other balanced and income-oriented funds. Its excellent track record and superior management mean that this is the choice for investors who want a conservative holding. Out of all the balanced funds reviewed in this book, IFA has the best overall track record for the past three, five, and ten years.

Massachusetts Financial Total Return

MFS Financial Services
500 Boylston Street
Boston, MA 02116
1/800-654-0266

total return	★ ★ ★ ★	
risk	★ ★ ★	
management	★ ★ ★	
current income	★ ★	
expenses	★ ★ ★ ★	
symbol MSFRX	16 points	

TOTAL RETURN ★ ★ ★ ★

Over the past five years, Massachusetts Financial Total Return has taken $10,000 and turned it into $16,100 ($14,400 over three years and $40,500 over the past ten years). This translates into an average annual return of 10 percent over five years, 13 percent over the past three years, and 15 percent for the decade.

RISK/VOLATILITY ★ ★ ★

Over the past five years, Total Return has been safer than over 60 percent of all mutual funds; but within its category it ranks in the bottom 40 percent. During the past ten years, the fund has had only one negative year. It has underperformed the S & P 500/bond index only once in the past five years.

MANAGEMENT ★ ★ ★

Richard E. Dahlberg has managed Massachusetts Financial Total Return since 1985. He joined MFS in 1968 as an industry specialist. Richard is a graduate of Wharton and is a Chartered Financial Analyst.

Management has four objectives: above-average income, growth of income, growth of capital, and price stability. On the equity side, Dahlberg looks for companies that have high dividend yields and that are selling at low price-to-book values. Often these firms are solid economic entities that have gone through a period of adversity. According to Richard, "Once a company's stock starts selling at or slightly below the company's book value, the chances diminish that the stock price will drop much lower—that is, if the company is still viable."

The stock-bond mix of the fund depends on management's perception of the economy. If the economy is speeding up, that is usually not good for bonds. If it is slowing, that is not good for stocks, and the fund may increase its bond holdings. Over a long period of time, stocks generally give a 10 percent total rate of return; the fund simply asks if the bond they are contemplating can give the same total return. Historically, the portfolio has been about two-thirds in stocks and one-third in bonds.

Dahlberg's equity portfolio is composed mostly of well-known blue chip stocks, with a small portion devoted to some of the more speculative issues. The bond portion, which is only half the size of the stock weighting, is made up of high-quality instruments with a short-term maturity.

There are ninety-five stocks in this $770 million portfolio. Close to 50 percent of the fund's holdings are in common stocks; most of the balance is in bonds. The median market capitalization of the portfolio's typical stock is $6.4 billion, 58 percent the size of the average stock in the S & P 500.

CURRENT INCOME   ★ ★
Over the past five years, Total Return has averaged an annual income stream of 5.9 percent, a little higher than the average balanced fund.

EXPENSES   ★ ★ ★ ★
The expense ratio for this fund has averaged 0.76 percent for the past three years, well below its peer group average of 1.2 percent.

SUMMARY
Massachusetts Total Return has had an excellent track record over the past three, five, and ten years. Unfortunately, its risk level is just slightly better than average. This is a fine choice for the investor who can accept a modest level of volatility. The patient shareholder should be highly rewarded.

National Total Income

NSR Distributors
2 Pickwick Plaza
Greenwich, CT 06839
1/800-356-5535

total return	★ ★ ★ ★	
risk	★ ★ ★ ★	
management	★ ★ ★ ★	
current income	★ ★	
expenses	★	
symbol NAINX	15 points	

TOTAL RETURN   ★ ★ ★ ★

Over the past five years, National Total Income has taken $10,000 and turned it into $16,900 ($14,400 over three years and $40,500 over the past ten years). This translates into an average annual return of 11 percent over five years, 13 percent over the past three years, and 15 percent for the decade.

RISK/VOLATILITY   ★ ★ ★ ★

Over the past five years, National Total Income has been safer than 70 percent of all mutual funds; within its category it ranks in the top 25 percent over the past three, five, and ten years. During the past ten years, this fund has had only one negative year. It has underperformed the S & P 500/bond index once in five years.

MANAGEMENT   ★ ★ ★ ★

Portfolio manager John Doney has only been at the helm of this fund since 1987. John has an MA in economics from Trinity College and over thirty years of investment experience. Prior to joining National Securities, he was with American Capital as chief investment officer. The overall fund group is not very appealing, but this member stands out.

The investment methodology of the fund is to purchase stocks judged to be undervalued based on relative financial ratios. Such stocks are deemed to have a high probability of favorable change in a one- or two-year period. The undervaluation will likely be because of a temporary deterioration in the business or a lack of investment favor.

There are thirty-five stocks in this $210 million portfolio. Close to 90 percent of the fund's holdings are evenly divided between bonds and common stocks; the balance is in cash. The stocks in the portfolio have an average dividend of 4 percent. The median market capitalization of the portfolio's typical stock is $6.6 billion, 59 percent the size of the average stock in the S & P 500.

CURRENT INCOME   ★ ★
Over the past three years, the fund's annual income of 6.1 percent is somewhat higher than that of the average balanced fund.

EXPENSES   ★
The annual expense ratio for Total Income has averaged 1 percent, making it slightly higher than any other balanced or income fund in this book but still lower than its industry average of 1.2 percent.

Over the past three years, the average balanced fund has had an average annual turnover rate of 101 percent. Total Income has enjoyed an extremely low turnover rate of only 25 percent.

SUMMARY
A rating of "excellent" in both return and risk makes this a tough choice to beat. National Total Income's less-than-perfect rating in other categories should be overshadowed by its risk management and performance. It has shown great consistency despite management changes throughout the past decade.

Phoenix Balanced

Phoenix Equity Planning
101 Munson Street
Greenfield, MA 01301
1/800-243-4361

total return	★ ★ ★ ★ ★	
risk	★ ★ ★ ★ ★	
management	★ ★ ★ ★ ★	
current income	★	
expenses	★ ★ ★	
symbol PHBLX	19 points	

TOTAL RETURN   ★ ★ ★ ★ ★

Over the past five years, Phoenix Balanced has taken $10,000 and turned it into $17,600 ($15,600 over three years and $52,300 over ten years). This translates into an average annual return of 12 percent over five years, 16 percent over the past three years, and 18 percent for the decade.

A $10,000 investment in the fund at its 1970 inception was worth over $225,000 at the beginning of 1991. This translates into an average compound rate of 17 percent per year.

RISK/VOLATILITY   ★ ★ ★ ★ ★

Over the past five years, Phoenix Balanced has been less risky than about 70 percent all mutual funds; 80 percent more stable than other mutual funds whose investment objective is "balanced" or "income." During the past five years, the fund has had no negative years but has underperformed the S & P 500 two of these five years.

MANAGEMENT   ★ ★ ★ ★ ★

The fund seeks reasonable income, preservation of capital, and long-term growth. It may invest in any kind or class of security. Usually management will commit the portfolio's assets to common stocks and bonds.

Patricia Bannon has overseen the fund since 1986. Currently she is positioning the fund in anticipation of investors seeking high-quality issues. Securites are targeted in the areas of health care, food, tobacco, and a handful of some of the less risky technology stocks.

There are twenty stocks in this $470 million portfolio. Close to 85 percent of the fund's holdings are divided equally between common stocks and bonds. The median market capitalization of the portfolio's typical stock is $13.5 billion, 123 percent the size of the average stock in the S & P 500.

CURRENT INCOME   ★

Over the past three years, the average balanced fund has averaged an annual income stream of 5 percent, identical to that of Phoenix Balanced. This interest and dividend rate helps to reduce overall volatility.

EXPENSES ★ ★ ★

The expense ratio for Phoenix Balanced has averaged about 0.9 percent for each of the last three years. Phoenix's expense level is close to one-fourth lower than that found with the typical balanced fund. Since expenses are taken off the top of shareholder profits, this significantly lower-than-average expense ratio helps to enhance the bottom line for investors.

Over the past three years, the average balanced fund has had an average turnover rate of 101 percent annually. Phoenix has had a significantly higher turnover rate of 181 percent, the second-worst in its category. A high turnover rate means increased transactions costs for a fund and can help decrease performance results. Despite such added costs, the fund posts the highest returns and risk management in its category.

SUMMARY

Phoenix Balanced must be commended for its tremendous track record, management, and risk reduction. The fund has strong, consistent performance resulting from management's strong convictions. This should be most investors' number one choice in the balanced category.

Phoenix Convertible

Phoenix Equity Planning
101 Munson Street
Greenfield, MA 01301
1/800-243-4361

total return	★ ★ ★ ★
risk	★ ★ ★ ★ ★
management	★ ★ ★ ★
current income	★ ★
expenses	★ ★
symbol PVOYX	17 points

TOTAL RETURN ★ ★ ★ ★

Over the past five years, Phoenix Convertible has taken $10,000 and turned it into $16,900 ($14,100 over three years and $40,500 over ten years). This translates into an average annual return of 11 percent over five years, 12 percent over the past three years, and 15 percent for the decade.

The fund began operations in 1976. A $10,000 investment in the fund at its inception was worth $18,000 by the beginning of 1990. This is the number one rated convertible bond fund over the past ten years.

RISK/VOLATILITY ★ ★ ★ ★ ★

Over the past three and five years, Phoenix Convertible has been safer than 70 percent of all mutual funds; within its category it ranks in the top 20 percent. During the past ten years the fund has not had a single negative year and has underperformed the S & P 500/bond index only once in the past five years.

MANAGEMENT ★ ★ ★ ★

Portfolio manager John G. Martin has overseen this fund since its inception in 1981. He is a graduate of Yale and has an MBA from Harvard. After graduation, he was a private placement officer at Mutual of New York. Martin joined the Phoenix Group in 1973 and in 1978 joined Connecticut Bank. He returned to Phoenix in 1981.

The fund is run very defensively. Martin seeks only investment-grade bonds and convertibles. This kind of quality is not found in any other convertible fund. Securities from the business services and nondurables are at the center of the fund's holdings. Martin likes to maintain a very high cash position, giving the fund a low level of risk. Management continues to stress growth over income.

There are fifty-five bonds in this $160 million portfolio. Close to 70 percent of the fund's holdings are in convertibles, with the remainder in common stocks, cash preferreds, and bonds. The average weighted maturity is 15.5 years, the average weighted coupon is 4 percent of par, and the average weighted price is 55 percent of par.

CURRENT INCOME ★★

Over the past three years, Convertible has averaged an annual income stream of 5.4 percent, compared to a "convertible bond" category average of 6 percent. This slightly lower-than-average income stream is particularly appealing for the diversified portfolio owner concerned with income taxes.

EXPENSES ★★

The expense ratio for this fund has averaged 1 percent for the last three years, well below the "convertible bond" category average of 1.4 percent. Unfortunately, this fund has had an extremely high turnover rate of 190 percent, the highest of any balanced, income, or convertible fund reviewed in this book.

SUMMARY

According to Value Line, a well-known neutral investment advisory service, convertible issues will outperform common stocks when they rise modestly or stay flat. When the market takes off, the convertible will not rise as rapidly but will later tack on virtually all of the gain. When the common stock retreats, the convertible bond will usually hold up better; the bond's interest rate is a floor holding up the security, since the rate is fixed.

Phoenix Convertible ranks as "superior" in both return and management, two of the three most important categories. Its risk control makes it an excellent choice. To Phoenix's credit, this is certainly the best of all *convertible* funds. The Phoenix family is to be congratulated for turning out one superior fund after another.

Corporate Bond Funds

Traditionally, bond funds are held by investors who require high current income and low risk. Interest income is normally paid on a monthly basis. Corporate bond funds are primarily made up of bonds issued by corporations; portfolio composition is almost always exclusively American issues.

Normally purchased because of their income stream, one's principal in a bond fund can flutuate. The major influence on bond prices, and therefore the value of the underlying fund, is interest rates. There is an *inverse* relationship between interest rates and bond values; whatever one does, the other does the opposite. If interest rates rise, the price of a bond fund will fall, and vice versa.

The amount of appreciation or loss of a corporate bond fund primarily depends upon the average maturity of the bonds in the portfolio; the cumulative amount of interest rate movement and the typical yield of the bonds in the fund's portfolio are distant secondary concerns. *Short-term* bond funds, comprising debt instruments with an average maturity of five years or less, are subject to very little interest rate risk or reward. *Medium-term* bond funds, with maturities averaging between six and fifteen years, are subject to one-third to one-half the risk level of long-term funds. A long-term corporate bond fund will average an 8 percent increase or decrease in share price for every cumulative 1 percent change in interest rates.

Often, investors can determine the type of corporate bond fund they are purchasing by its name. Unless the fund includes the term "short" in its title, chances are that it is a medium or long-term bond fund. The investors would be wise to contact the fund or counsel with an investment advisor to learn more about the portfolio's average maturity; most bond funds will dramatically reduce their portfolio's average maturity during periods of interest rate uncertainty.

The average weighted maturity for the bonds in these funds is ten years, the average coupon rate is 10.2 percent, and the average weighted price is $975, just under par. The average beta is 0.77 which means that the group is 23 percent less volatile than the S & P 500. During the past three years corporate funds have underperformed the SLH bond index by just under 3 percent per year; the figure drops to 2 percent annually for the past five years and 1.4 for the decade. Average turnover during the last three years has been 126 percent. The average corporate bond fund throws off an income stream of just under 9.5 percent annually. The typical annual expense ratio for this group is 1.05 percent.

Over the past fifteen years, corporate bonds have underperformed common stocks by almost a third. From 1976 to 1991, long-term corporate bonds have averaged 10 percent compounded per year, compared to 16 percent for common stocks and 18 percent for small stocks. A $10,000 investment in corporate bonds grew to $42,000 over the past fifteen years, while a similar initial investment in common stocks grew to $97,100, and in common stocks to $119,200.

Looking at a longer time frame, corporate bonds have only outpaced inflation on a pre-tax basis. A dollar invested in corporate bonds in 1941 grew to $10.96 by the beginning of 1991. This translates into an average compound return of 5 percent per year. During the same period, $1 inflated to $9.50; this translates into an average annual inflation rate of 4.5 percent. Over the past fifty years the worst year for long-term corporate bonds, on a *total return* basis (yield plus or minus principal appreciation or loss), was 1969, when a loss of 9 percent was suffered. The best year so far has been 1985, when corporate bonds posted a gain of 31 percent.

Sixty funds make up the category "corporate bonds." Total market capitalization of this category is $21 billion. Over the past three and five years, corporate bond funds have had an average compound return of 7.5 percent per year; the *annual* return for the past decade has been 11.5 percent. The standard deviation for corporate bond funds has been 1.4 percent over the past three years. This means these funds have been less volatile than any equity fund and similar to return variances with other kinds of bond funds.

Corporate bond funds are not for the speculative. They should make up no more than 40 percent of a *diversified*, conservative portfolio. A moderate portfolio should have less than 30 percent of its assets devoted to long-term corporate bonds.

The sample portfolio shown in a previous chapter recommends a 20 percent commitment to this category for the conservative investor and a 10 percent commitment for the moderate portfolio. In both of these cases it is assumed that the investor is in a low tax bracket or that such monies are sheltered from current income taxes. Higher-bracket taxpayers should look at municipal bonds instead. As is true with any category of mutual funds, whenever larger dollar amounts are involved, more than one fund per category should be used.

Bond Fund of America

American Funds Distributors
333 South Hope Street
Los Angeles, CA 90071
1/800-421-0180

total return	★ ★ ★ ★	
risk	★ ★ ★ ★	
management	★ ★ ★ ★ ★	
current income	★ ★ ★ ★ ★	
expenses	★ ★ ★ ★ ★	
symbol ABNDX	23 points	

TOTAL RETURN   ★ ★ ★ ★

Over the past five years, the Bond Fund of America (BFA) has taken $10,000 and turned it into $14,700 ($12,600 over three years and $34,000 over the past ten years). This translates into an average annual return of 8 percent over five years, 8 percent over the past three years, and 13 percent for the decade. Since its 1974 inception, the fund ranks number one in its category.

A $10,000 investment in the fund at its inception was worth $48,000 at the beginning of 1991. This translates into a compound return of 10 percent per year.

RISK/VOLATILITY   ★ ★ ★ ★

Over the past five years, BFA has been safer than 85 percent of all mutual funds; within its category this fund is more stable than 30 percent of its peers. Since its inception this fund has never had a negative year, quite an impressive feat for any bond fund greater than ten years old. The fund has underperformed the bond index only once in five years.

MANAGEMENT   ★ ★ ★ ★ ★

Capital Research has managed this fund since its inception over fourteen years ago. Management emphasizes moderation and consistency. For the past decade, BFA has beaten every other corporate bond fund.

The fund is broadly diversified and represents almost every major sector of the high-quality bond market. BFA is a high-quality-oriented bond fund. High quality and United States government issues make up over 80 percent of the portfolio's total holdings. Even the small portion of the fund that is in high-yield bonds is safe, with the fund sticking only to the high end.

There are 300 bonds in this $1.8 billion portfolio. Close to 90 percent of the fund's holdings are in bonds; the balance is in cash. The average maturity of the bonds in the portfolio is eleven years. Most of the securities are rated as "bank quality."

CURRENT INCOME   ★ ★ ★ ★ ★
Over the past three years, the BFA has averaged an annual income of 9.6 percent, slightly above the group's average of 9.4 percent. Over the past decade the income level of BFA has ranged from a low of 9.5 percent to a high of 14 percent.

EXPENSES   ★ ★ ★ ★ ★
The expense ratio for BFA has averaged 0.7 percent for the last three years, a figure over 30 percent lower than bond funds in general. Over the past three years the average annual turnover rate for this fund has been 83 percent, about one-third less than the typical bond fund.

SUMMARY
The American Funds family has done it once again with BFA. The combination of excellent management and superior performance make this perhaps the best choice within the corporate bond fund sector. It may well be the only bond fund fifteen years or older that has never experienced a negative year.

FPA New Income

Angeles Securities
10301 West Pico Boulevard
Los Angeles, CA 90064
1/800-421-4374

total return	★ ★ ★ ★ ★
risk	★ ★ ★ ★
management	★ ★ ★ ★ ★
current income	★ ★
expenses	★ ★ ★ ★
symbol FPNIX	20 points

TOTAL RETURN   ★ ★ ★ ★ ★

Over the past five years, FPA New Income has taken $10,000 and turned it into $16,100 ($13,300 over three years and $31,100 over the past ten years). This translates into an average annual return of 10 percent over five years, 10 percent over the past three years, and 12 percent for the decade.

RISK/VOLATILITY   ★ ★ ★ ★

Over the past five years, FPA has been safer than 90 percent of all mutual funds; 65 percent less risky than other corporate bond funds. During the past ten years the fund has not had a negative year. It has underperformed the bond index only once in the past five years.

MANAGEMENT   ★ ★ ★ ★ ★

Robert L. Rodriguez has been the fund's manager since 1984. Prior to joining FPA in 1983, Robert was a portfolio manager for Sun Life Insurance. From 1971 to 1979, he was involved with securities research. Robert has an MBA from the University of Southern California and is a Chartered Financial Analyst. He has over twenty years of investment experience.

Rodriguez tries to identify value within various sectors of the bond market. The prospectus limits management's flexibility, since at least 75 percent of its assets must be government or agency issues.

There are forty five bonds in this $35 million portfolio. Close to 80 percent of the fund's holdings are in bonds; the balance is in convertibles, common stock, and cash. The average maturity of the bonds in the portfolio is thirteen years. Most of the securities are United States government obligations; the balance is in investment-grade bonds.

CURRENT INCOME   ★ ★

Over the past three years, FPA New Income has averaged an annual income stream of 8.1 percent, compared to 9.4 percent for the average corporate bond fund.

EXPENSES   ★ ★ ★ ★

The expense ratio for FPA has been high, averaging 0.9 percent for the past three years—below the corporate bond fund average of 1 percent.

Over the past three years, FPA has had a very low turnover rate of 34 percent, making it the lowest, by a wide margin, of all corporate bond funds included in this book.

SUMMARY

FPA New Income rates as "superior" or "excellent" in the three most important categories: performance, risk reduction, and management. With such a large percentage of its portfolio constantly in governments and United States agencies, it may not be fair to call this a corporate bond fund.

Merrill Lynch Corporate High Quality A

Merrill Lynch Funds Distributor
P.O. Box 9011
Princeton, NJ 08543
1/800-637-3863

total return	★ ★ ★ ★
risk	★ ★ ★ ★
management	★ ★ ★ ★
current income	★ ★ ★ ★
expenses	★ ★ ★ ★ ★
symbol MLHQX	21 points

TOTAL RETURN ★ ★ ★ ★
Over the past five years, Merrill Lynch Corporate High Quality has taken $10,000 and turned it into $14,700 ($13,000 over three years and $34,000 over 10 years). This translates into an average annual return of 8 percent over five years, 9 percent over the past three years. The fund has averaged almost 13 percent annually for the decade.

RISK/VOLATILITY ★ ★ ★ ★
Over the past five years, Merrill has been safer than 90 percent of all mutual funds; it ranks as merely average among funds within its category. During the past decade, the fund has not had a single negative year. It has underperformed the bond index in three of the past five years.

MANAGEMENT ★ ★ ★ ★
Martha S. Reed has managed the fund since 1981. She has been with Merrill Lynch for over twenty-five years in the areas of municipal and corporate bonds. Reed graduated with honors from Mount Holyoke College.

There are ninety-five bonds in this $310 million portfolio. Close to 90 percent of the fund's holdings are in bonds; the balance is in cash. The average maturity of the bonds in the portfolio is ten years. All of the securities are rated as "bank quality."

CURRENT INCOME ★ ★ ★ ★
Over the past three years, the fund has averaged an annual income stream of 8.9 percent, slightly below the industry norm.

EXPENSES ★ ★ ★ ★ ★
The expense ratio for Merrill has averaged 0.62 percent annually for the last three years. This is a very low ratio, the lowest of any corporate bond fund in the book. Lower operating costs translate into higher returns for shareholders.

Over the past five years, the fund has had an average annual turnover rate of 171 percent, quite a bit higher than its peer group's average of 126 percent.

SUMMARY

Merrill Lynch Corporate High Quality consistently ranks as "superior" in all important categories. This is a fine choice for the investor who wants current income while remaining concerned with preservation of capital. The fund demonstrates a low degree of volatility and should be purchased by the conservative or moderate bond investor.

United Bond
Waddell & Reed
2400 Pershing Road, P.O. Box 418343
Kansas City, MO 64141
1/800-821-5664

total return	★ ★ ★ ★	
risk	★ ★ ★	
management	★ ★ ★	
current income	★ ★ ★	
expenses	★ ★ ★ ★ ★	
symbol UNBDX	18 points	

TOTAL RETURN ★ ★ ★ ★
Over the past five years, United Bond has taken $10,000 and turned it into $14,000 ($12,600 over three years and $34,000 over the past ten years). This translates into an average annual return of 7 percent over five years, 8 percent over the past three years, and 13 percent for the decade.

The fund began operations in 1964. A $10,000 investment at inception grew to over $68,000 by the beginning of 1991. This translates into an average compound rate of 7 percent per year.

RISK/VOLATILITY ★ ★ ★
Over the past five years, United Bond has been safer than 85 percent of all mutual funds; within its category this fund is considered more volatile than 60 percent of its peers. The fund has not had one negative year in the past decade. It has underperformed the bond index only once in five years.

MANAGEMENT ★ ★ ★
Robert Alley has managed this fund since 1984. He joined the parent company, Waddell & Reed, over nine years ago. Alley has over eighteen years of investment experience and has an MBA from the University of Missouri.

Management's strategy is to seek capital appreciation by purchasing medium- and long-term bonds when interest rates are trending downward. Alley keeps a high level of cash, thereby somewhat tempering the risk exposure found with long maturing bonds.

There are fifty-five bonds in this $415 million portfolio. Close to 80 percent of the fund's holdings are in bonds; the balance is in cash and convertibles. The average maturity of the bonds in the portfolio is fourteen years. Most of the securities are rated as "bank quality."

CURRENT INCOME ★ ★ ★
Over the past three years, United has averaged an annual income stream of 8.8 per-

cent, compared to 9.4 percent for corporate bond funds in general.

EXPENSES   ★ ★ ★ ★ ★

The annual expense ratio for United has averaged 0.66 percent for the last three years. This is the second-lowest expense ratio of any corporate bond fund in this book.

Over the past three years, United Bond has had an extremely high average annual turnover rate of 298 percent. This makes it the highest fund within its sector by a large margin.

SUMMARY

United Bond is a smart choice for the corporate bond investor. Its performance has been superior; its safety and management have been very good. Its track record should clearly override other considerations.

Government Bond Funds

These funds invest in direct and indirect United States government obligations. Government bond funds comprise one or more of the following: T-Bills, T-Notes, T-Bonds, GNMAs and FNMAs. Treasury Bills, Notes, and Bonds make up the entire marketable debt of the United States government. Such instruments are exempt from state income taxes.

GNMAs are considered an indirect obligation of the government, but are still backed by the full faith and credit of the United States. FNMAs are not issued by the government but are considered virtually identical in safety to GNMAs. Both are subject to state and local income taxes. *All* of the securities in a government bond fund are subject to federal income taxes.

The average maturity of a security found in a government bond fund ranges quite a bit, depending on the kind of fund and on management's perception of risk and the future direction of interest rates. A more thorough discussion of interest rates and the volatility of bond fund prices is given in the introductory pages of the corporate bond section.

Over the past fifteen years, government bonds have underperformed long-term corporate bonds only slightly, 9.5 percent versus 10 percent. A $10,000 investment in United States government bonds grew to $39,400 over the past fifteen years; a similar initial investment in corporate bonds grew to $42,000.

Looking at a longer time frame, government bonds have only slightly outperformed inflation. A dollar invested in government bonds in 1941 grew to $8.86 by the beginning of 1991. This translates into an average compound return of 4.5 percent per year. Over the past fifty years, the worst year for government bonds was 1967, when a loss of 9 percent was suffered. The best year so far has been 1982, when government bonds posted a gain of 40 percent. All of these figures are based on total return, current yield plus or minus any appreciation or loss of principal.

Over the past fifty years, there have been forty-one ten-year periods. On a pretax basis, government bonds have outperformed inflation only eleven times. Over the past half-century there have been thirty-one twenty-year periods. On a pre-tax basis, government bonds have outperformed inflation only five times. All five of those twenty-year periods were the most recent in time (1967-1986, 1968-1987, 1969-1988, 1970-1989, and 1971-1990).

Eighty-five funds make up the category "government bonds." Total market capitalization of this category is $122 billion.

Over the past three years, government funds have had an average compound return of 9 percent per year. The *annual* return for the past five years has been 8 percent; 11 percent for the past decade. The standard deviation for government bond funds has been 1.3 percent over the past three years. This means these funds have been less volatile than any other category except money market funds.

Government bond funds are the perfect choice for the conservative investor who wants to avoid any possibility of default. They should probably be avoided by most moderate investors and all aggressive portfolios. Up to 50 percent of an investor's holdings could be in government bonds; however, these securities should be avoided even by conservative investors who are in a high tax bracket or unable to shelter such an investment in a retirement plan or annuity. Such investors should look first at the advantages of municipal bond funds.

The prospective investor should always remember that government and corporate bonds are generally not good investments once inflation *and* taxes are factored in. The investor who appreciates the cumulative effects of even low levels of inflation should probably avoid government and corporate bonds except as part of a retirement plan.

The sample portfolio shown in a previous chapter recommends a 35 percent commitment to this category for the conservative investor and 10 percent for the moderate portfolio. As is true with any category of mutual funds, whenever larger dollar amounts are involved, more than one fund per category should be used.

Alliance Mortgage Securities Income
Alliance Fund Distributors
P.O. Box 1520
Secaucus, NJ 07096
1/800-227-4618

total return	★ ★ ★ ★
risk	★ ★
management	★ ★
current income	★ ★ ★ ★ ★
expenses	
symbol ALMSX	13 points

TOTAL RETURN ★ ★ ★ ★

Over the past five years, Alliance Mortgage Securities Income has taken $10,000 and turned it into $15,400 ($13,000 over three years). This translates into an average annual return of 9 percent over five years and 9 percent over the past three years.

RISK/VOLATILITY ★ ★

Over the past five years, Alliance Mortgage has been safer than 95 percent of all mutual funds; within its category it ranks in the top 80 percent. Since its 1984 inception the fund has not had a negative year. It has underperformed the bond index in two of the past five years.

MANAGEMENT ★ ★

Paul Zoschke has been the portfolio manager since 1987. Prior to joining Alliance, Zoscheke was director of fixed income at Century Capital Associates. He is a Chartered Financial Analyst and has an MBA from Columbia School of Business. Zoschke has had over twenty-four years of investment experience.

The portfolio is made up mostly of government and federal agency obligations: GNMAs, FHLMCs, Treasury Notes, and FNMAs, with 12 percent coupon rates. His management style includes the purchasing of call options that will benefit the portfolio when interest rates fall.

There are fifty-five mortgage-backed bonds in this $510 million portfolio. Close to 130 percent of the fund's holdings are in United States government agency issues; the fund is 30 percent leveraged. The average maturity of the bonds in the portfolio is sixteen years. All of the securities are rated as "bank quality."

CURRENT INCOME ★ ★ ★ ★ ★

Over the past three years, Alliance Mortgage has averaged an annual income stream of 10.2 percent, compared to an industry group average of just under 9 percent. This level of income makes it the highest of any government fund reviewed in this book.

EXPENSES

The expense ratio for Alliance Mortgage has averaged 1.1 percent for each of the last three years, almost identical to its group's average of 1 percent.

Over the past three years, the fund has had an average annual turnover rate of 259 percent, close to twice the level of its peer group average.

SUMMARY

Alliance Mortgage Securities Income is ideal for the income-oriented investor. It is safe and run by very good management. A favored pick when viewed as a total return vehicle, it is also a great choice for that large percentage of government fund investors who are more concerned with current yield.

Federated GNMA Trust

Federated Securities
Federated Investors Tower
Pittsburgh, PA 15222
1/800-245-5000

total return	★ ★ ★ ★ ★
risk	★
management	★ ★ ★ ★
current income	★ ★ ★
expenses	★ ★ ★ ★
symbol FGMAX	17 points

TOTAL RETURN   ★ ★ ★ ★ ★

Over the past five years, Federated GNMA Trust has taken $10,000 and turned it into $15,400 ($13,700 over three years). This translates into an average annual return of 9 percent over five years and 11 percent over the past three years.

RISK/VOLATILITY   ★

Over the past five years, Federated GNMA has been safer than 90 percent of all mutual funds; within its category it is less risky than 70 percent of its peers. Since its inception in 1982 this fund has not had a negative year. It has underperformed the bond index in two of these five years.

MANAGEMENT   ★ ★ ★ ★

Portfolio manager Gary Madich has overseen Federated GNMA since 1984. He is responsible for Federated's fixed income area, concentrating on agency and mortgage-backed securities. Prior to joining the firm, he was a fixed-income analyst with Mellon Bank. Madich has an MA from the University of Pittsburgh.

There are twenty mortgage-backed bonds in this $1.4 billion portfolio. Close to 100 percent of the fund's holdings are in GNMAs. The average maturity of the obligations in the portfolio is twelve years. All of the securities are backed by the United States government. Minimum initial investment in the fund is $25,000.

CURRENT INCOME   ★ ★ ★

Over the past three years, Federated GNMA has averaged an annual income stream of 9.3 percent, compared to an industry average of 8.8 percent.

EXPENSES   ★ ★ ★ ★

The annual expense ratio for this fund has averaged 0.5 percent for the last five years. This is half the rate normally incurred by a government bond fund.

Over the past three years, the average annual turnover rate for Federated GNMA has been 23 percent, well below its peer group's average. This fund has a lower turnover rate than any other government bond fund reviewed in the book.

SUMMARY
Federated GNMA Trust has superior management and an excellent track record. It is a fine choice, but limited to institutions and individuals willing to invest at least $25,000. It should only be considered by the risk averse or conservative institution or individual who owns another government or mortgage-backed securities fund.

Federated Income Trust

Federated Securities
Federated Investors Tower
Pittsburgh, PA 15222
1/800-245-5000

total return	★ ★ ★ ★
risk	★ ★ ★ ★ ★
management	★ ★ ★ ★ ★
current income	★ ★ ★
expenses	★ ★ ★ ★
symbol FICMX	21 points

TOTAL RETURN   ★ ★ ★ ★
Over the past five years, Federated Income Trust has taken $10,000 and turned it into $15,400 ($13,300 over three years). This translates into an average annual return of 9 percent over five years and 10 percent over the past three years.

RISK/VOLATILITY   ★ ★ ★ ★ ★
Over the past five years, Federated Income has been safer than 95 percent of all mutual funds; within its category it ranks in the top 5 percent for stability. Since its 1982 inception the fund has not had a negative year. It has underperformed the bond index in two of the past five years.

MANAGEMENT   ★ ★ ★ ★ ★
Portfolio manager Gary Madich has been with Federated Income since 1984. He is responsible for Federated's fixed income area, concentrating on agency and mortgage-backed securities. Prior to joining the firm he was a fixed income analyst with Mellon Bank. Madich has an MA from the University of Pittsburgh.

The fund requires a minimum investment of $25,000. It is made up mostly of United States government agency issues, such as FNMAs and FHLMCs. Management's goal is to generate high income while preserving capital. The portfolio's average maturity of only five years helps to ensure safety of principal.

Because of its modest maturity, the fund really shows its colors during a bear bond market (increasing interest rates), but has also fared well during some bull markets. By accepting close to half the interest rate risk found in a typical government bond portfolio, Madich has had to give up only a little current income.

There are forty mortgage-backed bonds in this $930 million portfolio. 100 percent of the fund's holdings are in United States government agency issues, such as FNMAs and FHLMCs. The average maturity of the bonds in the portfolio is twelve years. All of the securities are rated as "bank quality" and backed by government agencies.

CURRENT INCOME   ★ ★ ★

Over the past three years, Federated Income has averaged an annual income stream of 9.3 percent, compared to an industry average of 8.8 percent.

EXPENSES   ★ ★ ★ ★

The expense ratio for this fund has averaged 0.5 percent for the last three years. This is well below the group's average of 1 percent.

Over the past three years, the average mortgage bond fund has had an average turnover rate of 155 percent annually. Federated Income's turnover has averaged 71 percent.

SUMMARY

This is the best choice for the safety-conscious investor willing to make an initial investment of at least $25,000. The fund scores extremely well in all categories. Federated has again demonstrated that it excels at managing government bond funds.

Federated Intermediate Government Trust

Federated Securities
Federated Investors Tower
Pittsburgh, PA 15222
1/800-245-5000

total return	★ ★
risk	★ ★
management	★ ★
current income	★ ★
expenses	★ ★ ★ ★
symbol FIGTX	12 points

TOTAL RETURN   ★ ★

Over the past five years, Federated Intermediate Government Trust has taken $10,000 and turned it into $14,700 ($13,000 over three years). This translates into an average annual return of 8 percent over five years and 9 percent over the past three years.

RISK/VOLATILITY   ★ ★

Over the past five years, Federated Intermediate has been more stable than 95 percent of all mutual funds; within its category the fund is more volatile than 65 percent of all government bond funds. Since its inception in 1983 the fund has not had a negative year, but has underperformed the bond index three of the past five years.

MANAGEMENT   ★ ★

Portfolio manager Roger Early has overseen this fund since 1987. He is responsible for research and management in the fixed income area for all Federated funds. Prior to joining Federated he was the international finance manager for Rockwell and senior financial consultant for Touche Ross. Early has a BS from Wharton and an MBA from the University of Pennsylvania.

There are fifteen bonds in this $850 million portfolio. The fund is almost exclusively United States Treasury Notes, with the balance made up of cash. The average maturity is less than five years, which helps reduce interest rate risk dramatically. The fund requires a minimum initial investment of $25,000.

CURRENT INCOME   ★ ★

Over the past three years, the Federated Intermediate fund has averaged an annual income stream of 8.3 percent, making it the lowest of all government bond funds in this book. Bear in mind that the portfolio has a very short maturity; the lower returns are compensated for by an extremely consistent price per share.

EXPENSES ★ ★ ★ ★

The expense ratio for this fund has averaged 0.48 percent for the last three years, making it the second-most frugal within its group. This rate compares extremely favorably to the average government bond expense ratio of 1.3 percent.

Over the past three years, the average government fund has had an average annual turnover rate of 163 percent, compared to Federated's rate of 106 percent.

SUMMARY

Federated Intermediate Government Trust has had good returns, management, and risk control. This is a recommended choice for the institutional buyer or individual willing to make an initial commitment of $25,000.

Fund for U.S. Government Securities

Federated Securities
Federated Investors Tower
Pittsburgh, PA 15222
1/800-356-2805

total return	★ ★ ★	
risk	★ ★ ★	
management	★ ★ ★	
current income	★ ★ ★	
expenses	★	
symbol FUSGX	13 points	

TOTAL RETURN ★ ★ ★
Over the past five years, the Fund for U.S. Government Securities has taken $10,000 and turned it into $15,400 ($13,300 over three years and $31,100 over the past ten years). This translates into an average annual return of 9 percent over five years, 10 percent over the past three years, and 12 percent over the past decade.

RISK/VOLATILITY ★ ★ ★
Over the past five years, Fund for U.S. has been safer than 95 percent of all mutual funds; within its category it ranks in the top 5 percent. During the past ten years the fund has had only one negative year (off 2 percent in 1981). It has underperformed the bond index three of the past five years.

MANAGEMENT ★ ★ ★
Gary Madich has been managing this fund since 1984. He is responsible for Federated's fixed income area, concentrating on agency and mortgage-backed securities. Prior to joining the firm he was a fixed-income analyst with Mellon Bank. Madich has an MA from the University of Pittsburgh.

There are forty bonds in this $1.1 billion portfolio. Close to 100 percent of the fund's holdings are in United States government agency issues, such as T-Notes, GNMAs, FNMAs and FHLMCs. The average maturity of the bonds in the portfolio is ten years. All of the securities are backed by the United States government or its agencies. Unlike the other Federated fund managed by Madich, Federated Income, this one accepts accounts from anyone with as little as $500.

CURRENT INCOME ★ ★ ★
Over the past three years, the fund has had an average annual income stream of 9.3 percent. This is slightly higher than government securities funds in general.

EXPENSES ★
The expense ratio for Fund for U.S. has averaged 0.96 percent annually over the

past three years, slightly below its peer group average.

Over the past three years, the fund has had an average annual turnover rate of 84 percent annually. This turnover rate is close to half the rate seen by other government bond funds. Such a comparatively low rate often translates into higher total returns for the investors.

SUMMARY

The Fund for U.S. Government Securities is the fourth government securities fund offered by Federated Advisors that has made it into this book. It consistently ranks as "very good" in the four most important categories. Unlike three of its sister funds, this one is designed for the general public and does not require a large minimum investment. It is certainly a recommended choice.

Kemper U.S. Government Securities

Kemper Financial Services
120 South LaSalle Street
Chicago, IL 60603
1/800-621-1048

total return	★ ★ ★
risk	★
management	★ ★
current income	★ ★ ★ ★
expenses	★ ★ ★ ★
symbol KPGVX	14 points

TOTAL RETURN   ★ ★ ★

Over the past five years, Kemper U.S. Government Securities has taken $10,000 and turned it into $14,700 ($13,300 over three years and $31,100 over the past ten years). This translates into an average annual return of 8 percent over five years, 10 percent over the past three years, and 12 percent for the past decade. This is only one of two funds in this category to receive an "excellent" rating.

A $10,000 investment in the fund at its inception in 1979 was worth over $30,000 at the beginning of 1991. This translates into a compound return of 10 percent per year.

RISK/VOLATILITY   ★

Over the past five years, Kemper has been safer than 90 percent of all mutual funds; within its category it ranks in the bottom 40 percent. Since its inception in 1979, this fund has had one negative year (off 1 percent in 1980). It has underperformed the bond index only once in the past five years.

MANAGEMENT   ★ ★

Portfolio manager J. Patrick Beimford Jr. has been with the fund since 1981. Beimford joined Kemper Financial Services in 1976 as a fixed income portfolio manager. Previously, Beimford was a financial accountant with Inland Steel Company. He has an MBA from the University of Chicago and is a Chartered Financial Analyst.

Beimford's largest position is Treasury Notes, followed by government agency bonds from FNMA and FHLMC. The fund's average maturity is a conservative ten years. There are ten bonds in this $4.5 billion portfolio.

CURRENT INCOME   ★ ★ ★ ★

Over the past three years, Kemper's income has averaged 9.8 percent annually, making it one of the highest-yielding government funds.

EXPENSES ★ ★ ★ ★

The expense ratio for Kemper has averaged 0.5 percent for the last three years. This figure means that Kemper is able to operate for less than half the cost of a similar fund. Such costs are reflected in the fund's total return figures.

Over the past three years, the fund has had a disappointing average annual turnover rate of 257 percent. This rate is 58 percent greater than that found with the typical government fund.

SUMMARY

The combination of very good performance and good management makes Kemper U.S. Government Securities a worthy contender. The Kemper Group is known for its expertise with all kinds of fixed-income portfolios, and this fund is no exception.

Lord Abbett U.S. Government Securities

Lord Abbett
General Motors Building
767 Fifth Avenue
New York, NY 10153
1/800-874-3733

total return	★ ★ ★
risk	
management	★
current income	★ ★ ★ ★ ★
expenses	★ ★
symbol LAGVX	11 points

TOTAL RETURN ★ ★ ★

Over the past five years, Lord Abbett U.S. Government Securities has taken $10,000 and turned it into $14,700 ($13,000 over three years and $34,000 over the past ten years). This translates into an average annual return of 8 percent over five years, 9 percent over the past three years, and 13 percent for the decade.

RISK/VOLATILITY

Over the past five years, Lord Abbett has been safer than 80 percent of all mutual funds; within its category it ranks in the bottom 5 percent. During the past decade the fund has not had a negative year. It has underperformed the bond index in three of the past five years.

MANAGEMENT ★

Portfolio manager Carroll L. Coward has been with this fund since 1986. Prior to joining Lord Abbett & Company, she was the senior portfolio manager for the Bank of New York. Coward received her MA in economics from New York University in 1989.

One hundred percent of this fund is invested in bonds with an average weighted maturity of twelve years; over 60 percent of its assets are invested in four GNMAs. There are fifteen issues in this $1.5 billion portfolio. Coward has positioned the fund so that it will do very well on current income and total return if interest rates fall.

CURRENT INCOME ★ ★ ★ ★ ★

Over the past three years, the Lord Abbett U.S. Government Securities has averaged an annual income of 10.8 percent, the second-highest government bond listed in this book.

EXPENSES   ★ ★

The expense ratio for Lord Abbett has averaged 0.88 percent for the last three years, lower than its category's average of 1 percent.

Over the past three years, the average government fund has had an average annual turnover rate of 163 percentl. Lord Abbett has averaged 400 percent over the same period, making it the highest in this section.

SUMMARY

Lord Abbett U.S. Government Securities is designed for the investor seeking current income and only somewhat concerned with total return. It is only recommended for someone who can live with quite a bit of volatility.

Merrill Lynch Federal Securities

Merrill Lynch Funds Distributors
P.O. Box 9011
Princeton, NJ 08543
1/800-637-3863

total return	★ ★ ★ ★	
risk	★ ★ ★	
management	★ ★ ★	
current income	★ ★ ★	
expenses	★ ★	
symbol MLFSX	15 points	

TOTAL RETURN ★ ★ ★ ★

Over the past five years, Merrill Lynch Federal Securities has taken $10,000 and turned it into $15,400 ($13,300 over three years). This translates into an average annual return of 9 percent over five years and 10 percent over the past three years.

RISK/VOLATILITY ★ ★ ★

Over the past five years, Merrill Lynch has been safer than over 95 percent of all mutual funds; within its category it ranks in the top 25 percent. Since its inception in 1984 this fund has not had a negative year, but has underperformed the bond index in two of the past five years.

MANAGEMENT ★ ★ ★

Portfolio manager Gregory M. Maunz has been with this fund since 1984. He also manages five other funds for Merrill Lynch. Prior to joining Merrill Lynch, Maunz was an investment officer at Empire of America. He has an MBA from NYU.

The portfolio is comprised almost completely of mortgage-backed securities: FHLMCs, FNMAs, and GNMAs. The fund's average maturity is eleven years. There are forty issues in this $2.4 billion portfolio.

CURRENT INCOME ★ ★ ★

Over the past three years, Merrill Lynch Federal Securities has averaged an annual income stream of 9.3 percent, one of the lowest income levels for any government fund in this book. This rate is still higher than its industry norm of 8.8 percent.

EXPENSES ★ ★

The expense ratio over the past three years for Merrill has averaged 0.73 percent, about 30 percent less than its peers.

Over the past three years, the fund has had an average annual turnover rate of 287 percent. This figure is well above the government bond fund average of 163 percent and 155 percent for mortgage-backed portfolios.

SUMMARY

Merrill Lynch Federal Securities is a good performer in all categories. The returns for this fund are superior. It does not excel in any given area, but it is quite consistent.

Putnam U.S. Government Income
Putnam Financial Services
1 Post Office Square
Boston, MA 02109
1/800-225-1581

total return	★ ★ ★ ★	
risk	★ ★ ★ ★	
management	★ ★ ★ ★	
current income	★ ★ ★ ★	
expenses	★ ★ ★	
symbol PGSIX	19 points	

TOTAL RETURN ★ ★ ★ ★
Over the past five years, Putnam U.S. Government Income has taken $10,000 and turned it into $15,400 ($13,300 over three years). This translates into an average annual return of 9 percent over five years and 10 percent over the past three years.

RISK/VOLATILITY ★ ★ ★ ★
Over the past five years, Putnam has been safer than 95 percent of all mutual funds; within its category it ranks in the top 5 percent for stability. Since its inception in 1984 the fund has not had a negative year, but it has underperformed the bond index in four of the past five years.

MANAGEMENT ★ ★ ★ ★
Jaclyn S. Conrad has been the Putnam manager since 1987. She came to Putnam from the Colonial Group. Conrad is a Chartered Financial Analyst and has an MBA from Michigan State University. She has over twelve years of investment experience.

The prospectus restricts the fund to United States Treasuries and GNMAs. Close to 50 percent of the fund is invested in GNMAs, with the balance in T-Notes. Average maturity for this $1.6 billion portfolio is ten years. Conrad's main objective is current income and preservation of investors' capital.

CURRENT INCOME ★ ★ ★ ★
Over the past three years, Putnam U.S. Government has averaged an annual income stream of 9.8 percent, higher than its industry average of 8.8 percent.

EXPENSES ★ ★ ★
The expense ratio for this fund has averaged 0.61 percent annually for the last three years. This is almost half the level found with the typical government fund.

Over the past three years, Putnam has had an average annual turnover rate of 89 percent, making it one of the lowest within the government bond category.

SUMMARY

This is the perfect fund for the risk conscious investor. Virtually no other fund is rated so highly in the area of risk management. Overall fund management is also superior. Putnam U.S. Government Guaranteed Securities is designed for the conservative shareholder satisfied with a high current income and total return.

Vanguard Fixed-Income GNMA

Vanguard Group
Vanguard Financial Center
Valley Forge, PA 19482
1/800-662-7447

total return	★ ★ ★ ★ ★	
risk	★	
management	★ ★ ★ ★	
current income	★ ★ ★	
expenses	★ ★ ★ ★ ★	
symbol VFIIX	18 points	

TOTAL RETURN   ★ ★ ★ ★ ★

Over the past five years, Vanguard Fixed-Income GNMA has taken $10,000 and turned it into $15,400 ($13,700 over three years and $34,000 over ten years). This translates into an average annual return of 9 percent over five years, 11 percent over the past three years, and 13 percent for the decade.

RISK/VOLATILITY   ★

Over the past five years, Vanguard Fixed-Income GNMA has been safer than 90 percent of all mutual funds; within its category it ranks as "average." Since its 1980 inception, this fund has not had a single negative year. Over the past five years, it has underperformed the bond index twice.

MANAGEMENT   ★ ★ ★ ★

Portfolio manager Paul Sullivan has overseen the fund's operations since its inception in 1980. He has over twenty-six years of investment experience. Paul D. Kaplan is the fund's co-manager; he has an MS from MIT and over twelve years investment experience.

The fund is made up exclusively of GNMAs with an average life of twelve years. Sullivan plans to hold these mortgage-backed securities until maturity. There are twenty-five issues in this $2.3 billion portfolio.

Mortgage-backed securities such as GNMAs, which have coupons significantly higher than current market rates, are often prepaid. To reduce prepayment risk, management maintains an average coupon that is normally only slightly above the GNMA market's current coupon. This strategy allows the portfolio to maintain both a competitive yield and a reasonably predictable income stream.

CURRENT INCOME   ★ ★ ★

Over the past three years, Vanguard has averaged an annual income stream of 9.3 percent, a higher-than-average rate for the government and mortgage-backed funds.

EXPENSES   ★ ★ ★ ★ ★
The expense ratio for Vanguard Fixed-Income GNMA has averaged 0.34 percent annually for the last three years. This makes it the lowest of all government funds in the book.

Over the past three years, the fund has had an incredibly low average annual turnover rate of 13 percent. Such a rate is 50 percent less than its closest competitor.

SUMMARY
Investing in GNMA securities assures the timely payment of interest and principal but does not provide stability in either yield or price. In addition, interest rate changes affect the price of a GNMA far differently than they do a conventional bond. This difference is due to prepayment risk.

Each GNMA security consists of a pool of individual mortgages; the GNMA price reflects the rate at which the marketplace assumes the mortgages in the pool will be prepaid. Fluctuations in interest rates change the assumed prepayments, thereby changing the average maturity, and hence the price. It is because of prepayment risk, which is unique to mortgage securities, that GNMA securities offer a higher yield than other debt instruments with the full-faith backing of the United States government. Vanguard reduces such prepayment risk by the way in which it selects a GNMA.

Vanguard Fixed-Income GNMA demonstrates that you do not need much activity to create an excellent track record. This fund is not for the risk-wary investor, but ranks extremely well in all other categories. It is an ideal candidate for the portfolio looking for the highest possible total return

Growth Funds

These funds generally seek capital appreciation, with current income as a distant secondary concern. Growth funds typically invest in United States common stocks, do not deal in speculative issues, and avoid aggressive trading techniques. The goal of most of these funds is *long-term* growth. The approaches used to attain this appreciation can vary significantly among growth funds.

Over the past fifteen years, growth stocks have outperformed corporate and government bonds by a third. From 1975-1989, common stocks have averaged 14 percent compounded per year, versus 10 percent for bonds. A $10,000 investment in stocks grew to over $70,750 over the past fifteen years; a similar initial investment in corporate bonds grew to $42,000.

Growth stocks have outperformed bonds in every single decade. If George Washington had invested $1 in common stocks with an average return of 12 percent, his investment would be worth over $111 billion today. If George had been a little lucky and averaged 14 percent on his stock portfolio, his portfolio would be large enough to pay our national debt two-and-a-half times over!

Looking at a shorter time frame, common stocks have also fared quite well. A dollar invested in stocks in 1941 grew to over $285 by the beginning of 1991. This translates into an average compound return of 12 percent per year. Over the past fifty years the worst year for common stocks was 1974, when a loss of 26 percent was suffered. One year later, these same stocks posted a gain of 37 percent. The best year so far has been 1958, when growth stocks posted a gain of 43 percent.

There are 246 funds that make up the category "growth." Total market capitalization of this category is $80 billion.

Over the past three years, growth funds have had an average compound return of 12 percent per year. The *annual* return for the past five years has been 10 percent; 13 percent for the past ten years. The standard deviation for growth funds has been 4.4 percent over the past three years. This means these funds have been more volatile than any other category except aggressive growth and metals funds.

Growth funds should be a part of everyone's holdings. They should make up no more than 25 percent in a *diversified*, conservative portfolio, 50 percent for the moderate risk-taker, and 75 percent for the aggressive investor.

The sample portfolio shown in chapter VI recommends a 10 percent commitment to this category for the moderate and aggressive portfolio. As is true with any category of mutual funds, whenever larger dollar amounts are involved, more than one fund per category should be used.

AIM Weingarten

AIM Distributors
11 Greenway Plaza, Suite 1919
Houston, TX 77046
1/800-231-0803

total return	★ ★ ★ ★ ★
risk	
management	★ ★
current income	
expenses	★ ★
symbol WEINX	9 points

TOTAL RETURN   ★ ★ ★ ★ ★

Over the past five years, AIM Weingarten has taken $10,000 and turned it into $21,900 ($18,200 over three years and $52,300 for the past ten years). This translates into an average annual return of 17 percent over five years, 22 percent over the past three years, and 18 percent for the decade.

Over the past fifteen years, the fund's price has increased by almost 2,200 percent, compared to the S & P 500's 905 percent. Over the past ten years, the fund has gone up 600 percent, compared to 395 percent for the general stock market.

RISK/VOLATILITY

Over the past five years, AIM Weingarten has been *riskier* than 75 percent of all mutual funds; within its category it ranks in the bottom 40 percent. During this time, the fund has not had one negative year and has underperformed the S & P 500 only once.

MANAGEMENT   ★ ★

Harry Hutzler started the fund in 1969 and continues to manage it today. He has beaten the market by at least two-to-one, sometimes three-to-one, in every rolling ten-year period since 1969.

Hutzler does not care about the general economy or interest rates. He rejects the idea of picking industries and thinks market timing is a big mistake. He stays fully invested at all times. Hutzler believes there are imperfections in the efficient market theory (every company already trades for what it is worth; stocks are selling at their correct price because everything is known about the company) and is always looking for ways to detect them. A company's "earnings surprise" is one of the ways he picks stocks.

According to Hutzler, studies have show that about 65 percent of the time an "earnings surprise" is followed by another "earnings surprise" three months later. The theory also works the other way; when a company comes out with lower-than-expected growth, 70 percent of the time the following quarter is even worse.

The fund is evenly divided between blue chip stocks with long-term earnings records and issues that can can fluctuate widely. Management may look at more than a thousand different stocks before it settles on adding or replacing ten issues. Hutzler buys a stock with "the idea of holding it until something goes wrong. Sooner or later, something always does."

Management's philosophy can be summed up with a quote from Hutzler: "All I'm trying to do is be right more often than I'm wrong. If I'm right 55 percent to 60 percent of the time, I get very good results. That's all you can really hope for in this business."

The fund comprises ninety stocks with a total market capitalization of $800 million. The median market capitalization of the portfolio's typical stock is $5.4 billion, 49 percent the size of the average stock in the S & P 500. Over 95 percent of the company's holdings are in stocks, with the balance in cash. The stocks in the portfolio are from companies that, over the past decade, have grown much faster than the economy as a whole, very consistently, with earnings higher every year. Management concentrates on capital appreciation; dividend yield is unimportant. Such a strategy is very appealing to the moderate- and high-bracket taxpayer.

CURRENT INCOME
Over the past three years, the average growth fund has averaged an annual income stream of 2.4 percent, compared to Weingarten's income stream of 0.8 percent. This rate is lower than any other growth fund featured in the book. Fortunately for the fund, the vast majority of growth fund buyers are not concerned with dividends.

EXPENSES   ★ ★
The expense ratio for Weingarten has averaged 1.2 percent for the last three years. This is 20 percent less than its peer group average.

Over the past three years, the average growth fund has had an average turnover rate of 90 percent annually. Weingarten has had a slightly higher turnover rate of 96 percent.

SUMMARY
Do not let some of the low ratings fool you. AIM Weingarten has an exceptional track record for the past three, five, and ten years. In fact, there are few funds that can boast such performance. Because of its risk level, however, the fund should only be part of a diversified portfolio.

AMCAP

American Funds Distributors
333 South Hope Street
Los Angeles, CA 90071
1/800-421-0180

total return	★ ★ ★ ★	
risk	★	
management	★ ★ ★ ★	
current income	★ ★	
expenses	★ ★ ★ ★	
symbol AMCPX	15 points	

TOTAL RETURN   ★ ★ ★ ★

Over the past five years, the AMCAP has taken $10,000 and turned it into $18,400 ($15,200 over three years and $40,500 over the past decade). This translates into an average annual return of 13 percent over five years, 15 percent over the past three years, and 15 percent for the decade.

A $10,000 investment at the mid-1967 inception of the fund was worth over $140,000 by the beginning of 1991. This translates into an average compound return of 12 percent per year.

RISK/VOLATILITY   ★

Over the past five years, AMCAP has been more volatile than 65 percent of all mutual funds; within its category it ranks in the top 40 percent. During the past decade the fund has had only one negative year (off 1 percent in 1984). It has underperformed the S & P 500 four times over the past five years but outperformed the S & P 500 in every one of the thirteen ten-year periods since its inception.

MANAGEMENT   ★ ★ ★ ★

Capital Research has managed this fund since its 1967 inception. Management invests primarily in financially strong, rapidly growing companies. The fund can be quite defensive; its cash reserves have frequently been in the 20 percent range. Fund management is known for its conservative and consistent approach.

AMCAP is a member of the American Funds Group, a family of mutual funds managed by Capital Research and Management Company. The organization's roots reach back almost sixty years to 1931. Over this long span—years during which the world has seen war, peace, recession, depression, prosperity, inflation, and unprecedented political, social, and technological change—Capital Research has achieved superior long-term investment results.

Last year, AMCAP appeared on *Forbes* magazine's Honor Roll for the tenth consecutive year. That is longer than any other fund on the list. The list recognizes outstanding performance in up and down markets. There are ninety stocks in this

$1.9 billion portfolio. 90 percent of the fund's holdings are in common stocks, with the balance in cash and bonds. The median market capitalization of the portfolio's typical stock is $4.1 billion, 37 percent the size of the average stock in the S & P 500.

CURRENT INCOME   ★ ★

Over the past three years, AMCAP has averaged an annual income stream of 2.1 percent, similar to the growth fund average of 2.4 percent.

EXPENSES   ★ ★ ★ ★

The expense ratio for AMCAP has averaged 0.68 percent for the last five years. This is one of the lowest of any growth fund in the book.

Over the past three years, the fund has had an average annual turnover rate of 15 percent. This is an extremely low rate, the third lowest in the group.

SUMMARY

AMCAP Fund should be commended for its consistency. This is one of the few instances where more than just the numbers need to be reviewed. It is recommended without any hesitation. Management does not get any better than Capital Guardian. Risk management is excellent when viewed over a lengthy period.

Franklin Growth

Franklin Distributors
777 Mariners Island Boulevard
San Mateo, CA 94404
1/800-342-5236

total return	★ ★ ★ ★	
risk	★ ★ ★ ★	
management	★ ★ ★ ★	
current income	★ ★	
expenses	★ ★ ★ ★	
symbol FKGRX	18 points	

TOTAL RETURN ★ ★ ★ ★

Over the past five years, Franklin Growth has taken $10,000 and turned it into $19,300 ($14,800 over three years and $40,500 over the past ten years). This translates into an average annual return of 14 percent over five years, 14 percent over the past three years, and 15 percent for the decade.

The fund began operations in 1949. A $10,000 investment in the fund had grown to over $800,000 by the beginning of 1991. This translates into an average compound rate of 11 percent per year.

RISK/VOLATILITY ★ ★ ★ ★

Over the past five years, Franklin Growth Fund has been safer than over 60 percent of all mutual funds; within its category it ranks in the top 5 percent. During the past decade the fund has had only one negative year. Over the past five years, the fund has underperformed the S & P 500 three times.

MANAGEMENT ★ ★ ★ ★

Portfolio manager Jerry Palameri has been with Franklin since 1964. He received his BA in economics from Williams College. His management technique can be described as long-term quality investing. The fund likes to find the very best company in any given industry. Palameri looks at the long term, although you would not know it by looking at the fund's exceptional short- and medium-term performance.

There are seventy stocks in this $200 million portfolio. Such a small size translates into flexibility not found with other funds. Close to 90 percent of the fund's holdings are in common stocks, with the balance in cash. The median market capitalization of the portfolio's typical stock is $6.8 billion, 62 percent the size of the average stock in the S & P 500.

CURRENT INCOME ★ ★

Over the past three years, Franklin has averaged an annual income stream of 2.3 percent, identical to its peer group.

EXPENSES   ★ ★ ★ ★
The expense ratio for Franklin Growth has averaged 0.75 percent, half of what it normally costs to run a similar fund. Lower operating costs translate into higher net returns for investors.

Over the past three years, the fund has had an incredibly low turnover rate, averaging less than 1 percent per year. This is the lowest turnover rate of any growth fund by a wide margin. it is also the lowest of *any* fund in the book. This "buy-and-hold" strategy has paid off handsomely in the fund's total return figures.

SUMMARY
Franklin Growth fund should be seriously considered by any conservative investor who wants exposure in United States stocks. Management, risk reduction, and safety are superior.

Growth Fund of America

American Funds Distributors
333 South Hope St.
Los Angeles, CA 90071
1/800-421-0180

total return	★ ★ ★ ★ ★
risk	★
management	★ ★ ★ ★
current income	★ ★
expenses	★ ★ ★ ★
symbol AGTHX	16 points

TOTAL RETURN   ★ ★ ★ ★ ★

Over the past five years, Growth Fund of America (GFA) has taken $10,000 and turned it into $19,300 ($16,000 over three years and $40,500 over the past ten years). This translates into an average annual return of 14 percent over five years, 17 percent over the past three years, and 15 percent for the decade.

A $10,000 investment at the fund's inception in late 1973 grew to over $128,000 by the beginning of 1991. This translates into an average compound rate of 17 percent per year.

RISK/VOLATILITY   ★

Over the past five years, GFA has been riskier than 70 percent of all mutual funds. Within its category it is safer than 60 percent of its peers. During the past decade the fund has had only two negative years. It has underperformed the S & P 500 three times over the past five years.

There have been seven ten-year periods since GFA's inception. The fund has beat the S & P 500 in every one of those periods.

MANAGEMENT   ★ ★ ★ ★

As with other members of the American Funds family, GFA is run by a management team. Capital Research has overseen fund operations since its 1973 inception. The fund's track record reflects its success at selecting industry groups and its effective cash management skills. Cash reserves have sometimes been as high as 25 percent of the portfolio's total assets.

GFA invests in a variety of companies characterized by superior earnings growth. Recently it was named to *Forbes* magazine's Honor Roll for the sixth consecutive year in recognition of outstanding performance in up and down markets. GFA was one of only nineteen funds to make the list.

There are 110 stocks in this $2.1 billion portfolio. Close to 80 percent of the fund's holdings are in common stocks, with the balance in cash. The median market capitalization of the portfolio's typical stock is $3.7 billion, 34 percent the size of the average stock in the S & P 500.

CURRENT INCOME   ★ ★
Over the past three years, GFA's average annual income stream has averaged 2.4 percent, similar to the industry norm.

EXPENSES   ★ ★ ★ ★
The expense ratio for this fund has averaged 0.76 percent for each of the last five years. This is about half the average expense level for all growth funds.

Over the past five years, the average growth fund has had an average turnover rate of 90 percent annually. GFA has had a rate of 22 percent, one of the very lowest in the group.

SUMMARY
Growth Fund of America is another thoroughbred in the American Funds family stable. Its track record and management are excellent. Because of its only moderate safety level, it is recommended for the diversified portfolio. Despite this mild warning, it is still a top choice for a growth fund.

Guardian Park Avenue

Guardian Investor Services
201 Park Avenue South
New York, NY 10003
1/800-221-3253

total return	★ ★ ★	
risk	★	
management	★ ★	
current income	★ ★ ★ ★	
expenses	★ ★ ★ ★	
symbol GPAFX	14 points	

TOTAL RETURN ★ ★ ★

Over the past five years, Guardian Park Avenue has taken $10,000 and turned it into $16,100 ($13,700 over three years and $44,100 over the past ten years). This translates into an average annual return of 10 percent over five years, 11 percent over the past three years, and 16 percent for the decade.

A $10,000 investment at the fund's inception in 1972 was worth over $130,000 at the beginning of 1991. This translates into an average compound return of 15 percent per year.

RISK/VOLATILITY ★

Over the past five years, Guardian has been more volatile than 70 percent of all mutual funds; within its category it ranks in the top 60 percent for safety. During the past decade the fund has not had one negative year. The fund has shown positive returns every year except 1990 since its 1974 inception. Over the past five years it has underperformed the S & P 500 three times.

MANAGEMENT ★ ★

Charles E. Albers has been the fund's portfolio manager since its inception in 1972. Albers has an MBA from Columbia University and is a Chartered Financial Analyst. He was an analyst at Value Line before joining Guardian Life.

Albers subscribes to several research services and filters their opinions through his own home-brewed scoring system. He keeps an eye out for stocks that have fallen substantially from highs over the past five years. According to Albers, they tend to produce above-average results over the next one to two years.

Another favorite strategy employed by Albers is the "neglected stock effect." To measure this, he simply "counts noses" of analysts who follow a company and then ranks the stocks from least covered to most covered.

The fund selects individual securities for investing by analyzing a company's business fundamentals to determine whether the current stock price represents good relative value in the marketplace. A modest exposure to metals stocks, convertibles, and cash has helped Albers prepare for virtually any kind of market.

There are 175 stocks in this $220 million portfolio. Close to 80 percent of the fund's holdings are in common stocks, with the balance in convertibles and cash. The median market capitalization of the portfolio's typical stock is $600 million, a mere 6 percent the size of the average stock in the S & P 500.

CURRENT INCOME   ★ ★ ★ ★
Over the past three years, the fund has averaged an annual income stream of 3.4 percent, greater than its group average of 2.4 percent.

EXPENSES   ★ ★ ★ ★
The expense ratio for Guardian has averaged 0.69 percent annually for the last three years, half the cost of running the average growth fund. This is very impressive, particularly for such a small fund.

Over the past three years, Guardian has had an average turnover rate of 37 percent annually; this figure is 60 percent lower than its peer group average.

SUMMARY
Guardian Park Avenue should be noted for its consistency in producing above-market performance figures. The fund is a very good addition for the diversified investor.

IAI Regional

IAI Funds
1100 Dain Tower, P.O. Box 357
Minneapolis, MN 55440
1/612-371-7780

total return	★ ★ ★ ★ ★	
risk	★ ★ ★ ★	
management	★ ★ ★ ★	
current income	★	
expenses	★ ★ ★	
symbol IARGX	17 points	

TOTAL RETURN   ★ ★ ★ ★ ★
Over the past five years, IAI Regional has taken $10,000 and turned it into $21,000 ($16,900 over three years and $52,300 over 10 years.). This translates into an average annual return of 16 percent over five years, 19 percent over the past three years, and 18 percent over the decade.

RISK/VOLATILITY   ★ ★ ★ ★
Over the past five years, IAI Regional has been safer than half of all mutual funds; within its category it has been safer than 85 percent of its peers. Since its 1980 inception, the fund has had only one negative year (off 2 percent in 1984). It has underperformed the S & P 500 once in the past five years.

MANAGEMENT   ★ ★ ★ ★
Portfolio manager Bing Carlin has been with IAI Regional since its inception. Carlin concentrates exclusively on unassuming, medium-sized Midwestern growth companies in his own back yard, particular attention to company management. Thus management concentrates on fewer than 300 stocks located in one geographic area. Carlin is certainly a specialist.

IAI Regional invests at least 80 percent of its equity in companies headquartered in Minnesota, Wisconsin, Iowa, Nebraska, Montana, North Dakota, and South Dakota. There are fewer than seventy different issues in the portfolio. The fund can be quite defensive; cash holdings of 20 percent or more are not uncommon. Total fund value is close to $211 million, half the size of the average growth fund. The median market capitalization of the portfolio's typical stock is $660 million, 6 percent the size of the average stock in the S & P 500.

CURRENT INCOME   ★
Over the past three years, IAI Regional has averaged an annual income stream of 2 percent, a little lower than average for a growth fund.

EXPENSES   ★ ★ ★

The expense ratio for IAI has averaged 0.9 percent for the last three years. This is 60 percent of the average growth fund.

Over the past three years, the fund has had an average annual turnover rate of 98 percent, slightly higher than its group's average.

SUMMARY

The prospective investor should not bypass IAI Region because of its being rather specialized in scope. On the contrary, credit should be given to fund manager Carlin. He has the sensible approach of concentrating on areas in which he has expertise and keen insight, particularly in the area of corporate management. IAI has proven capable in providing solid returns along with preserving capital.

IDEX

Pioneer Western Distributors
201 Highland Avenue
Largo, FL 34640
1/800-237-3055

total return	★ ★ ★ ★ ★	
risk	★ ★	
management	★ ★	
current income	★	
expenses	★ ★	
symbol IDEFX	12 points	

TOTAL RETURN ★ ★ ★ ★ ★

Over the past five years, the IDEX Fund has taken $10,000 and turned it into $21,900 ($20,000 over three years). This translates into an average annual return of 17 percent over five years and 26 percent over the past three years.

RISK/VOLATILITY ★ ★

Over the past five years, IDEX has been more volatile than 60 percent of all mutual funds, 70 percent less risky than other mutual funds whose investment objective is "aggressive growth" or "small company." During the past five years the fund has had no negative years, but has underperformed the S & P 500 four of these five years.

MANAGEMENT ★ ★

The fund looks for stocks based on asset value, cash flow, and earnings per share. Management also looks at a company's revenue, as well as at its dividend record. Investment style can best be described as "fundamental."

IDEX has been overseen by Thomas F. Marisco since its 1985 inception. Janus Capital is the fund's sub-adviser. The fund's small size lets it enjoy flexibility not often found with a top-performing portfolio.

There are thirty stocks in this $105 million portfolio. Close to 65 percent of the fund's holdings are in common stocks, with the balance in cash. The median market capitalization of the portfolio's typical stock is $1.9 billion, 17 percent the size of the average stock in the S & P 500.

CURRENT INCOME ★

Over the past three years, the average aggressive growth fund has averaged an annual income stream of 2.4 percent, compared to IDEX's income stream of 1.2 percent. The lower-than-normal dividend rate helps to reduce tax liability. Growth funds should be purchased for capital appreciation purposes, not current income.

EXPENSES   ★ ★

The expense ratio for IDEX has averaged about 1.4 percent for each of the last three years. IDEX's expense level is slightly less than the ratio found with the typical growth fund. Since expenses are taken off the top of shareholder profits, this average expense ratio helps to enhance the bottom line for investors.

Over the past three years, the average growth fund has had an average turnover rate of 90 percent annually. IDEX has had a significantly higher turnover rate of 131 percent. A high turnover rate means increased transactions costs for a fund, slightly reducing performance results.

SUMMARY

IDEX must be commended for its strong performance since inception and its unique management style. Although difficult to define, this style has led to strong, consistent performance as a result of the decision-making ability of its management. It is to be congratulated for having done so well with only a modest amount of backing.

Janus

Janus Group
100 Fillmore St., Suite 300
Denver, CO 80206
1/800-525-3713

total return	★ ★ ★ ★ ★
risk	★ ★ ★ ★
management	★ ★ ★ ★
current income	★ ★ ★
expenses	★ ★ ★
symbol JANSX	19 points

TOTAL RETURN   ★ ★ ★ ★ ★

Over the past five years, Janus has taken $10,000 and turned it into $20,100 ($19,500 over three years and $52,300 over the past ten years). This translates into an average annual return of 15 percent over five years, 25 percent over the past three years, and 18 percent for the decade.

RISK/VOLATILITY   ★ ★ ★ ★

Over the past five years, Janus has been safer than half of all mutual funds; within its category it ranks in the top 10 percent. During the past ten years the fund has had only two negative years (off 0.1 percent in 1984 and 0.75 percent in 1990). It has underperformed the S & P 500 in two of the past five years.

MANAGEMENT   ★ ★ ★ ★

Portfolio manager James Craig has been the fund's manager since 1985. Prior to joining the Janus Group in 1983, Craig was an investment analyst with Trust Company of the West. He received his MBA at Wharton, where he was also a teaching assistant.

Janus' first goal is capital preservation. Management likes to buy stocks for the same reasons it would buy the company. It does not buy just because the market is going up. When the market is too high in the eyes of management, it will increase its cash position by selling off the full-valued holdings. Normally this strategy will protect the fund when downturns occur. Craig emphasizes that they are not market timers. He believes the chances of timing the market are about one in three, and that would give him an erratic record.

Instead, Janus prefers to emphasize stock picking, but within the context of the general economic environment. According to Craig: "We make money by finding things that haven't been exploited, where the market is inefficient, where there's a new development that's going to make someone own that stock in the future."

Interestingly, Craig does not change his risk level as the market gets higher. If he is in a period where he cannot find anything he likes, he will be 50 percent in cash, but the 50 percent that is invested will always be invested aggressively in equities he feels have high growth potential.

Management focuses almost all of its stock exposure to just four industry groups. Almost 25 percent of the total fund's assets are invested in just five stocks. The fund itself holds fewer than fifty stocks; total fund capitalization is over $1.2 billion. Close to 65 percent of the fund's holdings are in common stocks, with the balance in cash. The median market capitalization of the portfolio's typical stock is $2.9 billion, 26 percent the size of the average stock in the S & P 500.

CURRENT INCOME   ★ ★ ★
Over the past three years, Janus has averaged a high annual income stream of 2.93 percent.

EXPENSES   ★ ★ ★
The expense ratio for Janus has averaged just under 1 percent for the last three years, well below the industry average of 1.5 percent.

Over the past three years, the average annual turnover rate for the fund has been 229 percent, the second-highest level for any growth fund in this book.

SUMMARY
Janus has proven itself one of the strongest funds in its category, managing to turn out excellent results with superior risk reduction and management. The fund's high concentration in a few dozen stocks is somewhat disturbing, but you cannot argue with success. This fund is a great addition to most portfolios.

Mathers

Mather Fund
100 Corporate North Suite 201
Bannockburn, IL 60015
1/800-962-3863

total return	★ ★ ★ ★	
risk	★ ★ ★ ★ ★	
management	★ ★ ★ ★	
current income	★ ★ ★ ★	
expenses	★ ★ ★	
symbol MATRX	20 points	

TOTAL RETURN   ★ ★ ★ ★

Over the past five years, Mathers has taken $10,000 and turned it into $18,400 ($13,700 over three years and $28,400 over the past ten years). This translates into an average annual return of 13 percent over five years, 11 percent over the past three years, and 11 percent for the decade.

A $10,000 investment in the fund fifteen years ago is worth over $110,000 today. Since its inception twenty-four years ago the fund has appreciated over 2,900 percent, compared to 775 percent for the Dow Jones Industrial Average; over this time frame the Consumer Price Index (CPI) has risen close to 300 percent. The fund's compound annual rate of return since inception has been 15 percent, compared to 9 percent for the Dow and 5.9 percent for the CPI.

RISK/VOLATILITY   ★ ★ ★ ★ ★

Over the past five years, Mathers has been safer than 70 percent of all mutual funds; within its category it ranks in the top 5 percent. During the past five years, the fund has not had one negative year, but has underperformed the S & P 500 four times.

MANAGEMENT   ★ ★ ★ ★

Portfolio managers Henry G. Van der Eb and Robert J. Reynolds have been with Mathers since 1971. Both are Chartered Financial Analysts. Van der Eb received his MBA from Northwestern in 1970. Reynolds got his MBA from Harvard in 1977. Management also oversees investments for Indiana University and the University of Bridgeport.

Management technique incorporates a very, very defensive stance. At times the fund holds more than 70 percent of its assets in cash. The managers believe that there is no point in buying when stocks are fairly or overvalued. Favorable risk-adjusted return has been achieved by increasing cash reserves when the risk/reward ratio for stocks is high and reducing cash reserves when the ratio is low. The fund's style is risk-averse. It will trade short-term opportunity for long-term safety of principal, while striving for superior long-term returns.

There are only three stocks in this $300 million portfolio. Just 8 percent of the fund's holdings are in common stocks, with the balance in cash, 16 percent, and bonds, 76 percent. The median market capitalization of the portfolio's typical stock is $2.1 billion, 19 percent the size of the average stock in the S & P 500.

CURRENT INCOME   ★ ★ ★ ★
Over the past three years, Mathers has averaged an annual income stream of 3.3 percent, a rate over a point higher than the group's average.

EXPENSES   ★ ★ ★
The expense ratio for the fund has averaged a low 0.94 percent annually for the last three years. This is 40 percent less than average.

Unfortunately, the fund has an incredibly high turnover rate of 218 percent. Performance can suffer when a lot of buying and selling are going on; nevertheless, this fund's total return has suffered very little despite extraordinary transaction costs.

SUMMARY
Mathers fits the bill of a growth fund for the conservative investor. Despite its current sizable cash holdings, this fund has proven capable of producing double-digit returns on a consistent basis.

Merrill Lynch Basic Value—Class A

Merrill Lynch Funds Distributors
P.O. Box 9011
Princeton, NJ 08543
1/800-637-3863

total return	★
risk	★ ★ ★
management	★ ★ ★ ★
current income	★ ★ ★ ★ ★
expenses	★ ★ ★ ★ ★
symbol MVBVX	18 points

TOTAL RETURN ★

Over the past five years, Merrill Lynch Basic Value—Class A has taken $10,000 and turned it into $15,400 ($13,300 over three years and $40,500 over the past ten years). This translates into an average annual return of 9 percent over five years, 10 percent over the past three years, and 15 percent for the decade. Despite its "fair" rating in this category, the fund consistently outperforms two-thirds of all other growth funds.

RISK/VOLATILITY ★ ★ ★

Over the past five years, Basic Value has been safer than half of all mutual funds; within its category it is less volatile than 80 percent of its group. During the past decade, the fund has had only one negative year. It has underperformed the S & P 500 in three of the past five years.

MANAGEMENT ★ ★ ★ ★

Paul M. Hoffmann has managed the fund since its 1977 inception; he has been with Merrill Lynch since 1971. Prior to joining Merrill Hoffman was a securities analyst at Lehman Brothers. He has attended NYU Business School and graduated from Hofstra University.

Management's technique is one that relies on patience. Hoffmann would prefer holding on to cash until stocks with above-market yields can be found. A large cash position results in disappointing performance during hot markets but provides an added measure of safety.

There are eighty-five stocks in this $1.3 billion portfolio. Close to 90 percent of the fund's holdings are in common stocks, with the balance in cash. The median market capitalization of the portfolio's typical stock is $4.8 billion, 43 percent the size of the average stock in the S & P 500.

CURRENT INCOME ★ ★ ★ ★ ★

Over the past three years, Basic Value has averaged an annual income stream of 4.6 percent, the highest of any growth fund in the book.

EXPENSES   ★ ★ ★ ★ ★

The expense ratio for Basic Value has been a nimble 0.58 percent over the past three years, the lowest of any growth fund found in this book.

Over the past three years, the fund has had an average annual turnover rate of 13 percent, lower than any other fund except one.

SUMMARY

Merrill Lynch Basic Value—Class A is primarily for the patient investor able to deal with moderate returns during periods when the fund retains large cash reserves. The holdings of this fund are far from glamorous but do offer potential for expansion. This is a strong choice for the risk-conscious investor looking for superior management.

Mutual Beacon

Heine Securities
51 John F. Kennedy Parkway
Short Hills, NJ 07078
1/800-553-3014

total return	★ ★ ★	
risk	★ ★ ★ ★ ★	
management	★ ★ ★ ★	
current income	★ ★ ★ ★ ★	
expenses	★ ★ ★ ★	
symbol BEGRX	21 points	

TOTAL RETURN   ★ ★ ★

Over the past five years, Mutual Beacon has taken $10,000 and turned it into $18,400 ($13,700 over three years and $31,100 over the past ten years). This translates into an average annual return of 13 percent over five years, 11 percent over the past three years, and 12 percent for the decade.

RISK/VOLATILITY   ★ ★ ★ ★ ★

Over the past five years, Mutual Beacon has been safer than 70 percent of all mutual funds; within its category it ranks in the top 5 percent. During the past five years the fund has not had one negative year, but it has underperformed the S & P 500 three times.

MANAGEMENT   ★ ★ ★ ★

Michael Price has been with Beacon since 1985. Management focuses its attention on issues involving bankruptcies and turnarounds. Price's conservative stance performs best during bear markets, but has proved far from disappointing even during strong bull markets. Frequently the fund's cash position exceeds 25 percent of the portfolio's total value. Price actively looks for many of the smaller-capitalized stocks.

There are 290 stocks in this $390 million portfolio. Close to 50 percent of the fund's holdings are in common stocks, with the balance in cash and bonds. The median market capitalization of the portfolio's typical stock is $1.1 billion, 10 percent the size of the average stock in the S & P 500. This fund has an initial minimum investment requirement of $50,000.

CURRENT INCOME   ★ ★ ★ ★ ★

Over the past three years, Beacon has averaged an annual income stream of 4.6 percent, a rate almost double its group average.

EXPENSES   ★ ★ ★ ★
The expense ratio for Mutual Beacon has averaged 0.7 percent for the last three years, 50 percent less than the average growth fund.

Over the past three years, the fund has had an average annual turnover rate of 76 percent, slightly lower than average.

SUMMARY
Mutual Beacon should be seriously considered by the investor in search of an extremely conservative growth vehicle. This fund provides protection during down markets and has proved capable during strong markets. Mutual Beacon offers extremely low risk coupled with strong results. Because of its minimum investment requirement, the fund is not for everyone.

Mutual Benefit

Mutual Benefit Financial
520 Broad Street
Newark, NJ 07101
1/800-333-4726

total return	★ ★ ★ ★
risk	★ ★ ★ ★
management	★ ★ ★ ★
current income	★ ★
expenses	★
symbol MUBFX	15 points

TOTAL RETURN ★ ★ ★ ★
Over the past five years, Mutual Benefit has taken $10,000 and turned it into $17,600 ($15,600 over three years and $44,100 over the past ten years). This translates into an average annual return of 12 percent over five years, 16 percent over the past three years, and 16 percent for the decade.

RISK/VOLATILITY ★ ★ ★ ★
Over the past five years, Mutual Benefit has been safer than half of all mutual funds; within its category it ranks in the top 15 percent. During the past five years the fund has had one negative year (off 1 percent in 1987), and has underperformed the bond index twice.

MANAGEMENT ★ ★ ★ ★
The fund has been run since 1981 by a management team put together by Markston Investment Management. The management company is headed by John Stone and Michael Mullarkey. Stone, who has a PhD from Cornell, was previously employed at the Ford Foundation and as an economist for the Federal Reserve Bank of New York. Mullarkey has an MBA from Harvard; he was previously employed by the Ford Foundation and Goldman Sachs.

Stone ignores a stock's price-earnings ratio, which many investors regard as gospel. Instead, he looks at a company's assets and calculates the price at which it might be bought. If the market price is 50 percent below that level, he is interested. Further, he is attracted to companies with long-entrenched, competent management whose products are established. Stone also likes firms with a lot of cash to spend on research and dividends.

Mutual Benefit spends time monitoring the shelf space allocated to the brands produced by prospective companies and their competitors. They count ad pages in magazines. They pace off square footage of new retail stores and count customers waiting in checkout lines. They tour factories and visit real estate sites. The survivors are typically thirty or fewer companies.

There are fifty-five stocks in this $34 million portfolio. Close to 90 percent of the fund's holdings are in common stocks, with the balance in cash. The median market capitalization of the portfolio's typical stock is $2.1 billion, 19 percent the size of the average stock in the S & P 500.

CURRENT INCOME   ★ ★
Over the past three years, Mutual Benefit has averaged an annual income stream of 2.4 percent, a rate similar to the industry's average.

EXPENSES   ★
The expense ratio for Benefit has averaged 1.4 percent for the last three years. This is almost 10 percent less than that experienced by the average growth fund.

Over the past three years, the fund has had an average annual turnover rate of 18 percent, one of the very lowest rates within its group.

SUMMARY
Mutual Benefit's record speaks for itself. This fund offers one of the best risk-adjusted returns of all equity funds. The fund has succeeded in producing such results with its sensible investment techniques.

New Economy

American Funds Distributor
333 South Hope Street
Los Angeles, CA 90071
1/800-421-0180

total return	★ ★ ★ ★
risk	★ ★
management	★ ★ ★
current income	★
expenses	★ ★ ★
symbol ANEFX	13 points

TOTAL RETURN ★ ★ ★ ★

Over the past five years, New Economy has taken $10,000 and turned it into $16,900 ($14,800 over three years). This translates into an average annual return of 11 percent over five years and 14 percent over the past three years.

A $10,000 investment at the early 1984 inception of the fund was worth over $25,000 by the beginning of 1991. This translates into an average compound return of 14 percent per year.

RISK/VOLATILITY ★ ★

Over the past five years, New Economy has been more volatile than 60 percent of all mutual funds; within its category it ranks in the top 30 percent for safety. Since its inception the fund has had only one negative year. It has underperformed the S & P 500 four of the past five years.

MANAGEMENT ★ ★ ★

Capital Research has managed the fund since its 1984 inception. Management emphasizes securities of companies in the services and information sector of the United States and elsewhere. This sector has grown much faster than the American economy as a whole and has held up much better whenever business slowed. Cash reserves rise to 20 percent whenever sustained bull markets occur. By taking profits, the fund is able to lock in profits and reduce risk.

There are eighty stocks in this $800 million portfolio. Close to 80 percent of the fund's holdings are in common stocks, with the balance in cash. The median market capitalization of the portfolio's typical stock is $4.2 billion, 38 percent the size of the average stock in the S & P 500.

CURRENT INCOME ★

Over the past five years, the fund has averaged an annual income stream of 2.2 percent, a little less than normal. Like other equity funds managed by Capital Research tax consequences to investors are a concern. By focusing on total return and a low turnover rate, current income taxes are minimized.

EXPENSES   ★ ★ ★
The expense ratio for New Economy has averaged 0.85 percent annually for the last three years. This is just over half the cost incurred by similar growth funds.

Over the past three years, the fund has had an average annual turnover rate of 16 percent. This is 80 percent less than its peer group. By limiting transaction costs, investors make more money. Low turnover also results in reduced *recognized* capital gains, something any taxpayer can appreciate.

SUMMARY
Since New Economy concentrates on the areas of service and information, this fund would be best suited for the investor who is a believer in the continued strength of these sectors. This fund has kept pace with the expanding service and information sectors. It is an exceptional choice for a diversified portfolio.

New York Venture

Venture Advisors
124 East Marcy Street
Santa Fe, NM 87501
1/800-545-2098

total return	★ ★ ★ ★ ★
risk	★ ★ ★ ★
management	★ ★ ★ ★
current income	★ ★ ★
expenses	★ ★ ★
symbol NYVTX	19 points

TOTAL RETURN ★ ★ ★ ★ ★

Over the past five years, New York Venture has taken $10,000 and turned it into $18,400 ($17,300 over three years and $48,100 over the past ten years). This translates into an average annual return of 13 percent over five years, 20 percent over the past three years, and 17 percent for the decade.

A $10,000 investment at the 1969 inception of the fund was worth over $145,000 by the beginning of 1990. This translates into an average compound return of 14 percent per year. This is one of the few funds that has outperformed the growth fund group average for nine of the last eleven years.

RISK/VOLATILITY ★ ★ ★ ★

Over the past five years, New York Venture has shown more stability than half of all mutual funds; within its category it ranks in the top 15 percent for safety. During the past decade the fund has had one negative year (off 1 percent in 1987). It has underperformed the S & P 500 only once during the past five years.

MANAGEMENT ★ ★ ★ ★

Portfolio manager Shelby M.C. Davis has been with New York Venture since its inception in 1969. His management technique has been described as that of a moderate contrarian. Davis focuses on companies having solid growth potential coupled with relatively low multiples. He places a great deal of emphasis on identifying future market trends, and also seeks to identify individual issues with a high degree of insider ownership, solid cash flow, a strong market niche, and a high earnings retention rate.

There are eighty stocks in this $350 million portfolio. Close to 95 percent of the fund's holdings are in common stocks, with the balance in cash. The median market capitalization of the portfolio's typical stock is $8.2 billion, 75 percent the size of the average stock in the S & P 500.

CURRENT INCOME   ★ ★ ★

Over the past three years, Venture has averaged an annual income stream of 2.9 percent, slightly higher than its industry average.

EXPENSES   ★ ★ ★

The expense ratio for Venture has averaged 1 percent, close to one-third leaner than the average growth fund.

Over the past three years, the fund has had an average turnover rate of 48 percent. This rate is well below its peer group rate of 90 percent.

SUMMARY

New York Venture stands out, with performance figures that place it in the top fifteenth percentile over the last five and ten years. The fund's success can largely be attributed to its sensible management technique. New York Venture has also successfully outperformed the S & P 500 in eight of the last ten years.

Phoenix Growth

Phoenix Equity Planning
101 Munson Street
Greenfield, MA 01301
1/800-243-4361

total return	★ ★ ★ ★ ★
risk	★ ★ ★ ★ ★
management	★ ★ ★ ★ ★
current income	★ ★ ★ ★
expenses	★ ★ ★
symbol PHGRX	22 points

TOTAL RETURN ★ ★ ★ ★ ★

Over the past five years, Phoenix Growth has taken $10,000 and turned it into $19,300 ($16,400 over three years and $61,900 over the past ten years). This translates into an average annual return of 14 percent over five years, 18 percent over the past three years, and 20 percent for the decade.

The fund began operations in 1976. An investment of $10,000 at its inception grew to over $106,000 by the beginning of 1990. This translates into an average compound rate of 18 percent per year.

RISK/VOLATILITY ★ ★ ★ ★ ★

Over the past five years, Phoenix Growth has been safer than 60 percent of all mutual funds; within its category it ranks in the top 5 percent. During the past decade the fund has not had a single negative year. It has underperformed the S & P 500 in two of the past five years.

MANAGEMENT ★ ★ ★ ★ ★

Portfolio manager Robert Chesek has been with Phoenix Growth since 1980. He was in the Investment Department at Chemical Bank before joining the Phoenix Group in 1968. He left Phoenix in 1972 to work for Travelers Insurance, then rejoined the company in 1980. Chesek graduated from NYU.

Management begins by looking at the entire economy, inflation expectations, and labor demographics. Chesek's management technique is one of extreme defensiveness. The fund raises its cash reserves to 20 percent or more when it is felt that the market is topping. Blue chip, high quality stocks make up the equity portion of the portfolio. The fund's largest sector weighting is the drug and health care industries.

There are sixty-five stocks in this $750 million portfolio. Close to 80 percent of the fund's holdings are in common stocks, with the balance in cash and bonds. The median market capitalization of the portfolio's typical stock is $7.8 billion, 71 percent the size of the average stock in the S & P 500.

CURRENT INCOME   ★ ★ ★ ★
Over the past three years, Phoenix has averaged an annual income stream of 3.1 percent, one of the higher rates found with growth funds.

EXPENSES   ★ ★ ★
The expense ratio for Phoenix has averaged 1 percent annually for the last three years. This is one-third less than its peer group.

Over the past three years, the fund averaged an annual turnover rate of 193 percent. This is one of the highest rates of any growth fund in this book.

SUMMARY
Phoenix Growth is for the defensive investor. Its track record, management, and risk control are simply excellent. The Phoenix family includes a modest number of funds, funds that consistently rank at the top. This one ranks in the top 3 percent for performance and risk management for the past decade. It should be considered the number one or two choice for anyone seeking a growth fund.

Security Equity

Security Distributors
700 Harrison
Topeka, KS 66636
1/800-888-2461

total return	★ ★ ★ ★
risk	★ ★ ★
management	★ ★ ★
current income	★
expenses	★ ★ ★
symbol SECEX	14 points

TOTAL RETURN   ★ ★ ★ ★

Over the past five years, Security Equity has taken $10,000 and turned it into $17,600 ($16,400 over three years and $34,000 over the past ten years). This translates into an average annual return of 12 percent over five years, 18 percent over the past three years, and 13 percent for the decade.

A $10,000 investment at the inception of the fund would be worth $290,000 at the beginning of 1990.

RISK/VOLATILITY   ★ ★ ★

Over the past five years, Security Equity has been more volatile than 60 percent of all mutual funds; within its category it is safer than 60 percent of its peers. During the past five years the fund has had only one negative year and has underperformed the S & P 500 three times.

MANAGEMENT   ★ ★ ★

Portfolio manager Terry Milberger has been with Security Equity since 1982. He brings more than fifteen years of investment experience to the fund. Milberger began as an investment analyst in the insurance industry; he was later a pension fund manager for a Houston bank. He has an MBA from the University of Kansas and is a Chartered Financial Analyst.

Management's investment philosophy is based on patience and geared toward the long-term investor. The portfolio for Security is designed to stay healthy in a down market. The fund will generally be fully invested in a diversified selection of common stocks. Milberger places emphasis on value and earnings momentum. The fund rarely finishes at the top but avoids the bottom.

There are sixty-five stocks in this $250 million portfolio. Close to 90 percent of the fund's holdings are in common stocks, with the balance in cash. The median market capitalization of the portfolio's typical stock is $5.3 billion, 48 percent the size of the average stock in the S & P 500.

CURRENT INCOME ★

Over the past three years, Security has averaged an annual income stream of 1.8 percent, somewhat below the industry average.

EXPENSES ★ ★ ★

The expense ratio for Security has averaged 0.9 percent annually for the last three years. This is quite low for a growth fund.

Over the past three years, the average annual turnover rate for Security has been 114 percent, a little higher than the traditional growth fund.

SUMMARY

Security Equity is a fine choice; it has a superior track record. Its safety factor is very good, as a result of management's disciplined approach to security selection.

Shearson Appreciation

Shearson Lehman Hutton
31 West 52nd Street
New York, NY 10019
1/800-451-2010

total return	★ ★ ★ ★
risk	★ ★ ★ ★
management	★ ★ ★ ★
current income	★ ★ ★
expenses	★ ★ ★
symbol SHAPX	18 points

TOTAL RETURN ★ ★ ★ ★

Over the past five years, Shearson Appreciation has taken $10,000 and turned it into $18,400 ($15,600 over three years and $44,100 over the past ten years). This translates into an average annual return of 13 percent over five years, 16 percent over the past three years, and 16 percent for the decade.

An investment in the fund at its 1969 inception had grown by over 758 percent by the beginning of 1991; thus, a $10,000 investment grew to over $85,000. This translates into an average compound rate of 16 percent per year.

RISK/VOLATILITY ★ ★ ★ ★

Over the past five years, Shearson Appreciation has been safer than half of all mutual funds; within its category it ranks as safer than over 85 percent of other growth funds. During the past decade the fund has not had a negative year. It has underperformed the S & P 500 in two of the past five years.

MANAGEMENT ★ ★ ★ ★

Portfolio managers Harry Cohen and Harold Williamson Jr., have been with the fund since 1981. Cohen has a PhD from Tufts University and has been a portfolio manager since 1968. Williamson has been a research analyst since 1946. Their management technique centers on high-quality, balanced holdings, attractive portfolio statistics, and strong performance figures. The fund looks at the long term.

There are 140 stocks in this $1.1 billion portfolio. Close to 90 percent of the fund's holdings are in common stocks, with the balance in cash. The median market capitalization of the portfolio's typical stock is $8.5 billion, 77 percent the size of the average stock in the S & P 500.

CURRENT INCOME ★ ★ ★

Over the past three years, Shearson Appreciation has averaged an annual income stream of 3 percent, compared to an industry average of 2.4 percent.

EXPENSES   ★ ★ ★
The expense ratio for Shearson Appreciation has averaged 0.9 percent, well below an industry group average of 1.5 percent.

Over the past three years, the fund has averaged an annual turnover rate of 25 percent, lower than most other growth funds.

SUMMARY
The strength of this fund is easily recognized when looking at its attractive record. Success is largely due to Shearson Appreciation's portfolio of high-quality holdings, selected to weather all investment climates with an emphasis on the long term. Shearson Appreciation consistently ranks as a superior choice.

Thomson Growth B

Thomson Investor Services
One Station Place
Stamford, CT 06902
1/800-628-1237

total return	★ ★ ★ ★ ★
risk	★ ★ ★
management	★ ★ ★
current income	
expenses	
symbol TGWBX	11 points

TOTAL RETURN ★ ★ ★ ★ ★
Over the past five years, Thomson Growth B has taken $10,000 and turned it into $20,100 ($16,900 over three years). This translates into an average annual return of 15 percent over five years and 19 percent over the past three years.

RISK/VOLATILITY ★ ★ ★
Over the past five years, Thomson has been safer than half of all mutual funds; within its category it ranks in the top 20 percent. Since the fund's 1984 inception, it has not had one negative year. It has underperformed the S & P 500 in only one of the past five years.

MANAGEMENT ★ ★ ★
Portfolio manager Irwin Smith has been the fund's manager since 1986. His management technique is quite different from that of other growth funds described in the book; he is the only featured manager who uses call writing, a defensive option-writing strategy. During its entire history the fund has only significantly underperformed the market once.

There are forty-two stocks in the entire fund. Close to 85 percent of the fund's holdings are in common stocks, with the balance in cash. The median market capitalization of the portfolio's typical stock is $9.5 billion, 86 percent the size of the average stock in the S & P 500.

CURRENT INCOME
Over the past three years, Growth B has averaged an annual income stream of 0.8 percent, a rate lower than any other growth fund in the book. This makes the fund particularly attractive for medium- and high-bracket taxpayers.

EXPENSES
The annual expense ratio for Thomson has averaged 1.7 percent for the last three years. This rate is slightly higher than its group's average.

Over the past three years, the traditional growth fund has had an average annual turnover rate of 90 percent. Growth B's turnover has been 92 percent.

SUMMARY
Thomson Growth B is an exceptional performer with very good risk management. Investors should note this fund's emphasis on the long-term time frame. The fund's somewhat different management approach makes it an ideal candidate when combined with another growth fund.

United Accumulative

Waddell & Reed
2400 Pershing Road, P.O. Box 418343
Kansas City, MO 64141
1/800-821-5664

total return	★ ★ ★	
risk	★ ★ ★ ★	
management	★ ★ ★	
current income	★ ★ ★ ★ ★	
expenses	★ ★ ★ ★ ★	
symbol UNACX	20 points	

TOTAL RETURN   ★ ★ ★

Over the past five years, United Accumulative has taken $10,000 and turned it into $16,100 ($14,100 over three years and $40,500 over the past ten years). This translates into an average annual return of 10 percent over five years, 12 percent over the past three years, and 15 percent for the decade.

A $10,000 investment in the fund at its 1940 inception was worth over $1,608,000 at the beginning of 1991. This translates into an average compound rate of 10 percent per year.

RISK/VOLATILITY   ★ ★ ★ ★

Over the past five years, United Accumulative has been safer than half of all mutual funds; within its growth category it ranks in the top 15 percent. During the past decade the fund has had only one negative year (off 1 percent in 1981). Over the past five years it has underperformed the S & P 500 four times.

MANAGEMENT   ★ ★ ★

Portfolio manager Antonio Intagliata has been with United Accumulative since 1979. He has been with the parent company, Waddell & Reed, for over sixteen years. Intagliata has over twenty-three years of investment experience and an MA in finance from Washington University. His management technique relies on historical pricing and macro economic trends. This allows Intagliata to buy out-of-favor value plays. Once a stock reaches its targeted point and no suitable alternatives can be found, the fund will sell off large positions. This is evidenced by a cash reserve that has been greater than 30 percent in the past.

There are eighty stocks in this $770 million portfolio. 75 percent of the fund's holdings are in common stocks, with the balance in cash. The median market capitalization of the portfolio's typical stock is $5 billion, 45 percent the size of the average stock in the S & P 500.

CURRENT INCOME ★ ★ ★ ★ ★
Over the past three years, United has averaged an annual income stream of 4.1 percent, the second-highest rate of any growth fund in this book.

EXPENSES ★ ★ ★ ★ ★
The expense ratio for United has averaged 0.62 percent for each of the last five years. This is the second-lowest rate of any other growth fund in the book.

For the past three years, the fund has had an average annual turnover rate of 313 percent. This is higher than any other growth fund in the book by quite a wide margin. Higher turnover rates mean more recognized gains, something no taxpayer wants to see.

SUMMARY
United Accumulative does well in good times and bad. It has demonstrated less risk than virtually all of its peers over the past three, five, and ten years. Management and performance have been very good; risk reduction has been superior. This is a wise choice for the conservative, growth-oriented investor. Because of its high turnover rate, this fund is best suited for retirement accounts.

Growth & Income Funds

These funds attempt to produce both capital appreciation and current income with priority given to appreciation potential in the stocks purchased. Growth and income fund portfolios include seasoned, well-established firms that pay relatively high cash dividends. The goal of these funds is to provide long-term growth without excessive volatility in share price.

Portfolio composition is almost always exclusively United States stocks, with an emphasis on utility common stocks and convertible preferred stocks. By selecting securities with comparatively high yields, overall risk is reduced; dividends will help prop up the overall return of growth and income funds during negative market conditions.

Growth and income funds are the most cautious United States stock play an investor can make. Conservative investors should commit no more than 35 percent of their diversified portfolio to growth and income stock funds, moderate investors should invest no more than 60 percent, and aggressive investors will want to invest less than 50 percent of their total holdings to this category.

Over the past fifty years, common stocks have outperformed inflation: 70 percent of the time over one-year periods, 83 percent of the time over five-year periods, 88 percent of the time over ten-year periods, and 100 percent over any given twenty-year period.

Over the past fifty years, high quality, long-term corporate bonds have also outperformed inflation: 52 percent of the time over one-year periods, 43 percent of the time over five-year periods, 37 percent of the time over ten-year periods, and 32 percent over any given twenty-year period.

There are close to 125 funds making up the category of "growth and income." Another category, "equity-income" funds, has been combined with growth and income. Thus, for this section, there were a total of 155 possible candidates. Total market capitalization of these two categories combined is $80 billion.

Over the past three and five years, growth and income funds have had an average compound return of 10.5 percent per year. The average *annual* return for the past decade has been 12.7 percent; 11.2 percent for the past fifteen years. The standard deviation for growth and income funds has been 3.7 percent over the past three years. This means that these funds have been less volatile than any other category of equity funds.

The sample portfolio shown in a previous chapter recommends a 15 percent commitment to this category for the conservative investor, 10 percent for the moderate and aggressive portfolios. This is one of the few categories of mutual funds recommended for all kinds of portfolios. As is true with any category of mutual funds, whenever larger dollar amounts are involved, more than one fund per category should be used.

AIM Charter

AIM Advisors
11 Greenway Plaza, Suite 1919
Houston, TX 77046
1/800-347-1919

total return	★ ★ ★ ★ ★	
risk	★ ★ ★ ★	
management	★ ★ ★ ★	
current income	★ ★ ★	
expenses	★	
symbol CHTRX	17 points	

TOTAL RETURN   ★ ★ ★ ★ ★

Over the past five years, AIM Charter has taken $10,000 and turned it into $20,100 ($18,200 over three years and $37,100 over the past ten years). This translates into an average annual return of 15 percent over five years, 22 percent over the past three years, and 14 percent for the decade.

RISK/VOLATILITY   ★ ★ ★ ★

Over the past five years, Charter has been safer than half of all mutual funds; within its category it ranks in the top 35 percent. During the past decade, the fund has had only one negative year. It has underperformed the S & P 500 two of the past five years.

MANAGEMENT   ★ ★ ★ ★

Portfolio manager Julian A. Lemer has overseen the fund since its inception in 1968. The fund invests a substantial portion of its assets in dividend-paying common stocks. No more than 10 percent of Charter's stocks can be securities that are not currently paying dividends; investment in foreign securities is also limited to 10 percent of the fund's holdings. Lemer's recent performance can only be described as outstanding, posting close to a 40 percent gain in 1989 and close to a 10 percent return in 1990, a negative year for almost every other equity fund.

Lemer has a highly focused approach, concentrating on just a handful of industries. At the beginning of 1991 nearly half of his portfolio's assets were in brand-name nondurables. The balance of the portfolio is in telephone, electric utility, and consumer service stocks.

There are forty-five stocks in the entire fund. Close to 80 percent of the fund's holdings are in common stocks, with the balance in cash. The median market capitalization of the portfolio's typical stock is $7.7 billion, 69 percent the size of the average stock in the S & P 500.

CURRENT INCOME ★ ★ ★
Over the past three years, AIM has averaged an annual income stream of 3 percent, a half point lower than the average yield for a growth and income fund.

EXPENSES ★
The annual expense ratio for Charter has averaged 1.4 percent for the last three years. This rate is slightly higher than its group's average of 1.2 percent.

Over the past three years, the traditional growth fund has had an average annual turnover rate of 198 percent. This rate is the highest of any growth and income fund reviewed in the book. High turnover rates are not advantageous for high-bracket taxpayers.

SUMMARY
AIM Charter has demonstrated excellent performance, the best in its peer group. Management and risk reduction are excellent. Of all growth and income funds, this should be an investor's first or second choice, particularly if invested monies are in a sheltered vehicle such as an IRA, Keogh, or profit-sharing plan.

Colonial

Colonial Investment Services
1 Financial Center
Boston, MA 02111
1/800-248-2828

total return	★ ★ ★	
risk	★ ★ ★ ★	
management	★ ★ ★ ★	
current income	★ ★ ★ ★ ★	
expenses	★ ★ ★	
symbol COLFX	19 points	

TOTAL RETURN   ★ ★ ★

Over the past five years, Colonial has taken $10,000 and turned it into $16,100 ($13,700 over three years and $37,100 over the past ten years). This translates into an average annual return of 10 percent over five years, 11 percent over the past three years, and 14 percent for the decade.

RISK/VOLATILITY   ★ ★ ★ ★

Over the past five years, Colonial has been safer than over 60 percent of all mutual funds; within its category this fund is safer than 80 percent of its peers. During the last five years, the fund has had two negative years and has also underperformed the S & P 500 three times.

MANAGEMENT   ★ ★ ★ ★

Christian C. Bertelsen has managed Colonial Fund since 1986. Prior to joining Colonial in 1986, Bertelsen was a portfolio manager for Batterymarch Financial, specializing in tax-exempt accounts. He has an MBA from Boston University and over eighteen years of investment experience.

There are 285 stocks in this $310 million portfolio. Close to 80 percent of the fund's holdings are in common stocks, with the balance in cash. The median market capitalization of the portfolio's typical stock is $1.9 billion, 17 percent the size of the average stock in the S & P 500.

CURRENT INCOME   ★ ★ ★ ★ ★

Over the past three years, Colonial has averaged an annual income stream of 4.4 percent, the second highest for its group in this book.

EXPENSES   ★ ★ ★

The expense ratio for this fund has averaged 0.98 percent for the last three years. This is almost 25 percent less than the average growth and income fund.

Over the past three years, Colonial has had an average turnover rate of 32 percent annually. This rates very favorably in comparison to its industry average of 78 percent.

SUMMARY
The Colonial Fund offers higher current income than any other growth and income fund in the book. Its superior risk control and management make this a top choice. This fund is highly recommended.

Dean Witter Dividend Growth Securities

Dean Witter Reynolds
2 World Trade Center
New York, NY 10048
1/800-869-3863

total return	★ ★ ★	
risk	★ ★ ★	
management	★ ★	
current income	★ ★ ★ ★	
expenses		
symbol DWDVX	12 points	

TOTAL RETURN ★ ★ ★

Over the past five years, Dean Witter Dividend Growth Securities has taken $10,000 and turned it into $16,900 ($15,200 over the past three years). This translates into an average annual return of 11 percent over five years and 15 percent over the past three years.

RISK/VOLATILITY ★ ★ ★

Over the past five years, Dividend Growth has been safer than half of all mutual funds; within its category it ranks in the top 40 percent. Since the fund's 1981 inception the fund has had two negative years and has underperformed the S & P 500 in three of the past five years.

MANAGEMENT ★ ★

Portfolio manager Paul D. Vance has overseen this fund since its 1981 inception. Vance has been with Dean Witter since 1971 as a director of international operations and as an asset manager. He has over thirty years of investment experience and is a Chartered Financial Analyst.

The fund's portfolio mirrors the S & P 500. However, Vance tends to emphasize mature industries such as chemicals, telephones, foods, and utilities. Every stock in the fund pays a dividend. Management can best be described as conservative.

There are seventy stocks in this $2.8 billion portfolio. Close to 99 percent of the fund's holdings are in common stocks, with the balance in cash. The median market capitalization of the portfolio's typical stock is $6.1 billion, 55 percent the size of the average stock in the S & P 500.

CURRENT INCOME ★ ★ ★ ★

Over the past three years, Dividend Growth has averaged an annual income stream of 3.5 percent, virtually identical to its peer group average.

EXPENSES

The annual expense ratio for the fund has averaged a very high 1.5 percent for the last three years. This rate is almost 25 percent higher than the category average, giving this fund a higher expense ratio than any other growth and income fund listed in this book.

Over the past three years, the average annual turnover rate for Dividend Growth has been an incredibly low 6 percent, the lowest of its peer group. Low turnovers mean reduced fund expenses, costs that are not shown in a portfolio's expense column.

SUMMARY

Dean Witter Dividend Growth rates as "very good" in risk reduction and performance. Management is also considered to be good. It is a fine recommendation for the somewhat conservative investor.

FPA Perennial

Angeles Securities
10301 West Pico Blvd.
Los Angeles, CA 90064
1/800-421-4374

total return	★ ★ ★	
risk	★ ★ ★ ★ ★	
management	★ ★ ★	
current income	★ ★ ★ ★	
expenses	★ ★	
symbol FPPFX	17 points	

TOTAL RETURN   ★ ★ ★

Over the past five years, FPA Perennial has taken $10,000 and turned it into $17,600 ($14,800 over three years). This translates into an average annual return of 12 percent over five years and 14 percent over the past three years.

RISK/VOLATILITY   ★ ★ ★ ★ ★

Over the past five years, FPA has been safer than 70 percent of all mutual funds; within its category it ranks in the top 5 percent. Since the fund's 1984 inception, it has only had one negative year, off 1 percent in 1987. It has underperformed the S & P 500 in three of the past five years.

MANAGEMENT   ★ ★ ★

Portfolio manager Chris Linden has been with Perennial since its inception. Linden strongly favors very high-quality issues, but finds that value in high-quality issues is best found in the universe of medium-sized companies, corporations often ignored by other managers and analysts.

The fund is loaded heavily with securities from low-debt, highly profitable companies. Management avoids purchasing the stocks or convertibles of businesses they do not feel confident they understand.

There are forty stocks in the entire fund. Close to 65 percent of the fund's holdings are in common stocks, with the balance in cash and bonds. The median market capitalization of the portfolio's typical stock is $1.4 billion, 13 percent the size of the average stock in the S & P 500.

CURRENT INCOME   ★ ★ ★ ★

Over the past three years, FPA has averaged an annual income stream of 3.6 percent, a common yield for a growth and income fund.

EXPENSES   ★ ★

The annual expense ratio for Perennial has averaged 1.1 percent for the last three years. This rate is slightly better than its group's average of 1.2 percent.

Over the past three years, the traditional growth and income fund has had an average annual turnover rate of 78 percent. FPA's turnover has been a mere 28 percent. A small turnover rate helps bring about better return figures.

SUMMARY

FPA Perennial is a very good performer with excellent risk management. Investors should note this fund's emphasis on the long term. The fund's high concentration stocks of medium-sized companies makes this an ideal addition to almost any portfolio.

Fundamental Investors

American Funds Distributor
333 South Hope Street
Los Angeles, CA 90071
1/800-421-0180

total return	★ ★ ★ ★
risk	★
management	★ ★ ★ ★ ★
current income	★ ★ ★
expenses	★ ★ ★ ★ ★
symbol ANCFX	18 points

TOTAL RETURN ★ ★ ★ ★

Over the past five years, Fundamental Investors has taken $10,000 and turned it into $17,600 ($15,200 over three years and $44,100 over the past ten years). This translates into an average annual return of 12 percent over five years, 15 percent over the past three years, and 16 percent for the decade. The fund has outperformed both the S & P 500 and DJIA over the past ten years.

A $10,000 investment at the fund's mid-1978 inception grew to $53,000 by the beginning of 1991. This translates into an average compound rate of 16 percent per year.

RISK/VOLATILITY ★

Over the past five years, Fundamental has been more volatile than 70 percent of all mutual funds; within its category the fund ranks in the bottom 20 percent. During the past ten years the fund has had two negative years. Over the past five years it has underperformed the S & P 500 by only a slight margin.

MANAGEMENT ★ ★ ★ ★ ★

Capital Research has overseen this fund since it took it over in 1978. The fund itself has been around since 1932. Management has been extremely consistent and disciplined, focusing on long-term horizons. Capital Research seeks out-of-favor industry leaders selling at discounted prices. The people at Capital Research are unsurpassed in the area of portfolio management. Fundamental Investors has increased at nearly three times the rate of inflation over the past decade.

There are fifty-five stocks in this $830 million portfolio. Close to 80 percent of the fund's holdings are in common stocks, with the balance in cash. The median market capitalization of the portfolio's typical stock is $6.3 billion, 57 percent the size of the average stock in the S & P 500.

CURRENT INCOME ★ ★ ★

Over the past three years, Fundamental has averaged a modest annual income stream of 2.9 percent. This lower-than-average yield is ideal for the tax-conscious investor. Shareholder dividends have increased in eight of the past ten years.

EXPENSES   ★ ★ ★ ★ ★
The annual expense ratio for Fundamental has averaged 0.66 percent for the last three years. This cost factor is extremely low and is reflected in the fund's returns.

Over the past three years, the typical growth and income fund has had an average annual turnover rate of 78 percent. Fundamental's rate has been a low 13 percent over this same period.

SUMMARY
American Funds has done it again with Fundamental Investors. This fund possesses superior returns for short, medium, and long-term periods. Management is unsurpassed. Because of its risk level, it is only ideal for the diversified portfolio.

Investment Company of America

American Funds Distributor
333 South Hope Street
Los Angeles, CA 90071
1/800-421-0180

total return	★ ★ ★ ★ ★
risk	★ ★ ★ ★
management	★ ★ ★ ★ ★
current income	★ ★ ★ ★
expenses	★ ★ ★ ★ ★
symbol AIVSX	23 points

TOTAL RETURN ★ ★ ★ ★ ★

Over the past five years, Investment Company of America (ICA) has taken $10,000 and turned it into $18,400 ($16,000 over three years and $48,100 over the past ten years). This translates into an average annual return of 13 percent over five years, 17 percent over the past three years, and 17 percent for the decade. Since it began almost sixty years ago, ICA has regularly surpassed all of the major unmanaged stock market averages.

A $10,000 investment at the 1934 inception of the fund was worth over $10,000,000 by the beginning of 1991. This translates into an average compound return of 13 percent per year.

RISK/VOLATILITY ★ ★ ★ ★

Over the past five years, ICA has been safer than 60 percent of all mutual funds; within its category this fund ranks in the top 20 percent. Over the past decade the fund has not had a negative year. It has underperformed the S & P 500 three times in the last ten years. In the past thirty years, ICA has beat the S & P 500 in every one of twenty-one ten-year periods. There are only seven other funds that can claim this feat.

MANAGEMENT ★ ★ ★ ★ ★

Capital Research has managed this fund since its inception in 1933. The fund is designed to produce steady returns that add up to excellent returns over the medium- and long-term. Management concentrates on blue chips with above-average yields.

Capital Research has always looked at long-term horizons, buying quality stocks that are temporarily troubled. The fund seeks long-term growth of capital and income, *placing greater emphasis on future dividends than on current income.* ICA is one of the nation's oldest and largest investment companies, with an outstanding record of achievement. There have been forty-six ten-year periods since ICA's 1933 inception; the fund has just completed its best-ever performing decade.

There are 100 stocks in this $5.9 billion portfolio. Close to 80 percent of the fund's holdings are in common stocks, with the balance in cash and bonds. The median market capitalization of the portfolio's typical stock is $11.8 billion, 107 percent the size of the average stock in the S & P 500.

CURRENT INCOME   ★ ★ ★ ★
Over the past three years, ICA has averaged an annual income stream of 4 percent. Shareholder dividends have increased in twenty-eight of the past thirty years, not including special dividends to investors.

EXPENSES   ★ ★ ★ ★ ★
ICA's expense ratio is the lowest in its category, averaging an extremely low 0.52 percent annually over the past three years.

The turnover rate for this fund has also been an extremely low 15 percent. This is 80 percent less than the average growth and income fund.

SUMMARY
Investment Company of America is the premier choice for the investor looking for excellent performance and unsurpassed management. Risk reduction is superior; it is a highly favored choice. This is yet another example of the kind of quality found in the American Funds Group.

Merrill Lynch Capital A

Merrill Lynch Funds Distributor
P.O. Box 9011
Princeton, NJ 08543
1/800-637-3863

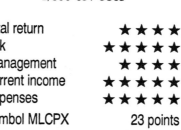

total return	★ ★ ★ ★	
risk	★ ★ ★ ★ ★	
management	★ ★ ★ ★	
current income	★ ★ ★ ★ ★	
expenses	★ ★ ★ ★ ★	
symbol MLCPX		23 points

TOTAL RETURN   ★ ★ ★ ★

Over the past five years, Merrill Lynch Capital A has taken $10,000 and turned it into $17,600 ($14,800 over three years and $44,100 over the past ten years). This translates into an average annual return of 12 percent over five years, 14 percent over the past three years, and 16 percent over the past decade.

RISK/VOLATILITY   ★ ★ ★ ★ ★

Over the past five years, Capital A has been less risky than 60 percent of all mutual funds; within its category it ranks in the top 5 percent. During the past decade the fund has not had one negative year. It has underperformed the S & P 500 two of the past five years.

MANAGEMENT   ★ ★ ★ ★

Ernest Watts has been the fund's manager since 1983. Prior to rejoining Merrill Lynch in 1983, Watts was a portfolio manager and senior analyst at J & W Seligman. From 1954 to 1969 he was a senior analyst and industry specialist at Merrill Lynch. Watts has a BS from the University of Maryland.

The fund has a very high cash position and moderately high bond exposure, traits not common for the typical growth and income fund. Management's strategy is to purchase stocks with a dividend yield approaching 5 percent. The fund takes on a defensive mode, loading up on bonds and cash, when stock yields fall to the 3 percent level.

There are eighty-five stocks in this $960 million portfolio. Close to 80 percent of the fund's holdings are in common stocks, with the balance in cash. The median market capitalization of the portfolio's typical stock is $6.9 billion, 62 percent the size of the average stock in the S & P 500.

CURRENT INCOME   ★ ★ ★ ★ ★

Over the past three years, Capital A has averaged an annual income stream of 4.4 percent, compared to an industry average of 3.5 percent. This gives Capital A the second-highest income stream within its category.

EXPENSES ★ ★ ★ ★ ★

The expense ratio for Capital A has averaged 0.61 percent annually for the past three years. This is close to half the rate incurred by similar funds.

The turnover rate for this fund has been 78 percent. This is virtually identical to the average growth and income fund.

SUMMARY

Merrill Lynch Capital A has demonstrated a superior record, particularly over the past five and ten years. Management is top quality and safety is excellent.

Putnam Fund for Growth & Income

Putnam Financial Services
1 Post Office Square
Boston, MA 02109
1/800-225-1581

total return	★ ★ ★ ★
risk	★ ★ ★ ★
management	★ ★ ★ ★
current income	★ ★ ★ ★ ★
expenses	★ ★ ★ ★
symbol IARCX	21 points

TOTAL RETURN ★ ★ ★ ★

Over the past five years, Putnam Fund for Growth & Income has taken $10,000 and turned it into $18,400 ($15,200 over three years and $40,500 over the past ten years). This translates into an average annual return of 13 percent over five years, 15 percent over the past three years, and 15 percent for the decade.

A $10,000 investment at the fund's inception in 1957 was worth over $590,000 by the beginning of 1991. This translates into a compound return of 13 percent per year.

RISK/VOLATILITY ★ ★ ★ ★

Over the past five years, Putnam has been safer than 60 percent of all mutual funds; within its category it ranks in the top 20 percent. During the past decade the fund has only had one negative year (off 3 percent in 1981). Over the past five years it has underperformed the S & P 500 twice.

MANAGEMENT ★ ★ ★ ★

Portfolio manager John Maurice has overseen this fund since 1968. Before joining Putnam, Maurice was manager of a stock fund at National Securities. He has an MBA from the University of Chicago and over thirty-six years of investment experience.

Management's style can be described as fast-paced. Maurice has been one of the very few managers to move successfully in and out of different blue chip stocks. Maurice is a value-oriented buyer.

There are eighty stocks in this $2.1 billion portfolio. Close to 70 percent of the fund's holdings are in common stocks, with the balance in cash. The median market capitalization of the portfolio's typical stock is $6.7 billion, 61 percent the size of the average stock in the S & P 500.

CURRENT INCOME ★ ★ ★ ★ ★

Over the past three years, this Putnam fund has averaged an annual income stream of 5 percent, making it the highest for its group. Such a high income helps to decrease fund risk and is a definite appeal to the income-oriented investor.

EXPENSES ★ ★ ★ ★

The annual expense ratio for Putnam has averaged 0.78 percent for the last three years. This means that the fund is able to do business for about two-thirds the cost of the typical growth and income fund.

The fund has had a somewhat greater-than-average annual turnover rate of 90 percent for the past three years. Fortunately, this has not had an adverse affect on the bottom line.

SUMMARY

Putnam Fund for Growth & Income is a superior choice. Its consistently high rankings make this an appropriate vehicle for virtually all investors who want a conservative exposure to the stock market.

SBSF Growth

SBSF Funds
45 Rockefeller Plaza
New York, NY 10111
1/800-422-7273

total return		★ ★
risk		★ ★ ★ ★ ★
management		★ ★ ★ ★
current income		★ ★
expenses		★ ★
symbol SBFFX	15 points	

TOTAL RETURN   ★ ★
Over the past five years, SBSF Growth has taken $10,000 and turned it into $16,100 ($15,600 over three years). This translates into an average annual return of 10 percent over five years and 16 percent over the past three years.

RISK/VOLATILITY   ★ ★ ★ ★ ★
Over the past five years, SBSF Growth has been safer than 60 percent of all mutual funds; within its category it ranks in the top 15 percent. During the fund's lifetime, it has had only one negative year. It has underperformed the S & P 500 three of the past five years.

MANAGEMENT   ★ ★ ★ ★
Portfolio manager Louis Benzak has been the fund's manager since its 1983 inception. His goal is to stay defensive: try not to get hurt and always expect the worst. Such an outlook enabled this fund to be one of the few within its group to outperform the S & P 500 during 1990's negative year.

Benzak's cautious approach means that the fund often holds a large cash position. The bulk of the portfolio's holdings are in financial, nondurable, and energy stocks.

There are thirty stocks in the entire fund. Close to 60 percent of the fund's holdings are in common stocks, with the balance in bonds and cash. The median market capitalization of the portfolio's typical stock is $8.9 billion, 81 percent the size of the average stock in the S & P 500.

CURRENT INCOME   ★ ★
Over the past three years, SBSF Growth has averaged an annual income stream of 2.6 percent, almost a full point lower than the typical growth and income fund.

EXPENSES   ★ ★
The annual expense ratio for SBSF has averaged 1.1 percent for the last three years. This rate is slightly better than its group's average.

Over the past three years, the traditional growth fund has had an average annual turnover rate of 78 percent. SBSF's turnover has been a modest 52 percent. A small turnover rate helps bring about better return figures.

SUMMARY

SBSF Growth is a good performer with superior risk management and exceptional risk control. Investors should note this fund's emphasis on the long-term. The fund's high concentration in just a few industries makes this an ideal candidate when combined with another growth fund.

Selected American Shares

Prescott Ball & Turben
230 West Monroe Street
Chicago, IL 60606
1/800-553-5533

total return	★ ★ ★ ★
risk	★
management	★ ★
current income	★
expenses	★ ★
symbol SLASX	10 points

TOTAL RETURN   ★ ★ ★ ★

Over the past five years, Selected American Shares has taken $10,000 and turned it into $18,400 ($16,400 over three years and $48,100 over the past ten years). This translates into an average annual return of 13 percent over five years, 18 percent over the past three years, and 17 percent for the decade.

A $10,000 investment in the fund thirty years ago was worth over $125,000 by the beginning of 1991. This translates into an average compound rate of 9 percent per year.

RISK/VOLATILITY   ★

Over the past five years, Selected has been more volatile than 60 percent of all mutual funds; within its category it ranks in the bottom 40 percent for safety. The fund has had only one negative year for the past ten years. It has underperformed the S & P 500 four of the past five years.

MANAGEMENT   ★ ★

Donald A. Yacktman has been the portfolio manager for Selected since 1983. Prior to joining Selected, Yacktman was a partner at SteinRoe for nine years. He is a Chartered Investment Counselor and has an MBA from Harvard. Management is generally pessimistic, which translates into a conservatively run portfolio.

Yacktman spends very little time thinking about broad economic trends. Nor does he forecast the direction of the stock market as a whole. Instead, he focuses on the outlook for individual stocks. He avoids less established companies and firms in the commodity-based and heavier industries with a large amount of fixed assets or union membership. Management favors companies that have a good market share and produce high-quality products.

There are thirty stocks in this $400 million portfolio. Close to 90 percent of the fund's holdings are in common stocks, with the balance in cash and convertibles. The median market capitalization of the portfolio's typical stock is $5.1 billion, 46 percent the size of the average stock in the S & P 500.

CURRENT INCOME   ★

Over the past three years, Selected has averaged a meager annual income stream of 2.4 percent, making it the lowest of any growth and income fund in this book. This makes the fund a very sensible selection for moderate and high income taxpayers.

EXPENSES   ★ ★

The annual expense ratio for Selected has averaged 1.2 percent, which is just under its peer group average for the last three years.

Over the past three years, the fund has had an average turnover rate of 43 percent annually. This rate is almost 45 percent lower than the industry norm.

SUMMARY

Selected American Shares has a superior track record. It rates as a top choice in the remaining categories. This is a fine and sensible choice for the growth and income investor who does not mind a certain amount of performance volatility.

Washington Mutual Investors

American Funds Distributor
333 South Hope Street
Los Angeles, CA 90071
1/800-421-0180

total return	★ ★ ★ ★
risk	★ ★ ★
management	★ ★ ★ ★ ★
current income	★ ★ ★ ★ ★
expenses	★ ★ ★ ★ ★
symbol AWSHX	22 points

TOTAL RETURN ★ ★ ★ ★

Over the past five years, Washington Mutual Investors has taken $10,000 and turned it into $17,600 ($15,200 over three years and $48,100 over the past ten years). This translates into an average annual return of 12 percent over five years, 15 percent over the past three years, and 17 percent for the decade.

A $10,000 investment in the fund at its 1952 inception was worth over $970,000 by the beginning of 1991. This translates into a compound rate of 13 percent per year.

RISK/VOLATILITY ★ ★ ★

Over the past five years, Washington Mutual has been safer than half of all other funds and half its peer group. During the past decade, the fund has only had a single negative year. It has underperformed the S & P 500 three times in the past decade.

In the past thirty years, Washington has beaten the S & P 500 in every one of twenty-one ten-year periods.

MANAGEMENT ★ ★ ★ ★ ★

Capital Research has managed Washington Mutual since its 1952 inception. Management seeks current income and opportunity for capital growth. The portfolio is dominated by mature industries such as energy, electric utilities, finance, and telecommunications.

There are ninety stocks in this $5.6 billion portfolio. Close to 95 percent of the fund's holdings are in common stocks, with the balance in cash. The median market capitalization of the portfolio's typical stock is $6.9 billion, 63 percent the size of the average stock in the S & P 500.

CURRENT INCOME ★ ★ ★ ★ ★

Over the past three years, Washington Mutual has averaged an annual income stream of 4.3 percent, nearly a point higher than its peer group average. Dividends to investors have increased every year since 1952.

EXPENSES   ★ ★ ★ ★ ★
The annual expense ratio for the fund has averaged 0.65 percent, the third-lowest of any growth and income fund in the book.

Over the past three years, Washington Mutual has had an average turnover rate of 13 percent annually. This is substantially lower than its group average and well under half the rate found with the typical growth and income fund in this book.

SUMMARY
This unusual fund is always fully invested in the stocks of American companies that meet strict standards originally established by the United States District Court for the investment of trust funds in the District of Columbia. It is the only fund that meets such criteria. Such exposure has not prevented it from showing nice returns during recent bear market years. Capital Research consistently ranks as the best in the area of management.

Washington Mutual Investors is yet another winner for the American Funds family. This group of funds continues on the high road; the longer the time frame, the better the different funds in this family look. Washington Mutual gets an almost perfect score. It is strongly recommended for all investors.

High-Yield Funds

Sometimes referred to as "junk bond" funds, these portfolios invest in corporate bonds rated lower than BBB or Baa. The world of bonds is divided into two general categories: "investment grade" and "high-yield." Investment grade, sometimes referred to as "bank quality," means that the bond issue has been rated AAA, AA, A or Baa. Certain institutions and fiduciaries are forbidden to invest their clients' monies in anything less than investment grade. Everything less than bank quality is considered "junk."

The world of bonds is not black and white. There are several categories of high-yield bonds. Junk bond funds contain issues that range from BBB to C; a rating less than single-C means that the bond is in default, and payment of interest and/or principal is in arrears. High-yield bond funds perform best during good economic times. Such issues should be avoided by traditional investors during recessionary periods, since the underlying corporations may have difficulty making interest and principal payments when business slows down.

Although junk bonds may exhibit greater volatility than their investment-grade peers, they are safer when it comes to *interest rate* risk. Since junk issues have high-yielding coupons and shorter maturities than high-quality corporate bond funds, they fluctuate less in value when interest rates change. Thus, during expansionary periods in the economy when interest rates are rising, high-yield funds will generally drop less in value than high-quality corporate or government bond funds. Conversely, when interest rates are falling, government and corporate bonds will appreciate more in value than junk funds.

The high end of the junk bond market, those debentures rated BBB and BB, have been able to withstand the general beating the junk bond market incurred during the late 1980s and early 1990s. Moderate and conservative investors who want high-yield bonds as part of their portfolio should focus on funds that have a high percentage of their assets in higher-rated bonds, BB or better.

There are forty-one funds in the category "high-yield." Total market capitalization of this category is $19 billion.

Over the past three years, high-yield corporate bond funds have had an average compound total return of -1 percent per year. The *annual* return for the past five years has been 3 percent; 9 percent per year for the past decade. The standard deviation for high-yield bond funds has been 2.2 percent over the past three years. This means that these funds have been less volatile than any equity fund and similar in return variances with other kinds of bond funds.

A cautious investor should have no more than 20 percent of her diversified holdings in a high-yield bond fund. Moderate investors should have less than 40 percent, and aggressive investors would not want more than 30 percent of their assets in this one category.

The sample portfolios shown in a previous chapter recommend that only moderate investors consider making a 10 percent commitment to this category. Conservative and aggressive investors should probably avoid high-yield funds. As is true with any category of mutual funds, whenever larger dollar amounts are involved, more than one fund per category should be used.

CIGNA High Yield

CIGNA Capital Brokerage
1 Financial Plaza
Springfield, MA 01103
1/800-562-4462

total return	★ ★ ★ ★
risk	★ ★
management	★ ★ ★
current income	★ ★ ★ ★
expenses	★ ★ ★
symbol INAHX	16 points

TOTAL RETURN ★ ★ ★ ★
Over the past five years, CIGNA High Yield has taken $10,000 and turned it into $14,000 ($11,600 over three years and $31,100 over the past ten years). This translates into an average annual return of 7 percent over five years, 5 percent over the past three years, and 12 percent for the decade.

RISK/VOLATILITY ★ ★
Over the past five years, CIGNA has been more stable than 70 percent of all mutual funds; within its category it ranks in the top 60 percent. During the past decade, the fund has not had one negative year; it has underperformed the bond index in two of the past five years.

MANAGEMENT ★ ★ ★
Portfolio manager Alan C. Petersen has been with CIGNA High Yield since 1982. Petersen began his career at CIGNA in 1978 as a bond analyst. In 1981 he was appointed Director of Fixed Income Research. Prior to joining CIGNA, he spent four years at Northwestern Life Insurance as an equity and fixed-income specialist. He has an MBA from Northwestern University and is a Chartered Financial Analyst.

Petersen's management technique has proven successful in avoiding major mistakes. He likes to focus on the least vulnerable sectors of the junk bond market. According to Peterson, the junk bond market is alive and well. "The remarkable strength of the market is largely due to broad-based, growing participation by institutional investors. During the last decade, the institutional market for high-yield securities grew to $160 billion—more than 20 percent of the U.S. corporate bond market . . . . This appeal is driven by two factors: One, that adjusted for default losses, returns compare very favorably to more traditional investment sectors; and two, the diversification provided by this new investment vehicle, which has demonstrated a low correlation of returns with other asset classes."

There are seventy-five bonds in this $220 million portfolio. Close to 90 percent of the fund's holdings are in bonds, with the balance in cash. The average maturity of the bonds in the portfolio is ten years. Most of the bonds in the portfolio are single-B rated.

CURRENT INCOME   ★ ★ ★ ★
Over the past three years, the fund has averaged an annual income stream of 12 percent, slightly lower than the industry's average of 12.6 percent.

EXPENSES   ★ ★ ★
The annual expense ratio for CIGNA has averaged 0.96 percent for the last three years. This is a little lower than the typical high-yield bond fund.

Over the past three years, the fund has had an average annual turnover rate of 64 percent, slightly lower than its group's average.

SUMMARY
CIGNA High Yield is rated as a solid junk bond fund. It consistently rates as "very good" in every important category. The fund's success is the result of its emphasis on quality issues.

Merrill Lynch Corporate Bond High Income Portfolio

Merrill Lynch Funds Distributor
P.O. Box 9011
Princeton, NJ 08543
1/800-637-3863

total return	★ ★ ★ ★ ★
risk	★ ★ ★ ★
management	★ ★ ★ ★ ★
current income	★ ★ ★ ★ ★
expenses	★ ★ ★ ★ ★
symbol MLHIX	24 points

TOTAL RETURN ★ ★ ★ ★ ★

Over the past five years, Merrill Lynch Corporate Bond High Income Portfolio has taken $10,000 and turned it into $14,700 ($12,300 over three years and $31,100 over the past ten years). This translates into an average annual return of 8 percent over five years, 7 percent over the past three years, and 12 percent for the decade.

RISK/VOLATILITY ★ ★ ★ ★

Over the past five years, Merrill Lynch Corporate Bond High Income Portfolio has been safer than 75 percent of all mutual funds; within its category it ranks in the top 15 percent for safety. During the past decade, the fund has only had one negative year. Over the past five years the fund has underperformed the bond index three times.

MANAGEMENT ★ ★ ★ ★ ★

Vincent T. Lansbury has been the fund's manager since 1979, two months after the fund's inception. He is considered one of the most seasoned and savvy securities managers in the business.

The fund's premier concern is to obtain a high current income without sustaining principal erosion. The fund has gained a reputation as the junk bond portfolio of choice during bad markets.

There are 115 bonds in this $490 million portfolio. Close to 85 percent of the fund's holdings are in bonds, with the balance in cash and convertibles. The average maturity of the bonds in the portfolio is nine years, with an average weighted price that is at a 17 percent discount to par. Such a discount provides some nice appreciation potential. Most of the bonds in the portfolio are not rated; single-B rated issues make up the bulk of the fund's assets.

CURRENT INCOME ★ ★ ★ ★ ★

Over the past three years, Merrill's High Income Portfolio has averaged an annual income stream of close to 13 percent, making it the highest in the book.

EXPENSES   ★ ★ ★ ★ ★

The expense ratio for Merrill has averaged 0.7 percent for the last three years. This is lower than any other high-yield fund in the book.

Over the past three years, the fund has had an average turnover rate of 51 percent, lower than any other high-yield corporate bond fund in the book.

SUMMARY

Merrill Lynch Corporate Bond High Income Portfolio is one of the very few high-yield funds whose total return has been excellent over the past three, five, and ten years. Investors seeking the highest possible current income should strongly consider this fund. This is one of the few cases where you can get a great current income while still preserving principal later. This is one of the very best junk bond funds.

Oppenheimer High Yield

Oppenheimer Fund Management
P.O. Box 300
Denver, CO 80201
1/800-525-7048

total return	★ ★ ★ ★ ★
risk	★ ★ ★ ★ ★
management	★ ★ ★ ★ ★
current income	★ ★ ★ ★ ★
expenses	★ ★ ★
symbol OPPHX	23 points

TOTAL RETURN   ★ ★ ★ ★ ★
Over the past five years, Oppenheimer High Yield has taken $10,000 and turned it into $14,700 ($12,300 over three years and $28,400 over ten years). This translates into an average annual return of 8 percent over five years, 7 percent over the past three years, and 11 percent over the past decade.

RISK/VOLATILITY   ★ ★ ★ ★ ★
Over the past five years, Oppenheimer High Yield has been more secure than 80 percent of all mutual funds; within its category it ranks in the top 5 percent.

MANAGEMENT   ★ ★ ★ ★ ★
Portfolio manager Ralph Stellmacher has been with the fund since 1987; the fund began operations in 1978. Stellmacher favors bonds from companies with strong balance sheets and decent liquidity. He believes that an issue selling at too high a discount is dangerous.

The fund's thrust is on high current income from those bonds selling only at a moderate discount. The fund invests primarily in unrated or BBB-rated or lower issues. The portfolio is well known for its strong downmarket performance..

There are 115 bonds in this $590 million portfolio. Ninety-five percent of the fund's holdings are in bonds, with the balance in cash, common stock, and convertibles. The average maturity of the bonds in the portfolio is nine years. Most of the bonds in the portfolio are single-B rated.

CURRENT INCOME   ★ ★ ★ ★ ★
Over the past three years, Oppenheimer has averaged an annual income stream of 12.6 percent, identical to its group's average of 12.6 percent.

EXPENSES   ★ ★ ★
The expense ratio for Oppenheimer High Yield has averaged 0.9 percent annually for the last three years. This is 10 percent less than the typical high-yield bond fund.

Over the past three years, the fund has had an average annual turnover rate of 55 percent, close to one-third less than traditional junk funds.

SUMMARY

Investors should note that high-yield bonds react differently than high-grade bonds in different economic environments. For example, high grade bonds will typically out-return high-yields significantly in a weakening economy, while high-yields will outperform in a strong economy.

Oppenheimer High Yield is one of only four junk bond funds recommended in this book. It is the only fund that receives excellent marks in the areas of current income, risk control, and management. Such a tremendous overall rating should make this the income investor's first or second choice.

Phoenix High Yield Fund Series

Phoenix Equity Planning
101 Munson Street
Greenfield, MA 01301
1/800-243-4361

total return	★ ★ ★ ★ ★	
risk	★ ★ ★ ★	
management	★ ★ ★ ★	
current income	★ ★ ★	
expenses	★ ★ ★ ★	
symbol PHCHX	20 points	

TOTAL RETURN　　　　　　　　　　　　　　　★ ★ ★ ★ ★

Over the past five years, Phoenix High Yield has taken $10,000 and turned it into $13,400 ($11,600 over three years and $28,400 over the past ten years). This translates into an average annual return of 6 percent over five years, 5 percent over the past three years, and 11 percent for the decade.

RISK/VOLATILITY　　　　　　　　　　　　　　　★ ★ ★ ★

Over the past five years, Phoenix High Yield has been more stable than 75 percent of all mutual funds; within its category it ranks in the top 15 percent.

MANAGEMENT　　　　　　　　　　　　　　　★ ★ ★ ★

Curtiss O. Barrows has been the portfolio's manager since 1985, the year the fund began operations. One of his favorite sayings is, "He who panics first panics best." Before purchasing any bond, Barrows sits down with management and asks simply, "How are you paying me back (interest and principal)?"

Management's focus is on "blue chip" junk. Virtually the entire portfolio is made up of issues rated single B or higher. Current income is its first objective, with growth a distant, secondary concern. Bonds from grocery store chains, oil, natural gas, electric and telephone utilities, and United States Treasuries dominate the portfolio.

There are thirty-eight bonds in this $90 million portfolio. 95 percent of the fund's holdings are in bonds, with the balance in cash. The average maturity of the bonds in the portfolio is nine years. Most of the bonds in the portfolio are single-B rated.

CURRENT INCOME　　　　　　　　　　　　　　　★ ★ ★

Over the past three years, Phoenix High Yield has averaged an annual income stream of 11.5 percent, close to a full point lower than its peer group average.

EXPENSES　　　　　　　　　　　　　　　★ ★ ★ ★

The annual expense ratio for Phoenix has averaged 0.8 percent for the last three years, lower than most high-yield funds.

Over the past three years, the fund has had an average annual turnover rate of 276 percent. This average rate reflects management's strategy of going to cash when the market looks troubled. The turnover rate demonstrated by the fund is almost four times greater than its industry's average.

SUMMARY

Phoenix High Yield clearly stands out as one of the two best junk bond funds. It ranks a very high score, particularly in the crucial areas of performance, management, and risk reduction. The Phoenix Group is known for its superior management across the board. It may well be the best medium-sized mutual fund group in the nation, doing something that very few other fund groups, large or small, have been able to do: excel in bonds, convertibles, and stocks.

International Bond Funds

International, also referred to as "foreign," funds purchase securities issued in a foreign currency, such as the Japanese yen or the British pound. Prospective investors need to be aware of the potential changes in the value of the foreign currency relative to the United States dollar. As an example, if you were to invest in Australian dollar-denominated bonds that had a current yield of 15 percent, and the Aussie currency appreciated 12 percent against the United States dollar, your total return for the year would be 27 percent. Conversely, if the Australian dollar declined by 20 percent against the United States dollar, your total return would be –6 percent.

International funds invest in securities issued all over the world, including the United States. A global bond fund usually invests in bonds issued by stable governments from a handful of countries. These funds try to avoid purchasing foreign government debt instruments from politically or economically unstable nations.

International bond funds seek higher interest rates, no matter where the search may take them. Inclusion in the fund portfolio depends on management's perception of interest rates, the country's projected currency strength against the United States dollar, and the country's political and economic stability.

Since foreign markets do not necessarily move in tandem with United States markets, each country represents varying investment opportunities at different times. The current value of the world bond market is estimated to be close to $8 trillion. Half of this marketplace is made up of United States bonds; Japan ranks second by taking up 20 percent of the pie.

Over the past twenty-five years, global bonds have outperformed United States bonds, United States stocks, and inflation. The Non-United States Bond Index has *outperformed* the United States Bond Index in *every* one of twenty-five ten-year periods since 1960.

There are only thirteen funds in the category "international bonds." Total market capitalization of this category is $4 billion.

Over the past three years, global bond funds have had an average compound return of 8.8 percent per year; the *annual* return for the past five years has been 16.4 percent. The standard deviation for global bond funds has been 1.9 percent over the past three years. This means these funds have been less volatile than any equity fund but slightly greater than the return variances found with other kinds of bond funds.

Global bond funds, particularly those that have a high concentration in foreign issues, are an excellent risk-reduction tool that should be used by the vast majority of investors. Traditional portfolios should have no more than 50 percent of their diversified holdings in global bonds, moderates should have no more than 30 percent, and aggressive investors no more than 20 percent.

The sample portfolio shown in a previous chapter recommends that conservative, moderate, and aggressive investors all have exactly 10 percent of their overall holdings in international bond funds. As is true with any category of mutual funds, whenever larger dollar amounts are involved, more than one fund per category should be used.

MFS Worldwide Governments Trust

MFS Financial Services
500 Boylston Street
Boston, MA 02116
1/800-654-0266

total return	★ ★ ★	
risk	★ ★ ★	
management	★ ★ ★	
current income	★ ★ ★	
expenses	★ ★ ★ ★	
symbol MFIBX	16 points	

TOTAL RETURN ★ ★ ★

Over the past five years, MFS Worldwide Governments Trust has taken $10,000 and turned it into $18,400 ($12,600 over three years and $40,500 over the 10 years). This translates into an average annual return of 13 percent over five years, 8 percent over the past three years, and 15 percent over the past decade. The fund's 13 percent five-year return tops the Salomon Brothers' World Bond Index by more than eight percentage points.

RISK/VOLATILITY ★ ★ ★

Over the past five years, MFS Worldwide has been safer than 70 percent of all mutual funds; within its category it ranks as one of the best. Since its 1982 inception the fund has not had one negative year, something few funds can claim. Over the past five years it has underperformed the bond index three times.

MANAGEMENT ★ ★ ★

Portfolio manager Leslie J. Nanberg has been the fund's manager since 1984. Nanberg joined MFS in 1983. He is a graduate of Northwestern Graduate School and is a Chartered Financial Analyst.

Nanberg focuses on government bonds, especially those of countries whose real rates of return, interest rates net of inflation, are the highest. Nanberg's theory is that countries with the highest real interest rates are not as likely to overheat as are those where real returns are low. Says Nanberg, "Over time, the high level of real rates makes those bonds undervalued relative to other markets." When he believes interest rates are on the rise, Nanberg will protect the fund's principal by staying invested in securities with maturities of one year or less.

There are fewer than twenty different bonds in the portfolio. The five largest country holdings in this $140 million fund are the United States, Canada, France, Denmark, and the United Kingdom. The average maturity of the bonds in the portfolio is less than six years. A modest maturity range helps to reduce risk. Ninety-five percent of the portfolio's holdings are in bonds, with the balance in cash.

CURRENT INCOME   ★ ★ ★
Over the past three years, MFS Worldwide has averaged an average annual income stream of 8 percent, a rate virtually identical to the average international bond fund.

EXPENSES   ★ ★ ★ ★
The expense ratio for MFS has averaged 1.2 percent for the last three years. This means that the fund is able to operate for 20 percent less than its peer group average.

Over the past three years, the fund has had an average annual turnover rate of almost 300 percent. What may appear as an exceedingly high rate is not that out of line for a category that traditionally averages well over 200 percent annually.

SUMMARY
MFS Worldwide Governments Trust is the oldest global bond fund. It has a better track record than any other international debt portfolio for the moderate- and long-term. Management and the safety factor are very good. This is a convincing choice for the investor who wants to see consistently positive and lengthy performance.

Foreign bonds can act as an important risk reduction tool. American investors have very little exposure in this area. This is unfortunate when one realizes that foreign government bonds have outperformed United States bonds in every ten-year rolling period over the past twenty-five years. When properly hedged (insured against a strong United States dollar), they are 50 percent safer than their United States counterparts; unhedged they are 30 percent riskier. Foreign bonds should be a part of most people's portfolios; MFS Worldwide Governments provides a top choice.

Van Eck World Income

Van Eck Securities
122 East 42nd Street, 42nd Floor
New York, NY 10168
1/800-221-2220

total return	★ ★ ★ ★ ★
risk	★ ★ ★ ★ ★
management	★ ★ ★ ★ ★
current income	★ ★ ★ ★ ★
expenses	★ ★ ★ ★ ★
symbol WIFRX	25 points

TOTAL RETURN ★ ★ ★ ★ ★

Over the past three years, Van Eck World Income has taken $10,000 and turned it into $14,300. This translates into an average annual return of almost 13 percent.

RISK/VOLATILITY ★ ★ ★ ★ ★

Over the past three years, Van Eck has been safer than 95 percent of all mutual funds; within its category it ranks in the top 10 percent. Since its inception, the fund has not had a single negative year and has underperformed the bond index only once.

MANAGEMENT ★ ★ ★ ★ ★

Portfolio managers Kenerson and Buescher have overseen the fund since its 1986 inception. So far, management has shown an almost uncanny ability to predict interest rates and currency values, two of the most important ingredients in global bond selection.

There is no limit as to the amount that can be invested in any one country. The portfolio can invest in government as well as corporate debt instruments.

There are fewer than ten different bonds in this $55 million portfolio. The four largest positions in the fund are Spain, Canada, New Zealand, and the United States. The portfolio is divided up into 88 percent bonds and 12 percent cash. The average weighted maturity is a mere three years. Such a short-term exposure means that investors are not subject to the wide price swings sustained by interest rate movements.

CURRENT INCOME ★ ★ ★ ★ ★

Over the past three years, Van Eck has had an average annual income stream of just under 10 percent, a rate over one-and-a-half points higher than its category norm.

EXPENSES ★ ★ ★ ★ ★

The expense ratio for Van Eck has averaged less than 1 percent for the last three years. This is 50 percent less than the typical international bond fund.

Over the past three years, the fund has had an average annual turnover rate of 330 percent; this rate is 50 percent greater than its industry average. Normally, such rates are cause for concern, but sterling results in every other category make such a comment moot.

SUMMARY

This is one of the few funds in the book that rates a perfect score. It is the ideal choice for conservative investors who want foreign exposure in their bond holdings. The Van Eck Group, best known for their expertise in managing gold mining stocks, is well thought of throughout the world for their knowledge of foreign and domestic markets.

American investors need to realize that foreign government bonds have come close to equaling the performance of American stocks over the past twenty-five years. Foreign bonds have outperformed their American counterparts by a ratio of two-to-one over the same time frame. Equally important, a global bond portfolio, one comprising American as well as foreign securities, is much safer than one of United States bonds alone.

More investors need to open their eyes to debt instruments issued outside the United States. Van Eck is perhaps the top choice.

International Equity Funds

International, also known as "foreign," funds invest only in stocks of foreign companies, while global funds invest in both foreign and U.S. stocks. For purposes of this book, the universe of international funds shown encompasses foreign and global portfolios.

It is wise to consider investing abroad, since different economies experience prosperity and recession at different times. During the 1980s, foreign stocks were the number one performing investment, averaging a compound return of over 22 percent per year, versus 17 percent for American stocks and 9 percent for residential real estate.

The economic outlook of foreign countries is the important factor in management's decision as to which nations and industries are to be favored. A secondary concern is the future anticipated value of the United States dollar relative to foreign currencies. A strong or weak dollar can detract or add to an international fund's overall performance. A strong dollar will lower a foreign portfolio's return; a weak dollar will enhance international performance. Trying to gauge the direction of any currency is as difficult as trying to figure out what the American stock market will do tomorrow, next week, or the following year.

Investors who do not wish to be subjected to currency swings may wish to use a fund family that practices "currency hedging" for its foreign holdings. Currency hedging means that management is buying a kind of "insurance policy" that pays off in the event of a strong U.S. dollar. Basically, the foreign or international fund that is being hurt by the dollar is making a killing in currency futures contracts. When hedging is done properly, the gains in the futures contracts offset most or all security losses attributed to a strong dollar. Some people may feel that buying currency contracts is risky business for the fund; it is not.

Like automobile insurance, currency hedging only pays off if there is an "accident," that is, if the United States dollar increases in value against the currencies represented by the portfolio's securities. If the dollar remains level or decreases in value, so much the better; the foreign securities increase in value and the currency contracts become virtually worthless. The price of these contracts becomes a cost of doing business; just like car insurance, the protection is simply renewed. In the case of a currency contract, the contract expires and a new one is purchased, covering another period of time.

Many mutual fund prospectuses mention that they have the ability to use currency hedging. Unfortunately, only one fund family uses hedging extensively. Fortunately for the reader, one of its funds has made our "100 best" list, and other family members will likely be in the next edition of this book.

To give you a tangible idea of how important currency hedging is on a *risk-adjusted* basis, consider how a foreign and United States stock portfolio fare against each other. Over the past ten years, American stocks have had a risk level of almost 16.5, versus just over 17 for foreign equities. Yet, during this same period, foreign stocks have outperformed their American counterparts by about 40 percent annually. Most readers would agree that the slightly greater risk of investing overseas is worth the vastly greater return.

The example described above becomes more dramatic when currency hedging is added to the foreign portfolio. When this is done, the international risk level drops to a level of thirteen, while the United States level stays at almost 16.5. The returns for the foreign portfolio drop only slightly with the added cost of "insurance": after hedging returns are still a *third greater* than those of American stocks. In short, a *hedged* foreign stock portfolio has 20 percent less risk than a United States stock fund while still providing a 33 percent greater return. This is truly the best of both worlds: less risk and greater returns.

During the past decade, Japan has had the number one performing stock market, with returns in excess of 1,000 percent. Sweden ranks number two, with returns close to 780 percent; Italy is a distant third with a gain of 480 percent. The United States ranks eleventh out of the eighteen *major* stock markets around the world. If smaller markets were included, the American position would be even lower. All of these figures are United States dollar adjusted and *do not include* the receipt or reinvestment of dividends.

If you were to construct a grid of the top performing stock markets around the world, ranked first through fifth place covering the past twelve years, you would have a total of sixty different slots. On this entire grid, the United States would appear only once. In 1982 the United States had the second-best performing stock market in the world.

Seventy-seven funds make up the category "international equities." Total market capitalization of this category is $25 billion.

Over the past three years, international equity funds have had an average compound return of 8 percent per year. The *annual* return for the past five years has been 13 percent; 14.5 percent for the past ten years. The standard deviation for global equity funds has been 4.9 percent over the past three years. This means that these funds have been slightly more volatile than the average growth fund but have delivered greater returns.

International, or foreign, funds should be part of everyone's portfolio. They provide superior returns and reduce overall portfolio risk. Conservative investors should have no more than 40 percent of their holdings in foreign stocks. Moderate portfolios should have no more than 65 percent of their holdings committed to international equities; aggressive candidates should limit their holdings to no more than 80 percent.

As with any other fund category, this one should not be looked at in a vacuum. The real beauty of foreign funds shines through when they are combined with other categories of United States equities. According to a Stanford University study, one's overall risk level is cut in half when a *global* portfolio of stocks is used instead of one based on United States issues alone. And, as already demonstrated, returns are also greater when we look for opportunities worldwide instead of just domestically.

The sample portfolio shown in a previous chapter recommends a 10 percent commitment to this category for the conservative investor, 25 percent for the moderate, and 30 percent for the aggressive portfolio. As is true with any category of mutual funds, whenever larger dollar amounts are involved, more than one fund per category should be used.

EuroPacific Growth

American Funds Distributor
333 South Hope Street
Los Angeles, CA 90071
1/800-421-0180

total return	★ ★ ★	
risk	★ ★ ★ ★	
management	★ ★ ★ ★	
current income	★ ★	
expenses	★ ★ ★ ★	
symbol AEPGX	17 points	

TOTAL RETURN ★ ★ ★

Over the past five years, EuroPacific Growth has taken $10,000 and turned it into $20,100 ($14,800 over three years). This translates into an average annual return of 15 percent over five years and 14 percent over the past three years.

A $10,000 investment at the mid-1984 inception of the fund was worth over $27,000 by the beginning of 1991. This translates into an average compound return of 18 percent per year.

RISK/VOLATILITY ★ ★ ★ ★

Over the past five years, EuroPacific Growth has been safer than 55 percent of all mutual funds; within its category it ranks in the top 20 percent. Since its inception the fund has had only one negative year. Over the past five years it has underperformed the S & P 500 only once.

MANAGEMENT ★ ★ ★ ★

Capital Research has managed EuroPacific since its 1984 inception. Management follows a combination of the team approach and star system. It has managed foreign securities for close to twenty years. Its sister company compiles indices seen in leading publications for every major world stock market. It also edits and compiles Morgan Stanley Capital International Perspective, which provides detailed financial and market information on more than 2,200 companies all over the globe.

In the tradition of the other American Funds, EuroPacific follows a conservative line. The fund seeks long-term appreciation of capital by investing in the securities of companies based outside of the United States.

The fund is broadly diversified across countries and industries. Its five largest holdings by country are Japan, the United Kingdom, West Germany, Australia, and Hong Kong. The largest industry groups are electronics, health care, publishing, and broadcasting. The fund does not intend to invest more than 20 percent of its holdings in developing countries.

There are 140 stocks in this $930 million portfolio. 75 percent of the fund's holdings are in stocks, with the balance in cash and bonds. The median market capitalization of the portfolio's typical stock is $4.2 billion, 38 percent the size of the average stock in the S & P 500.

CURRENT INCOME   ★ ★
Over the past three years, the average international equities fund has averaged an annual income stream of 0.9 percent, compared to EuroPacific's income stream of 1.9 percent.

EXPENSES   ★ ★ ★ ★
The annual expense ratio for EuroPacific Growth has averaged 1.3 percent for the last three years. This is almost 70 percent lower than the typical international equity fund.

Over the past three years, the average international equities fund has had an average annual turnover rate of 87 percent. EuroPacific Growth has had a much lower turnover rate of 30 percent. A low turnover rate translates into less taxable gains and a higher return for investors.

SUMMARY
EuroPacific Growth has a very good track record. The fund's safety level is superior. Its management, Capital Research, is widely known for its consistency and conservative approach. This global fund is one of the best.

G.T. Pacific Growth

G.T. Global Financial Services
50 California Street, 27th Floor
San Francisco, CA 94111
1/800-824-1580

total return	★ ★ ★ ★ ★
risk	★ ★
management	★ ★ ★
current income	
expenses	★ ★
symbol GTPAX	12 points

TOTAL RETURN ★ ★ ★ ★ ★

Over the past five years, G.T. Pacific Growth has taken $10,000 and turned it into $27,000 ($16,400 over three years and $44,100 over the past 10 years). This translates into an average annual return of 22 percent over five years, 18 percent over the past three years, and 16 percent over the last decade.

RISK/VOLATILITY ★ ★

Over the past five years, G.T. Pacific Growth was at the bottom 40 percent of all mutual funds for risk; within its category it ranks as "average." During the past five years the fund has had only one negative year and has underperformed the S & P 500 only once.

MANAGEMENT ★ ★ ★

The fund has been managed by Christian Wignall since its inception over a decade ago. Wignall favors stocks from economies classified as historically cheap and fast-growing. The fund attempts to invest at least 80 percent of its assets in firms domiciled in Japan, Hong Kong, Singapore, Malaysia, the Philippines, Australia, and New Zealand.

All of the G.T. Global funds in existence since 1985 rank in the top 6 percent of all mutual funds. Each is less volatile than the S & P 500. Each has been managed by the same manager since its inception.

G.T. funds make extensive use of currency hedging, reducing their exposure to currency swings. G.T. is the only fund group in this book that uses currency hedging extensively.

There are approximately seventy-five stocks in this $240 million portfolio. Close to 80 percent of the fund's holdings are in stocks, with the balance in cash and bonds. The median market capitalization of the portfolio's typical stock is $280 million, only 3 percent the size of the average stock in the S & P 500. The five geographic areas most heavily represented in the fund are West Germany, France, Norway, the United Kingdom, and Spain.

CURRENT INCOME

Over the past three years, the traditional international equities fund has averaged an annual income stream of just under 1 percent, compared to G.T.'s income stream of almost zero. Such a low income stream is ideal for the investor concerned with reducing income tax liability.

EXPENSES ★ ★

The expense ratio for G.T. Europe has averaged 2 percent for the last three years. This rate is slightly higher than the typical international equity fund.

Over the past three years, the group's average annual turnover rate has been 87 percent. G.T. Europe has had a slightly lower turnover rate of 77 percent.

SUMMARY

The G.T. group is known for its performance. Because of the somewhat specialized nature of several of its funds, returns can be rather extreme, but fortunately, most of these performance swings are in a positive direction. This is probably the best mutual fund that specializes in the Pacific Basin.

New Perspective

American Funds Distributor
333 South Hope Street
Los Angeles, CA 90071
1/800-421-0180

total return	★ ★ ★
risk	★ ★ ★ ★
management	★ ★ ★ ★
current income	★ ★ ★
expenses	★ ★ ★ ★ ★
symbol ANWPX	19 points

TOTAL RETURN   ★ ★ ★

Over the past five years, New Perspective has taken $10,000 and turned it into $19,300 ($14,400 over three years and $44,100 over the past ten years). This translates into an average annual return of 14 percent over five years, 13 percent over the past three years, and 16 percent for the decade. During the fund's seventeen-year life it has recorded a gain of over 1,000 percent, far outpacing comparable United States market indices.

RISK/VOLATILITY   ★ ★ ★ ★

Over the past five years, New Perspective has been safer than 60 percent of all mutual funds; within its category it ranks in the top 10 percent. During the past decade the fund has had only one negative year. It has underperformed the S & P 500 in two of the past five years.

MANAGEMENT   ★ ★ ★ ★

Capital Research & Management has overseen this fund since its 1973 inception. Management is noted for its conservative approach, focusing on long-term fundamental trends. Like other American Funds, New Perspective relies on a team management approach; assets are distributed to the fund's portfolio managers and stock analysts based on their respective areas of expertise.

Over ten years or more, every single common stock fund managed by Capital Research has consistently done better than leading American indices such as the Dow Jones Industrials and the S & P 500. An investment in New Perspective has gone up for ten consecutive years.

The fund's cautious approach has enabled it to outperform its peer group average with significantly less risk. There are over a 100 different issues in the portfolio. This fund can invest in both American and foreign securities. Close to a third of the fund's holdings are in United States securities. West Germany, the United Kingdom, Australia, and Japan are the next largest holdings, each representing about 7 percent of the fund's holdings. Cash reserves are close to 20 percent in this $1.8 billion portfolio.

Capital Research spends over $20 million a year on research. They have offices in Los Angeles, San Francisco, New York, Washington, D.C., London, Geneva, Singapore, Hong Kong, and Tokyo. Their analysts travel millions of miles a year. They have made over 2,500 research calls, about half outside the United States in more than thirty-six countries.

There are 110 stocks in the fund. Close to 80 percent of the fund's holdings are in stocks, with the balance in cash, bonds, and convertibles. The median market capitalization of the portfolio's typical stock is $8.4 billion, 76 percent the size of the average stock in the S & P 500.

CURRENT INCOME ★ ★ ★
Over the past three years, the fund has averaged an annual income stream of 2.6 percent, a rate almost three times greater than its peer group average. A higher-than-average dividend stream helps to reduce overall risk.

EXPENSES ★ ★ ★ ★ ★
The expense ratio for New Perspective has averaged 0.8 percent for each of the last three years. This is a considerably lower ratio than that of the average international equities fund.

Over the past three years, the fund's average annual turnover rate has averaged 21 percent, versus its peer group average of 87 percent.

SUMMARY
New Perspective is perfect for the conservative, globally oriented investor who seeks an efficiently managed fund. Like other funds managed by Capital Research, this one is overseen by a superior group. This fund is a great choice for someone seeking broad diversification and the opportunity to participate in foreign markets to a moderate degree. Its overall ratings would be higher if ten- or fifteen-year time frames were used.

Oppenheimer Global

Oppenheimer Fund Management
P.O. Box 300
Denver, CO 80201
1/800-525-7048

total return	★ ★ ★ ★
risk	★ ★
management	★ ★ ★
current income	
expenses	★ ★ ★
symbol OPPAX	12 points

TOTAL RETURN   ★ ★ ★ ★

Over the past five years, Oppenheimer Global has taken $10,000 and turned it into $20,100 ($16,400 over three years and $40,500 over the past ten years). This translates into an average annual return of 15 percent over five years, 18 percent over the past three years, and 15 percent for the decade.

RISK/VOLATILITY   ★ ★

Over the past five years, Oppenheimer Global has been more volatile than 60 percent of all mutual funds; within its category it ranks in the top 40 percent. It has underperformed the S & P 500 only once in the past five years.

MANAGEMENT   ★ ★ ★

Portfolio management has been by Ken Oberman since 1981. He is considered one of the top stars at Oppenheimer. Oberman looks for "themes": industries that have good growth prospects. He is not afraid to concentrate on a particular sector. The themes Oberman is attracted to are not the trendy; he often defies conventional wisdom in the international world.

Management currently favors the United States and Europe, almost to the complete exclusion of the Pacific Basin. Pharmaceutical, medical care, and biotechnology companies make up close to one-third of the portfolio.

There are 110 stocks in the entire fund. Close to 90 percent of the fund's holdings are in common stocks, with the balance in cash, preferreds, and convertibles. The median market capitalization of the portfolio's typical stock is $790 million, 7 percent the size of the average stock in the S & P 500.

CURRENT INCOME

Over the past three years, Oppenheimer has averaged an annual income stream of practically zero, versus a group average of almost 1 percent.

EXPENSES   ★ ★ ★
The annual expense ratio for Oppenheimer has averaged 1.9 percent for the last three years. This rate is slightly higher than average for its category.

Over the past three years, the traditional international equities fund has had an average annual turnover rate of 87 percent. Oppenheimer's turnover has been a modest 46 percent. A small turnover rate helps bring about better return figures.

SUMMARY
Oppenheimer Global Fund is a superior performer with very good risk management. Investors should note that this fund has a high percentage of its holdings in United States securities. Since this is not a pure foreign play, it is an ideal choice for the investor who does not already own a diversified global stock portfolio.

SoGen International

SoGen Securities
50 Rockefeller Plaza
New York, NY 10020
1/800-334-2143

total return	★ ★
risk	★ ★ ★ ★ ★
management	★ ★ ★ ★
current income	★ ★ ★ ★ ★
expenses	★ ★ ★ ★
symbol SGENX	20 points

TOTAL RETURN   ★ ★

Over the past five years, SoGen International has taken $10,000 and turned it into $17,600 ($13,300 over three years and $48,100 over the past ten years). This translates into an average annual return of 12 percent over five years, 10 percent over the past three years, and 17 percent for the decade.

RISK/VOLATILITY   ★ ★ ★ ★ ★

Over the past five and ten years, SoGen has been safer than 70 percent of all mutual funds; within its category it has been more stable than 97 percent of its peers. During the past decade the fund has had only one slightly negative year. Over the past five years it has underperformed the S & P 500 only once.

The fund can best be described as a balanced global fund, investing in stocks, bonds, and money market instruments issued around the world. Historically, the fund has participated only moderately in strong markets but has done very well in flat or declining markets.

MANAGEMENT   ★ ★ ★ ★

Portfolio manager Jean-Marie Eveillard, has been president and portfolio manager of SoGen since 1979. He graduated from HEC, a French business school. Eveillard combines a global perspective with deep concern for preserving capital. The portfolio is very creative; it appears ready for every contingency. Management appears to almost always be pessimistic. Eveillard believes that defensiveness ultimately leads to solid returns. There has been no turnover of security analysts in the company for the past eleven years. The company does not run any other mutual funds.

Management can best be described as original. Eveillard looks for the obscure. According to him, there is greater likelihood that such a security will be mispriced. It seldom happens that a big stock is unduly depressed. There are just too many analysts and major portfolio managers on the lookout for the larger issues. Eveillard feels that big stocks are generally either up to 20 percent undervalued or up to 20 percent overvalued.

There are over 150 stocks in this $210 million portfolio. Composition of the fund is as follows: 32 percent U.S. stocks, 22 percent cash, 14 percent foreign stocks, 14 percent United States bonds, 9 percent foreign bonds, and 9 percent gold-related securities. The median market capitalization of the portfolio's typical stock is $650 million, 6 percent the size of the average stock in the S & P 500. The five geographic areas most heavily represented in the fund are the United States, Switzerland, Germany, the United Kingdom, and France. The fund has frequently appeared on the *Forbes* magazine Mutual Fund Honor Roll.

CURRENT INCOME ★ ★ ★ ★ ★
Over the past three years, the fund has averaged an annual income stream of 3.9 percent. This return is higher than any other international equity fund in the book. Higher dividends translate into lower risk.

EXPENSES ★ ★ ★ ★
The expense ratio for SoGen has averaged 1.4 percent for the last three years. This expense ratio level is lower than the average international equities fund.

Over the past three years, the fund has had an average annual turnover rate of 36 percent, less than half the rate found with the typical international equity fund.

SUMMARY
Without any hesitation, SoGen International is *the* choice for the pessimistic investor. It turns out steady, positive returns each year. This fund is the perfect selection for investors who want a worry-free place to put their money. It is also an ideal place to invest for a child's future educational expenses. If there exists the perfect "all-weather fund," this is it.

Templeton Foreign

Securities Fund Investors
700 Central Avenue
St. Petersburg, FL 33733
1/800-237-0738

total return	★ ★ ★ ★
risk	★ ★ ★ ★ ★
management	★ ★ ★ ★ ★
current income	★ ★ ★ ★
expenses	★ ★ ★ ★ ★
symbol TEMF	23 points

TOTAL RETURN   ★ ★ ★ ★

Over the past five years, Templeton Foreign has taken $10,000 and turned it into $22,900 ($15,200 over three years). This translates into an average annual return of 18 percent over five years and 15 percent over the past three years.

RISK/VOLATILITY   ★ ★ ★ ★ ★

Over the past five years, Templeton Foreign has been safer than 65 percent of all mutual funds; within its category it ranks in the top 5 percent. Since its inception the fund has only had two negative years. It has underperformed the S & P 500 only once in five years.

MANAGEMENT   ★ ★ ★ ★ ★

Portfolio manager Mark Holowesko has overseen the fund since 1986. Holowesko has received extensive training from Sir John Templeton, who has managed securities for almost fifty years.

Holowesko's management technique is based on the time-honored value criteria. He acts on conviction based upon the conclusions derived from strict value analysis. According to Sir John, "Not everyone stops to think that you can't get a stock at a bargain price when it's popular. If you want to buy the same stocks that other people are buying, you'll not have a superior record . . . they have already pushed the price up. The only hope you've got to produce a superior investment record is do something different from what the crowd is doing." The genius of John Templeton is known throughout the financial world. Holowesko is certainly following in the master's footsteps.

The fund's objective is long-term capital growth, and any income realized will be considered incidental. The fund does not hold any United States stocks. There are 115 different stocks in this $940 million dollar portfolio. Cash reserves make up close to 20 percent of the fund's total market capitalization of $7.3 billion, 66 percent the size of the average stock in the S & P 500. The five largest countries represented by the fund are the United Kingdom, Canada, Switzerland, Hong Kong, and Australia.

CURRENT INCOME ★ ★ ★ ★

Over the past three years, the fund's average annual income stream has been 3 percent, over three times greater than that seen by the typical international equity fund.

EXPENSES ★ ★ ★ ★ ★

The annual expense ratio for Templeton Foreign has averaged 0.8 percent for the last three years. This is half the rate incurred by the fund's group average.

Over the past three years, the fund has had an average annual turnover rate of 17 percent, the second-lowest of any international equity fund in the book.

SUMMARY

Templeton Foreign is about as close as one can get to a perfect fund in the areas of risk, management, and performance. This has been, and continues to be, a favored choice for the risk-conscious investor.

Templeton Growth

Securities Fund Investors
700 Central Avenue
St. Petersburg, FL 33733
1/800-237-0738

total return	★ ★
risk	★ ★ ★ ★
management	★ ★ ★ ★
current income	★ ★ ★ ★ ★
expenses	★ ★ ★ ★ ★
symbol TEPLX	20 points

TOTAL RETURN   ★ ★

Over the past five years, Templeton Growth has taken $10,000 and turned it into $16,900 ($14,400 over three years and $37,100 over the past ten years). This translates into an average annual return of 11 percent over five years, 13 percent over the past three years, and 14 percent for the decade.

A $10,000 investment at the late-1954 inception of the fund was worth over $1,300,000 by the beginning of 1990. This translates into an average compound return of 16 percent per year. Over the same period of time, $10,000 became inflated to $47,000. Thus, the fund has dramatically outperformed the Consumer Price Index over the past thirty-six years.

There are approximately one hundred equity funds that are at least thirty years old. Fewer than twenty-five of these funds have outperformed the S & P 500 over this time frame. Templeton Growth has been the best performer by over a two-to-one margin. Over the past thirty-two years, the fund was up over 11,720 percent.

RISK/VOLATILITY   ★ ★ ★ ★

Over the past five years, Templeton Growth has been safer than half of all mutual funds; within its category it ranks in the top 20 percent. During the past decade, the fund has had only one negative year. It has underperformed the S & P 500 in three of the past five years.

MANAGEMENT   ★ ★ ★ ★

Portfolio manager Sir John Templeton, well known for his achievements in the realm of global investing, has overseen the fund since its 1954 inception. He is a graduate of Yale and is also a Chartered Financial Analyst. His management technique is strongly value oriented, borne out by the fact that Templeton refuses to pay a premium for stocks.

The Templeton Group believes in common sense. According to Templeton, "It just stands to reason that if you're looking all over the world, you will find better bargains than if you're looking in only one nation. The U.S. is so large and we're so accustomed to thinking in terms of our own nation, that it is really unusual to know much about stocks anywhere else. But let's suppose you lived in Switzerland instead, would you dream of having 100 percent of your assets in one country?" There is almost always some stock market that is going to do better than the American market.

Templeton has over 35 percent of the fund's assets invested in American stocks. The next three largest country holdings are Canada, the United Kingdom and Australia. Financial service, energy, chemicals and paper stocks still dominate the portfolio. There are over 150 different issues in this $2.3 billion dollar portfolio. Close to 90 percent of the fund's holdings are in stocks, with the balance in cash. The median market capitalization of the portfolio's typical stock is $4.9 billion, 44 percent the size of the average stock in the S & P 500.

CURRENT INCOME   ★ ★ ★ ★ ★
Over the past three years, the typical international equities fund has averaged an annual income stream of just under 1 percent, compared to Templeton Growth's income stream of 3.5 percent. This rate is the second-highest of any global equity fund in this book.

EXPENSES   ★ ★ ★ ★ ★
The annual expense ratio for Templeton Growth has averaged 0.7 percent for the last three years. This is lower than any other international stock fund in the book. Over the past three years, the fund has had an average annual turnover rate of 14 percent, lower than any other of its kind.

SUMMARY
Templeton Growth has proven itself to be a solid, consistently performing global fund. Out of all equity funds thirty years or older, Templeton Growth rates as number one by quite a margin. As suggested by its very low turnover ratio, the fund's overall posture does not change very much from year to year. Templeton is very bullish on the future; the fund currently has more equity exposure than at any other time in the past several years. John Templeton is a patient genius. This is a great choice for the conservative investor.

Templeton World

Securities Fund Investors
700 Central Avenue
St. Petersburg, FL 33733
1/800-237-0738

total return	★
risk	★ ★ ★
management	★ ★ ★
current income	★ ★ ★ ★
expenses	★ ★ ★ ★ ★
symbol TEMWX	16 points

TOTAL RETURN   ★
Over the past five years, Templeton World has taken $10,000 and turned it into
$15,400 ($13,000 over three years and $37,100 over the past ten years). This trans-
lates into an average annual return of 9 percent over five years, 9 percent over the
past three years, and 14 percent for the decade.

RISK/VOLATILITY   ★ ★ ★
Over the past five years, Templeton World has been safer than half of all mutual
funds; within its category it has been more stable than 75 percent of its peers.

MANAGEMENT   ★ ★ ★
Portfolio manager John Templeton, well known for his achievements in the realm
of global investing, has overseen the fund since its 1978 inception. He is a graduate
of Yale and is also a Chartered Financial Analyst. His management technique is
strongly value-oriented, borne out by the fact that Templeton refuses to pay a
premium for stocks. The fund is co-managed by Galbraith and Hansberger.

The Templeton Group believes in common sense. According to Templeton, "It
just stands to reason that if you're looking all over the world, you will find better
bargains than if you're looking in only one nation. The U.S. is so large and we're
so accustomed to thinking in terms of our own nation, that it is really unusual to
know much about stock anywhere else. But, let's suppose you lived in Switzerland
instead, would you dream of having 100 percent of your assets in one country?"
There is almost always some stock market that is going to do better than the
American market.

There are over 180 different issues in this $3.7 billion dollar portfolio. Close
to 90 percent of the fund's holdings are in stocks, with the balance in cash and
bonds. The median market capitalization of the portfolio's typical stock is $4.7 bil-
lion, 43 percent the size of the average stock in the S & P 500. Close to 40 percent
of the fund's holdings are in United States stocks. The United Kingdom, Canada,
Australia, and Switzerland collectively account for another 25 percent.

CURRENT INCOME   ★ ★ ★ ★

Over the past three years, the typical international equities fund has averaged an annual income stream of almost 1 percent, compared to Templeton World's 3 percent. This rate is one of the highest in the industry.

EXPENSES   ★ ★ ★ ★ ★

The annual expense ratio for Templeton Growth has averaged a low 0.7 percent for the last three years. This is over a full point lower than the typical international stock fund and the second-lowest in the book.

Over the past three years, the fund has had an average annual turnover rate of 19 percent, lower than any other non-Templeton international or global equity fund.

SUMMARY

Templeton Growth has proven itself to be a solid, consistently performing global fund. As suggested by its very low turnover ratio, the fund's overall posture does not change very much from year to year. Templeton is very bullish on the future, particularly as far as the United States is concerned. John Templeton is a patient genius. This is a nice choice for the conservative investor who is more concerned with risk reduction than returns.

Metals Funds

These funds purchase metals in one or more of the following ways: bullion, South African gold stocks, and non-South African mining stocks. The United States, Canada, and Australia are the three major *stock-issuing* producers of metals outside of South Africa. Metals, also referred to as gold funds, often own minor positions in other precious metals stocks such as silver and platinum.

The proportion and kind of metal held by a fund can have a great impact on its performance and volatility. Outright ownership of gold bullion is almost always less volatile than owning stock of a gold mining company. Thus, much greater gains or losses occur in metals funds purchasing only gold stocks compared to funds that hold high levels of bullion and stock. Silver has nearly twice the volatility of gold, yet has not had any greater return over the long terms.

Gold or metals, funds do particularly well during periods of political uncertainty and inflationary concerns. Over the past several hundred years, gold and silver have been a hedge against inflation. Most readers will be surprised to learn that historically, both metals have outperformed inflation by less than one percent annually.

Metals funds are the riskiest category of mutual funds described in this book. This is true regardless of the composition of the gold fund. Although this is a high-risk investment when viewed alone, ownership of a metals fund can actually reduce a portfolio's overall risk level and often enhance its total return. This is because gold usually has a negative correlation to other investments. That is, when one investment goes down in value, gold will often go up. Thus, a portfolio comprising strictly government bonds will actually exhibit more risk *and* less return than one made up of 90 percent government bonds and 10 percent metals.

Metals funds should be avoided by anyone who can not tolerate wide price swings in any *single* part of his portfolio. These funds are designed as an integral part of a diversified portfolio, that is, for the investor who looks at the *overall* return of her holdings. Conservative investors should have no more than 20 percent of their holdings in gold funds. Moderate shareholders should limit their holdings to no more than 30 percent, and aggressive portfolios should devote no more than 40 percent to metals funds.

There are twenty-four funds in the category of "metals." Total market capitalization of this category is $3.4 billion.

Over the past three years, metals funds have had an average compound return of –5 percent per year. The *annual* return for the past five years has been 7 percent; –1 percent in the past decade. The standard deviation for gold funds has been 6.8 percent over the past three years. This means that these funds have been even more volatile than aggressive growth funds.

The sample portfolio shown in a previous chapter recommends a 5 percent commitment to this category for the moderate investor and 10 percent for the aggressive portfolio. As is true with any category of mutual funds, whenever larger dollar amounts are involved, more than one fund per category should be used.

Franklin Gold

Franklin Funds
777 Mariners Island Boulevard
San Mateo, CA 94404
1/800-342-5236

total return	★ ★ ★ ★	
risk	★ ★ ★	
management	★ ★ ★ ★	
current income	★ ★ ★ ★ ★	
expenses	★ ★ ★ ★ ★	
symbol FKRCX	21 points	

TOTAL RETURN   ★ ★ ★ ★

Over the past five years, Franklin Gold has taken $10,000 and turned it into $17,600 ($10,600 over three years and $19,700 over the past ten years). This translates into an average annual return of 12 percent over five years, 2 percent over the past three years, and 7 percent for the decade. The fund began operations in 1969.

Over the past ten years, inflation has increased 66 percent while Franklin Gold wen up over 327 percent. Over the past fifteen years, inflation has gone up 145 percent compared to 532 percent for the fund.

RISK/VOLATILITY   ★ ★ ★

Over the past five years, Franklin Gold has been more volatile than 98 percent of all other mutual funds; within its category it ranks in the top half. During the past five years the fund has had two negative years. It has underperformed the S & P 500 in two of the past five years.

Investing in any metals fund involves a high level of volatility. Franklin's volatility remains lower than the group's average because of its ability to do well during periods of gold-price weakness. This fund possesses only half the risk of the typical metals fund.

MANAGEMENT   ★ ★ ★ ★

Martin Wiskemann, with Franklin since 1972, believes in keeping transaction costs down. He has been in the securities business for more than thirty years. Wiskemann is a recognized authority on gold mining stocks and precious metals. Prior to joining Franklin, Martin was an investment manager with Winfield & Company. He received a degree in business from Handelsschule in Switzerland.

Wiskemann does not adjust the portfolio in response to near-term considerations. Instead, he keeps the fund fully invested at all times. Management likes to buy stocks of companies whose mines are mature. Most of these companies have more than one operating mine; this reduces risk in the even of a disaster. Wiskemann believes that investors should have somewhere between 5 percent and 8 percent of their portfolio in metals.

The portfolio is made up of stocks in medium- and long-life mines in South Africa, Canada, Australia, and the United States, mines that have a remaining productive life of fifteen or twenty years, compared to the five years that some of the Australian mines have. Management favors large gold mining companies that produce 100,000 ounces or more annually. For further diversification, close to 10 percent of the fund is invested in companies that also mine silver and other strategic metals.

There are fifty stocks in this portfolio. Cash reserves account for 20 percent of the fund's $310 million, while stocks account for most of the remainder. The median market capitalization of the portfolio's typical stock is $3 billion, 27 percent the size of the average stock in the S & P 500.

CURRENT INCOME   ★ ★ ★ ★ ★
Over the past three years, the typical precious metals fund has averaged an annual income stream of less than 2 percent, compared to Franklin Gold's income stream of 3.5 percent.

EXPENSES   ★ ★ ★ ★ ★
The expense ratio for Franklin Gold has averaged 0.8 percent for the last three years. This is half the rate normally incurred by a metals funds.

Over the past three years, the fund has had an average annual turnover rate of less than 7 percent. This is one of the lowest turnover rates found in the entire book.

SUMMARY
Franklin Gold has been able to combine superior returns with a moderate level of risk. This is very impressive in light of the tremendous risk associated with gold funds. The Franklin Group is known for its conservative approach, and this fund is much safer than most metals funds. Of over two dozen metals funds, this is one of the only two that are recommended.

Oppenheimer Gold and Special Minerals

Oppenheimer Funds
2 World Trade Center
New York, NY 10048
1/800-525-7048

total return	★ ★ ★ ★ ★
risk	★ ★ ★ ★ ★
management	★ ★ ★ ★ ★
current income	★ ★ ★ ★
expenses	★ ★ ★ ★
symbol OPGSX	23 points

TOTAL RETURN   ★ ★ ★ ★ ★

Over the past five years, Oppenheimer Gold and Special Minerals has taken $10,000 and turned it into $21,000 ($9,900 over three years). This translates into an average annual return of 16 percent over five years and -0.3 percent over the past three years.

RISK/VOLATILITY   ★ ★ ★ ★ ★

Over the past five years, Oppenheimer Gold and Special Minerals has been riskier than 90 percent of all mutual funds; within its category it ranks in the top 15 percent for safety. During the past five years, the fund has had one negative year. It has underperformed the S & P 500 in two of the past five years.

It is important to recognize the high level of volatility that comes along with metals funds. Such funds serve best as hedges in a portfolio. Precious metals have a negative correlation to virtually all investments. A negative correlation means that the investment will typically move in the opposite direction to other assets. Such movement reduces a portfolio's *overall* risk.

Oppenheimer Gold is unique in that it will invest as much as 70 percent of its assets in non-precious metals if the outlook for gold is not promising. This approach can offer significant exposure to gold with much less volatility than its group's average.

There are forty different mining stocks in the portfolio. Cash reserves stand at close to 15 percent of this $150 million portfolio. The median market capitalization of the portfolio's typical stock is $1.6 billion, 20 percent the size of the average stock in the S & P 500.

MANAGEMENT   ★ ★ ★ ★ ★

Portfolio manager Ken Oberman has overseen this fund since 1987; the fund began operations in 1983. His management technique is simple: concentrate on mining companies that are not highly leveraged. The bulk of the fund's portfolio is in mining stocks of North America, South Africa, and Australia.

There are thirty-five stocks in this $170 million dollar portfolio. Nearly 80 percent of the fund's holdings are in stocks, with the rest in cash. The median market capitalization of the portfolio's typical stock is $960 million, 9 percent the size of the average stock in the S & P 500.

CURRENT INCOME   ★ ★ ★ ★
Over the past three years, the fund has had an annual income stream of 2 percent, slightly higher than its group's average.

EXPENSES   ★ ★ ★ ★
The annual expense ratio for Oppenheimer Gold has averaged 1.3 percent for the last three years. This is 20 percent lower than the typical metals fund.

Over the past three years, the fund has had an average turnover ratio of 121 percent. This is over twice the level of the typical gold fund.

SUMMARY
Oppenheimer Gold and Special Minerals has demonstrated excellent performance, safety, and superior management. All metals funds are very volatile, but this one demonstrates much better risk control than its peers. Making this Oppenheimer fund one's choice for gold exposure is a wise decision.

Money Market Funds

These funds invest in securities that mature in less than one year. Money market funds are made up of one or more of the following instruments: Treasury bills, certificates of deposit, commercial paper, Euro-dollar CDs, and notes. There are four different categories of money market funds: all-purpose, government-backed, federally tax-free, and doubly tax-exempt.

All-purpose funds are the most popular and make up the bulk of the money market universe. These funds are fully taxable and are composed of securities such as CDs, commercial paper, and T-bills. *Government-backed* money funds invest only in short-term paper directly or indirectly backed by the U.S. government. These funds are technically safer than the all-purpose variety, but no money market fund has ever defaulted. The yield on government-backed funds is somewhat lower than its all-purpose peers.

Federally tax-free funds are made up of municipal notes. Investors in these funds do not have to pay federal income taxes on the interest earned. The before-tax yield on these funds is certainly lower than those found with all-purpose and government-backed funds, but the after-tax return can be higher for the moderate or high-tax-bracket investor. *Double tax-exempt* funds invest in municipal obligations of a specific state. You must be a resident of that state in order to avoid paying state income taxes on any interest earned. *Non-resident* investors will still receive a federal tax exemption.

All money market funds are safer than any other mutual fund or category of funds in this book. They have a perfect track record—investors can only *make* money in these interest-bearing accounts. The rate of return earned in a money market is dependent upon the average maturity of the fund's paper, the kinds of securities held, the quality rating of that paper, and how efficiently the fund is operated. A lean fund will almost always outperform a similar fund with high operating costs.

Investments such as United States Treasury Bills and, for all practical purposes, money market funds, are often referred to as "risk-free." These kinds of investments are free from price swings and default risk, because of either their composition or history. However, as we have come to learn, there is more than one form of risk. Money market funds should never be considered a place to invest one's money for a medium or long-term period. The *real* return on this investment is poor. An investment's real return takes into account the effects of inflation and income taxes. During virtually every period of time, the after-tax, after-inflation return on all money market funds has been near zero or *negative.*

Over the past fifty years, United States Treasury bills—an index often used as a substitute for money market funds—have outperformed inflation on average 50 percent of the time over one-year periods, 61 percent of the time over five-year periods, 56 percent of the time over ten-year periods, and 59 percent over any given twenty-year period of time. These figures are not adjusted for income taxes. Money market funds have rarely outperformed inflation on an after-tax basis when looking at five-, ten-, or twenty-year holding positions.

Investors look back to the "good old days" of the early 1980s when money market funds averaged 18 percent and wish such times would come again. Well, those were not good times. During the early 1980s the top tax bracket, state and federal combined, was 55 percent. If you began with an 18 percent return and deducted taxes, many taxpayers saw their 18 percent return knocked down to about 9 percent. This may look great, especially for a "risk-free' investment, but we are not done yet. During the year in which money market accounts paid 18 percent, inflation was 12 percent. Now, take the 9 percent return and *subtract* another 12 percent. You are left with a real rate of return or -3 percent for the year. So much for the "good old days."

Money market funds are the best place to park your money while you are looking at other investment alternatives or if you will be using the money during the next year. These funds can provide the convenience of check-writing and a yield that is highly competitive with interest rates in general. These incredibly safe funds should only be considered for short-term periods of time or for regular expenditures, the way you would use a savings or checking account.

Over the past fifteen years, money market funds have had an average annual return of just over 8 percent, compared to an inflation rate of almost 7 percent. A $10,000 investment in a typical money market fund grew to $38,000 *on a pre-tax basis* over the past 15 years; $10,000 worth of goods and services "inflated" to $28,000 over this same period.

Money market funds came into existence for the general public in the mid-1970s. In order to view their performance over a long period of time, Treasury Bills are used as a substitute. Since 1940, a dollar ($1.22) invested in T-bills grew to eight dollars by the beginning of 1990. During this same period of time, $1 also inflated to $8.

There are close to 550 funds that make up the category "money market." Total market capitalization of this category is $450 billion.

Over the past three years, United States Treasury Bills—again, similar in return to money market funds—have had an average compound return of 7 percent per year. The *annual* return for the past five years has been 7 percent; 9 percent for the past ten years. The standard deviation for money market funds is lower than any other mutual fund category. This means that these funds have had less return variances than any other group.

No more than 60 percent of a conservative investor's portfolio should be devoted to money market funds. Moderate investors should have no more than 40 percent of their money tied up in money funds; aggressive portfolios should have no more than 30 percent committed to such funds.

The sample portfolio shown in a previous chapter recommends a 10 percent commitment to this category for the conservative investor only. Money market funds are not recommended for the moderate or aggressive portfolios as an *investment*; they are the perfect choice for all kinds of investors who are studying investment alternatives or are afraid of current market and/or interest rate conditions. Moderate- and high-tax-bracket investors looking for a temporary place for their monies should first look at tax-free money market funds.

Cash Equivalent: Government Securities Portfolio

Kemper Financial Services
120 LaSalle Street
Chicago, IL 60603
1/800-621-1148

total return	★ ★ ★ ★ ★
risk	★ ★ ★ ★ ★
management	★ ★ ★ ★ ★
expenses	★ ★
Symbol CQGXX	17 points

TOTAL RETURN   ★ ★ ★ ★ ★

Over the past three years, Cash Equivalent has taken $10,000 and turned it into $12,586 ($10,753 over one year and $14,200 over five years). This translates into an average annual return of 8 percent over three years, 7.5 percent over the past year, and 7.3 percent over five years.

A $10,000 investment in the fund at its inception in 1979 was worth over $27,000 at the beginning of 1991. This translates into a compound return of 10 percent per year.

RISK/VOLATILITY   ★ ★ ★ ★ ★

Over the past year, Cash Equivalent's yield has ranged from a high of 9.3 percent to a low of 7.9 percent. This is an average range for a government money market fund.

MANAGEMENT   ★ ★ ★ ★ ★

John W. Stuebe has been the fund's manager since 1981. He joined Kemper in 1979 as a money market trader. Stuebe has a BS in Finance and an MS in economics from DePaul. Stuebe has almost twenty years of investment experience.

The fund has close to $3 billion in assets. Approximately 73 percent of the portfolio is in repurchase agreements and short-term bills, notes, and bonds. The balance is in corporate repurchase agreements. Average maturity for the fund's securities is thirteen days.

This money market fund provides check writing privileges. The minimum amount per check is $250. Investors may use the telephone exchange privilege to make exchanges into other funds within the family.

EXPENSES   ★ ★

The expense ratio for the fund over the past year has been 0.7 percent. This is above average for a money market fund in this book.

SUMMARY

The Cash Equivalent is rated as the number three performing government securities fund for the past three and five years. This is an excellent choice for the extremely conservative investor who wants to be in government-backed obligations.

Federated Master Trust

Federated Research
Federated Investors Tower
Pittsburgh, PA 15222
1/800-245-5000

total return	★ ★ ★ ★ ★	
risk	★ ★ ★ ★ ★	
management	★ ★ ★ ★ ★	
expenses	★ ★ ★	
symbol FMTXX	18 points	

TOTAL RETURN   ★ ★ ★ ★ ★

Over the past three years, Federated Master Trust has taken $10,000 and turned it into $12,688 ($10,781 over one year, $14,383 over five years, and $24,178 over the past ten years). This translates into an average annual return of 8.3 percent over three years, 7.8 percent over the past year, 7.5 percent over five years, and 9.2 percent for the decade.

RISK/VOLATILITY   ★ ★ ★ ★ ★

Over the past year, Federated's yield has ranged from a high of 9.5 percent to a low of 8.2 percent.

MANAGEMENT   ★ ★ ★ ★ ★

The Master Trust is managed by a Federated management team. The fund has close to $2.5 billion in assets. The quality rating of the portfolio is primarily A1- and P1-rated commercial paper. Average maturity for the fund's securities is thirty-five days.

This money market fund does not provide check writing privileges. Investors may use the telephone exchange privilege to make exchanges into other funds within the family.

EXPENSES   ★ ★ ★

The expense ratio for the fund over the past year has been 0.4 percent. This is average for a money market fund in this book but lower than other money funds.

SUMMARY

Federated Master Trust is rated as one of the best performing money market funds over the past year. More importantly, it ranks as number seven for three years, fifth for five years and ten years. This is an extremely impressive and consistent track record. This fund is highly recommended as a general-purpose money market account.

Federated Money Market Trust

Federated Research
Federated Investors Tower
Pittsburgh, PA 15222
1/800-245-5000

total return	★ ★ ★ ★ ★
risk	★ ★ ★ ★ ★
management	★ ★ ★ ★ ★
expenses	★ ★ ★ ★ ★
symbol MMTXX	20 points

TOTAL RETURN ★ ★ ★ ★ ★
Over the past three years, Federated Money Market Trust has taken $10,000 and turned it into $11,776 ($10,550 over one year, $12,763 over five years, and $16,920 over the past ten years). This translates into an average annual return of 5.6 percent over three years, 5.5 percent over the past year, 5 percent over five years, and 5.4 percent for the decade.

RISK/VOLATILITY ★ ★ ★ ★ ★
Over the past year, Federated's yield has ranged from a high of 9.5 percent to a low of 8.2 percent. This is about an average range for a money market fund.

MANAGEMENT ★ ★ ★ ★ ★
The Money Market Trust is managed by a Federated management team. The fund has close to $1.5 billion in assets. The bulk of the portfolio is made up of commercial paper from domestic banks and variable rate CDs. Average maturity for the fund's securities is forty-five days.

This money market fund does not provide check writing privileges. Investors may use the telephone exchange privilege to make exchanges into other funds within the family.

EXPENSES ★ ★ ★ ★ ★
The expense ratio for the fund over the past year has been 0.4 percent. This is average for a money market fund in this book but lower than other money funds.

SUMMARY
Federated Money Market Trust is rated as one of the top performing general-purpose money market funds over the past year. Equally impressive, it ranks as number six for five years and tenth for three, five, and ten years. Since there are close to 1,500 different money market funds, this is quite a feat.

Kemper Government Money Market
Kemper Financial Services
120 South LaSalle Street
Chicago, IL 60603
1/800-621-1048

total return	★ ★ ★ ★ ★	
risk	★ ★ ★ ★ ★	
management	★ ★ ★ ★ ★	
expenses	★ ★ ★	
symbol KEGXX	18 points	

TOTAL RETURN   ★ ★ ★ ★ ★
Over the past three years, Kemper Government Money Market has taken $10,000 and turned it into $12,667 ($10,780 over one year and $14,290 over the past five years). This translates into an average annual return of 8.2 percent over three years, 7.8 percent over the past year, and 7.4 percent over five years.

RISK/VOLATILITY   ★ ★ ★ ★ ★
Over the past year, Kemper's yield has ranged from a high of 9.5 percent to a loss of 8.2 percent. This is an average range for a government money market fund.

MANAGEMENT   ★ ★ ★ ★ ★
Frank J. Rachwalski has been the fund's manager since its inception in 1981. Rachwalski has been with Kemper since 1973. He has an MBA from Loyola and is a Chartered Financial Analyst.

The fund has close to $650 million in assets. The entire portfolio is made up of repurchase agreements and federal agency paper. Average maturity for the fund's securities is 16 days.

This money market fund provides check writing privileges. The minimum amount per check is $500. Investors may use the telephone exchange privilege to make exchanges into other funds within the family.

EXPENSES   ★ ★ ★
The expense ratio for the fund over the past year has been 0.49 percent. This is just slightly above average for money market funds in the book but still well below the average money fund.

SUMMARY
Kemper Government Money Market is the number one rated government money market fund for the past year. It ranks as number five for the past five years. This is yet another example of Kemper's expertise in managing debt instruments. This fund is highly recommended.

Kemper Money Market Portfolio

Kemper Financial Services
120 South LaSalle Street
Chicago, IL 60603
1/800-621-1048

total return	★ ★ ★ ★ ★
risk	★ ★ ★ ★ ★
management	★ ★ ★ ★ ★
expenses	★ ★ ★ ★
symbol KMMXX	19 points

TOTAL RETURN ★ ★ ★ ★ ★

Over the past three years, Kemper Money Market Portfolio has taken $10,000 and turned it into $11,843 ($10,560 over one year). This translates into an average annual return of 5.8 percent over three years and 5.6 percent over the past year.

RISK/VOLATILITY ★ ★ ★ ★ ★

Over the past year, Kemper's yield has ranged from a high of 9.6 percent to a low of 8.3 percent. This is an average range for a money market fund in this book.

MANAGEMENT ★ ★ ★ ★ ★

Frank J. Rachwalski has been the fund's manager since its inception in 1981. Rachwalski has been with Kemper since 1973. He has an MBA from Loyola and is a Chartered Financial Analyst.

The fund has close to $7.5 billion in assets. The portfolio is mostly in A-rated paper. The balance is in United States CDs, Euro CDs, and Canadian CDs. Average maturity for the fund's securities is forty-eight days.

This money market fund provides check writing privileges. The minimum amount per check is $500. Investors may use the telephone exchange privilege to make exchanges into other funds within the family.

EXPENSES ★ ★ ★ ★

The expense ratio for the fund over the past year has been 0.49 percent. This is slightly above average for a money market fund in the book but still well below the typical charges incurred by most money funds.

SUMMARY

Kemper Money Market Portfolio rates as a top performer over the past year. It ranks as fifth for three years, fourth for five years, and number one for ten years. This general-purpose money market fund is highly recommended. It is one of the few money market funds that has been in existence for at least ten years.

Liquid Cash Trust

Federated Research
Federated Investors Tower
Pittsburgh, PA 15222
1/800-245-5000

total return	★ ★ ★ ★ ★
risk	★ ★ ★ ★ ★
management	★ ★ ★ ★ ★
expenses	★ ★ ★ ★ ★
symbol LCTXX	20 points

TOTAL RETURN　★ ★ ★ ★ ★

Over the past three years, Liquid Cash Trust has taken $10,000 and turned it into $12,808 ($10,790 over one year and $14,625 over the past five years). This translates into an average annual return of 8.6 percent over three years, 7.9 percent over the past year, and 7.9 percent over five years.

RISK/VOLATILITY　★ ★ ★ ★ ★

Over the past year, Liquid's yield has ranged from a high of 9.9 percent to a low of 8.5 percent. This is a higher range than that of any other money market fund in the book.

MANAGEMENT　★ ★ ★ ★ ★

The Liquid Cash Trust is managed by a Federated management team. The fund has close to $850 million in assets. The quality rating of the portfolio is made up of repurchase agreements and federal funds. Average maturity for the fund's securities is one day. The Liquid Cash Trust is set up only for institutional accounts.

EXPENSES　★ ★ ★ ★ ★

The expense ratio for the fund over the past year has been 0.1 percent. This is the lowest ratio in the entire book.

SUMMARY

Liquid Cash Trust is run leaner than any other money market fund. It ranks as number three for the past year, number one for the past three years, and number two for the past five years. This is an incredible track record. This is the most highly recommended general-purpose money market fund in the book. Unfortunately, it is only designed for institutional shareholders.

Nuveen Tax Exempt

John Nuveen
333 West Wacker Drive
Chicago, IL 60606
1/800-621-7227

total return	★ ★ ★ ★ ★
risk	★ ★ ★ ★ ★
management	★ ★ ★ ★ ★
expenses	★ ★ ★ ★
symbol NUVXX	19 points

TOTAL RETURN ★ ★ ★ ★ ★
Over the past three years, Nuveen Tax Exempt has taken $10,000 and turned it into $11,843 ($10,570 over one year and $12,946 over the past five years). This translates into an average annual return of 5.8 percent over three years, 5.7 percent over the past year, and 5.3 percent over five years.

RISK/VOLATILITY ★ ★ ★ ★ ★
Over the past year, Nuveen's yield has ranged from a high of 6.7 percent to a low of 5.8 percent. This is better than the range found with the typical *tax-free* money market fund.

MANAGEMENT ★ ★ ★ ★ ★
Stephen A. Barry has been the fund's manager since 1983. His prior experience includes more than twelve years with a major Chicago bank, supervising municipal underwriting and research. Barry received his undergraduate degree from the University of Illinois.

The fund has $2 billion in assets. All of the paper in the portfolio is in very highly rated issues. Average maturity for the fund's securities is thirty days.

This money market fund does not provide check writing privileges. Investors may use the telephone exchange privilege to make exchanges into other funds within the family.

EXPENSES ★ ★ ★ ★
The expense ratio for the fund over the past year has been 0.51 percent. This is slightly above average for a tax-free money market fund.

SUMMARY
Tax-free money market funds are often overlooked by high-tax-bracket investors. This is a mistake, since the net return on such portfolios can far surpass the after-tax yield on taxable money and checking accounts.

Nuveen has more than ninety years of municipal bond experience. Founded in

1898, it is the oldest and largest firm specializing in municipal securities. It is a top performer over the past year. It ranks number four for the past three years and third for the past five years. This is a highly recommended *tax-free* money market fund.

Trust for U.S. Treasury Obligations
Federated Research
Federated Investors Tower
Pittsburgh, PA 15222
1/800-245-5000

total return	★ ★ ★ ★ ★	
risk	★ ★ ★ ★ ★	
management	★ ★ ★ ★ ★	
expenses	★ ★ ★ ★	
symbol TTOXX	19 points	

TOTAL RETURN ★ ★ ★ ★ ★
Over the past three years, Trust U.S. Treasury Obligations has taken $10,000 and turned it into $12,632 ($10,760 over one year, $14,223 over five years, and $23,243 over the past ten years). This translates into an average annual return of 8.1 percent over three years, 7.6 percent over the past year, 7.3 percent over five years, and 8.8 percent for the decade.

RISK/VOLATILITY ★ ★ ★ ★ ★
Over the past year, Trust's yield has ranged from a high of 9.5 percent to a low of 8.2 percent. This is normal for a government money market fund in this book.

MANAGEMENT ★ ★ ★ ★ ★
Roger Early has been the fund's manager since 1985. Prior to joining Federated, he was the international finance manager for Rockwell and senior financial consultant for Touche Ross. Early has a BS from Wharton and an MBA from the University of Pennsylvania.

The fund has close to $6 billion in assets. The portfolio is made up of government agency paper. Average maturity for the fund's securities is thirty-three days.

The fund is set up for institutional use only. There is a minimum investment of $25,000. Investors may use the telephone exchange privilege to make exchanges into other funds within the family.

EXPENSES ★ ★ ★ ★
The expense ratio for the fund over the past year has been 0.45 percent. This is average for a government money market fund.

SUMMARY
Trust U.S. Treasury Obligations is yet another member of the Federated Research family. This group has demonstrated, over and over again, their expertise in managing United States government obligations. This fund ranks number six for

the past year, number four for the past five years, and number one for the decade. This is a highly recommended choice for investors who want to be in a money market fund comprising only government securities.

Vanguard Money Reserves: Federal Portfolio

Vanguard Group
Vanguard Financial Center
P.O. Box 2600
Valley Forge, PA 19482
1/800-662-7447

total return	★ ★ ★ ★ ★
risk	★ ★ ★ ★ ★
management	★ ★ ★ ★ ★
expenses	★ ★ ★ ★ ★
symbol VMFXX	20 points

TOTAL RETURN   ★ ★ ★ ★ ★
Over the past three years, Vanguard Money Reserves: Federal Portfolio has taken $10,000 and turned it into $12,667 ($10,780 over one year and $14,356 over the past five years). This translates into an average annual return of 8.2 percent over three years, 7.8 percent over the past year, and 7.5 percent over five years.

RISK/VOLATILITY   ★ ★ ★ ★ ★
Over the past year, Vanguard Federal Portfolio has had a high yield of 9.5 percent and a low yield of 8.1 percent. This is an average range for a government money market fund.

MANAGEMENT   ★ ★ ★ ★ ★
Vanguard Money Reserves, which consists of separate funds, Prime, Federal, and U.S. Treasury, seeks the maximum current income consistent with preservation of capital and liquidity. These funds are managed by a team, with Ian A. MacKinnon and Robert F. Auwaerter heading the group. MacKinnon has fifteen years' fixed income experience and has an MBA from Pennsylvania State University. Auwaerter has eleven years' fixed income experience and an MBA from Northwestern. Both have been managers of the fund since 1981.

The fund has close to $2 billion in assets. The portfolio is made up of United States government obligations. Average maturity for the fund's securities is forty-one days.

This money market fund provides check writing privileges. The minimum amount per check is $250. Investors may use the telephone exchange privilege to make exchanges into other funds within the family.

EXPENSES   ★ ★ ★ ★ ★
The expense ratio for the fund over the past year has been 0.28 percent. This is the lowest ratio found among similar money market funds.

SUMMARY

Vanguard Money Reserves: Federal Portfolio is rated as the number two performing government money market fund for the past year. It ranks number one for the past five years. Its extremely low costs of operation help give investors a higher return. This is an excellent choice for anyone who wants to be in a money fund comprising exclusively government securities.

Vanguard Money Reserves: Prime Portfolio

Vanguard Group
Vanguard Financial Center
P.O. Box 2600
Valley Forge, PA 19482
1/800-662-7447

total return	★ ★ ★ ★ ★
risk	★ ★ ★ ★ ★
management	★ ★ ★ ★ ★
expenses	★ ★ ★ ★ ★
symbol VMMXX	20 points

TOTAL RETURN ★ ★ ★ ★ ★

Over the past three years, Vanguard Money Reserves: Prime Portfolio has taken $10,000 and turned it into $12,738 ($10,800 over one year, $14,449 over five years, and $24,112 over the past ten years). This translates into an average annual return of 8.4 percent over three years, 8 percent over the past year, 7.7 percent over five years, and 9.2 percent over ten years.

RISK/VOLATILITY ★ ★ ★ ★ ★

Over the past year, Vanguard's yield has ranged from a high of 9.7 percent to a low of 8.3 percent. This is better than the range found with the typical money market fund.

MANAGEMENT ★ ★ ★ ★ ★

Ian Mackinnon and Robert Auwaerter have been the fund's managers since 1981. MacKinnon has fifteen years' fixed income experience and has an MBA from Pennsylvania State University. He is the manager of twenty-one Vanguard fixed-income funds. Auwaerter has eleven years' fixed income experience and an MBA from Northwestern.

The fund has close to $12.5 billion in assets. Over 77 percent of the portfolio is in highly rated P1-rated commercial paper. The balance is in CDs, United States Government obligations, Eurodollars, and banker's acceptances. Average maturity for the fund's securities is forty-four days.

This money market fund provides check writing privileges. The minimum amount per check is $250. Investors may use the telephone exchange privilege to make exchanges into other funds within the family.

EXPENSES ★ ★ ★ ★ ★

The expense ratio for the fund over the past year has been 0.28 percent. This is below average for a money market fund.

SUMMARY

Vanguard Money Reserves: Prime Portfolio is rated as the fifth-best-performing general-purpose money market fund for the past year. It rates as number two for the past three years and number three for the past five years. This is another example of Vanguard's expertise in managing money market instruments. The group knows how to run such funds with minimal costs to its investors.

Zweig Cash Fund: Government Securities
Zweig Securities
25 Broadway, 12th Floor
New York, NY 10004
1/800-272-2700

total return	★ ★ ★ ★ ★
risk	★ ★ ★ ★
management	★ ★ ★ ★ ★
expenses	★ ★
symbol DBGSX	16 points

TOTAL RETURN ★ ★ ★ ★ ★
Over the past three years, Zweig Cash Government Securities has taken $10,000 and turned it into $12,527 ($10,730 over one year and $14,157 over the past five years). This translates into an average annual return of 7.8 percent over three years, 7.3 percent over the past year, and 7.2 percent over five years.

RISK/VOLATILITY ★ ★ ★ ★
Over the past year, Zweig's yield has ranged from a high of 8.8 percent to a low of 7.6 percent. This is slightly below average for the government money market fund group.

MANAGEMENT ★ ★ ★ ★ ★
Bruce Trottier has been the fund's manager since the fund's 1984 inception. Prior to joining Zweig, he was chief investment advisor for Drexel Burnham for almost ten years. Before joining Drexel, he was a money manager and economist for Equitable Life Insurance.

The fund has close to $162 million in assets. The quality rating of the portfolio is all single-A rated paper or better. Average maturity for the fund's securities is thirty days.

This money market fund provides check writing privileges. The minimum amount per check is $500. Investors may use the telephone exchange privilege to make exchanges into other funds within the family.

EXPENSES ★ ★
The expense ratio for the fund over the past year has been 0.74 percent. This is higher than that of any other money market fund in the book.

SUMMARY
Zweig Cash Fund: Government Securities rates as a top performer over the past year. It is ranked as the sixth-best performer for the past five years. This is a fine choice for someone looking for a money market fund made up of government obligations, despite the fund's somewhat high operating costs.

Municipal Bond Funds

These funds invest in securities issued by municipalities, political subdivisions, and United States Territories. The kind of security issued is either a note or bond, both of which are interest-bearing instruments exempt from federal income taxes. There are three different categories of municipal bond funds: national, state-free, and high-yield.

National municipal bond funds are debt instruments issued by a wide range of states. These funds are exempt from federal income taxes only. To determine what small percentage is also exempt from state income taxes, consult the fund's prospectus and look for the weighting of United States Territory issues (e.g., the Virgin Islands, Guam, Puerto Rico), District of Columbia items, and obligations from your state of residence.

State-free, sometimes referred to as "double tax-free," funds invest only in bonds and notes issued in a particular state. You must be a legal resident of that state in order to avoid paying state income taxes on the fund's return. As an example, most California residents in a high tax bracket will only want to consider purchasing a municipal bond fund with the name "California" in it. Residents of New York who purchase a California tax-free fund will escape federal income taxes but not state and any local taxes.

High-yield tax-free funds invest in the same kinds of issues found in a national municipal bond fund but with one important difference. By seeking higher returns, high-yield funds look for lower-rated issues and bonds that are not rated. A municipality may not obtain a rating for its issue because of the costs involved compared to the relatively small size of the bond or note being floated. Many non-rated issues are very safe. These kinds of municipal bond funds are relatively new but should not be overlooked by the tax-conscious investor. High-yield tax-free funds have demonstrated less volatility and higher return than their other tax-free counterparts.

Prospective investors need to compare tax-free bond yields to *after-tax* yields on corporate or government bond funds. To determine which of these three fund categories is best for you, use your marginal tax bracket, subtract this amount from one, and multiply the resulting figure by the taxable investment. As an example, suppose you were in the 35 percent bracket, state and federal combined. By subtracting this figure from one, you are left with 0.65. Multiply 0.65 by the fully taxable yield you could get—let us say 9 percent. Sixty-five percent of 9 percent is 5.85 percent. The 5.85 percent represents what you get on a 9 percent investment *after* you have paid state and federal income taxes on it. This means that if you can get 5.85 percent or higher from a *tax-free* investment, take it.

Municipal bond funds are not for investors in a low tax bracket. Such investors who want to be in bonds are better off in corporate or government issues. Furthermore, municipal bonds should never be used in a retirement plan. There is only one way to make tax-free income taxable, and that is to put it into an IRA, pension, or profit-sharing plan. Everything that comes out of these plans is fully taxable by the Feds.

Over the past three years, the typical municipal bond fund has had an average compounded annual return of 8.6 percent. These funds have averaged a total annual return of 8.4 percent over the past five years and 10.75 percent annually for the decade. Looking at the same time periods, *high-yield* municipal bond funds have averaged 9.1 percent annually for the past three years, 8.6 percent for five years, and 11.5 percent for the past decade.

No more than 80 percent of a conservative investor's portfolio should be devoted to municipal bond funds. Moderate investors should have no more than 70 percent of their money tied up in money funds, and aggressive portfolios should have no more than 50 percent committed to such funds.

The sample portfolio shown in a previous chapter recommends a 20 percent commitment to this category for the conservative investor and 10 percent for the moderate investor. As is true with any category of mutual funds, whenever larger dollar amounts are involved, more than one fund per category should be used.

Calvert Tax-Free Reserves Limited-Term Portfolio

Calvert Securities
1700 Pennsylvania Avenue NW
Washington, DC 20006
1/800-368-2745

total return	★
risk	★ ★ ★ ★ ★
management	★ ★ ★ ★
current income	★ ★
expenses	★ ★ ★
symbol CTFLX	15 points

TOTAL RETURN ★
Over the past five years, Calvert Tax-Free Reserves Limited-Term Portfolio has taken $10,000 and turned it into $13,700 ($12,200 over three years). This translates into an average annual return of 6.5 percent over five years and 6.8 percent over the past three years.

RISK/VOLATILITY ★ ★ ★ ★ ★
Over the past five years, Calvert Tax-Free has been more stable than 99 percent of all other mutual funds and safer than 99 percent of its peers.

MANAGEMENT ★ ★ ★ ★
Rochat has been the fund's manager since its 1981 inception. Reno Martini came on-board as co-manager in 1983. The prospectus requires holdings in the fund to have a maturity of three years or less, eliminating almost any concern over interest rate risk.

The fund invests primarily in medium- and high-grade municipal obligations. Close to two-thirds of the portfolio's assets are in issues rated single-A or higher. There are 50 bonds in this $140 million portfolio. Close to 95 percent of the fund's holdings are in bonds, with the balance in cash. The average maturity of the bonds in the portfolio is one year.

CURRENT INCOME ★ ★
Over the past three years, Calvert has had an average annual yield of 6.1 percent, lower than any other tax-free fund in this book.

EXPENSES ★ ★ ★
The expense ration for the fund has averaged 0.8 percent annually over the past three years, virtually identical to the typical tax-free bond fund. The average annual turnover rate for the last three years has been 47 percent, approximately 40 percent less than its group's average. The low turnover rate helps reduce overall fund expenses and helps increase total return.

SUMMARY

Calvert Tax-Free Reserves Limited-Term Portfolio is the number one choice for someone looking for a very low risk tax-free bond fund. The performance ranking would be excellent if this fund were compared to a *money market* fund, which is perhaps how it should be judged, based on the short-term nature of the securities in the portfolio. Nevertheless, this is a very good choice for municipal *bond* buyers.

Delaware Tax-Free Income—USA Series

Delaware Distributors
10 Penn Center Plaza
Philadelphia, PA 19103
1/800-523-4640

total return	★ ★ ★ ★
risk	★ ★ ★
management	★ ★ ★ ★
current income	★ ★ ★ ★
expenses	★ ★ ★
symbol DMTFX	18 points

TOTAL RETURN ★ ★ ★ ★

Over the past five years, Delaware Tax-Free Income—USA Series has taken $10,000 and turned it into $15,700 ($13,100 over three years). This translates into an average annual return of 9 percent over past three and five years. Its returns have been higher than any other municipal bond fund in the book except two *high yield* tax-free funds.

RISK/VOLATILITY ★ ★ ★

Over the past five years, Delaware Tax-Free has been safer than 85 percent of all mutual funds; within its category it ranks in the top 65 percent. Since its 1984 inception the fund has had only one negative year (off 2 percent in 1987) and has underperformed the bond index twice.

MANAGEMENT ★ ★ ★ ★

J. Michael Pokorny has been the fund's manager since its inception. Prior to joining Delaware in 1978, Pokorny was a corporate bond specialist for eight years with Salomon Brothers and Kidder Peabody. Currently he manages all of the Delaware Group's municipal and high-yield corporate bond funds.

There are 180 bonds in this $620 million portfolio. Close to 100 percent of the fund's holdings are in bonds, with the balance in cash. The average maturity of the bonds in the portfolio is twenty-five years. Approximately 50 percent of the portfolio is invested in A-rated bonds or better, with the balance in BBB-rated issues.

CURRENT INCOME ★ ★ ★ ★

Over the past three years, Delaware Tax-Free has had an average annual yield of 7.41 percent, higher than any other tax-free fund in this book.

EXPENSES ★ ★ ★

The expense ratio for the fund has averaged 0.77 percent annually over the past three years, slightly less than the typical tax-free fund.

The average annual turnover rate for the last three years has been a low 16 percent, approximately 40 percent less than its group's average. The low turnover rate helps reduce overall fund expenses and increase the fund's total return.

SUMMARY

Delaware Tax-Free Income—USA Series earns a perfect score for total return. Its track record, current income stream, and management are excellent. The safety factor of the fund is superior. This portfolio would be a great addition to anyone seeking tax-free income.

Kemper California Tax-Free Income Fund

Kemper Financial Services
120 South LaSalle Street
Chicago, IL 60603
1/800-621-1048

total return	★ ★ ★
risk	★ ★
management	★ ★ ★
current income	★ ★ ★
expenses	★ ★ ★ ★
symbol KCTFX	15 points

TOTAL RETURN ★ ★ ★
Over the past five years, Kemper California—Tax-Free Income Fund has taken $10,000 and turned it into $14,700 ($13,000 over three years). This translates into an average annual return of 8 percent over five years and 9 percent over the past three years.

A $10,000 investment in the fund at its 1983 inception was worth over $20,000 at the beginning of 1990. This translates into a compound return of 11 percent.

RISK/VOLATILITY ★ ★
Over the past five years, Kemper was safer than 85 percent of all mutual funds; within its category it ranks in the top 40 percent. Since its inception in 1983, the fund has not had a negative year. Over the past five years it has underperformed the bond index twice.

MANAGEMENT ★ ★ ★
J. Patrick Beimford has managed the fund since 1985. Beimford joined Kemper Financial Services in 1976 as a fixed-income portfolio manager. Prior to coming to Kemper, Beimford was a financial accountant with Inland Steel Company. He has an MBA from the University of Chicago and is a Chartered Financial Analyst.

The fund is managed with an eye toward total return, not just current yield. Such an approach is crucial for preservation of principal. The average maturity of the fund is just under twenty-five years. Virtually all of the fund's bonds are invested in AAA, AA, and single-A issues, with the bulk in AAA-rated items. There are close to 200 different issues in the portfolio.

There are 190 bonds in this $750 million portfolio. Close to 100 percent of the fund's holdings are in bonds, with the balance in cash. The average maturity of the bonds in the portfolio is twenty-four years.

CURRENT INCOME ★ ★ ★
Over the past three years, Kemper California has averaged an annual income

stream of 7 percent, normal for its group but somewhat on the high side for a single-state fund.

EXPENSES   ★ ★ ★ ★
The average annual expense ratio for Kemper California has been 0.64 percent over the past three years. This rate is a little less than average for its category.

Over the past three years, the fund has had a very low average annual turnover rate of 32 percent. Such a low rate translates into an efficiently run operation and a high total return.

SUMMARY
Kemper California Tax-Free Income Fund rates as a very good choice for the tax-free investor. However, since the fund's income is exempt from California state as well as federal taxes, it is most appropriate for that state's residents. In fact, it is certainly a top choice for the Californian.

MFS Managed Municipal Bond Trust

MFS Financial Services
500 Boylston Street
Boston, MA 02116
1/800-654-0266

total return	★ ★ ★ ★
risk	★
management	★ ★
current income	★ ★ ★
expenses	★ ★ ★ ★
symbol MMBFX	14 points

TOTAL RETURN ★ ★ ★ ★

Over the past five years, MFS Managed Municipal Bond Trust has taken $10,000 and turned it into $14,700 ($13,000 over three years and $34,000 over the past ten years). This translates into an average annual return of 8 percent over five years, 9 percent over the past three years, and 13 percent for the decade.

RISK/VOLATILITY ★

Over the past five years, MFS Managed has been safer than 80 percent of all mutual funds; within its category it ranks in the top 40 percent. During the past decade the fund has not had a negative year, but has underperformed the bond index three times.

MANAGEMENT ★ ★

Portfolio manager Robert A. Dennis has run the fund since 1984. He joined MFS in 1980. Dennis is a graduate of MIT and is a Chartered Financial Analyst.

The fund has done well in down as well as up markets. Management style can best be described as very active. According to Dennis, "We don't just keep our fund invested in long municipal bonds of great volatility at all times." He sees his main job as adjusting the interest-rate sensitivity of the portfolio, reducing it as rates rise and increasing it as yields fall.

The tax-exempt market is not homogeneous. That means selection is very important. Sectors of the market like tax-supported general obligation bonds, turnpike revenue issues, and different geographic areas trade differently depending on their supply and demand and on how their credit quality is perceived. As a former budgetary officer for New York City, Dennis is very sensitive to these issues.

There are over 170 different bonds in this $1.4 billion portfolio. Close to 90 percent of the fund's holdings are in bonds, with the balance in cash. The average maturity of the bonds in the portfolio is twenty-three years; all of the bonds are rated single-A or higher.

CURRENT INCOME   ★ ★ ★
Over the past three years, MFS Managed has averaged an annual income stream of 7 percent, typical for its group.

EXPENSES   ★ ★ ★ ★
The annual expense ratio for MFS has averaged 0.64 percent, somewhat lower than its peers.

Over the past three years, average annual turnover has been a disappointing 202 percent. This high level makes it the second-worst in its group.

SUMMARY
MFS Managed Municipal Bond Trust is in somewhat of an unfortunate position. On the one hand it ranks at least "good" in all categories but does not score as high as some other tax-free funds in the book. On the other hand, its track record places it above 80 percent of all other municipal bond funds. If a ten-year time horizon were used, the fund would rank as "excellent" in the areas of return and risk.

Nuveen Municipal Bond

John Nuveen
333 West Wacker Drive
Chicago, IL 60606
1/800-621-7227

total return	★ ★ ★ ★
risk	★ ★ ★ ★
management	★ ★ ★ ★
current income	★ ★ ★
expenses .	★ ★ ★ ★
symbol NUVBX	19 points

TOTAL RETURN ★ ★ ★ ★

Over the past five years, Nuveen Municipal Bond has taken $10,000 and turned it into $14,700 ($13,000 over three years and $28,400 over the past ten years). This translates into an average annual return of 8 percent over five years, 9 percent over the past three years, and 11 percent for the decade.

RISK/VOLATILITY ★ ★ ★ ★

Over the past five years, Nuveen Municipal has been safer than over 90 percent of all mutual funds; within its category it ranks in the top 80 percent. During the past five years the fund has not had a negative year. It has underperformed the bond index twice.

MANAGEMENT ★ ★ ★ ★

Thomas C. Spalding Jr., has been with the fund since 1978, a very long time for a municipal bond fund manager. Spalding joined Nuveen in 1976 as a portfolio manager for some of their unit trusts. He was previously with Lincoln National Life as a bond research analyst. He has an MBA from the University of Michigan and is a Chartered Financial Analyst.

Nuveen maintains the largest research department in the investment banking industry devoted exclusively to municipal bonds. Using resources like this, Nuveen looks for bonds whose credit situations are improving. It also tries to find unrated bonds that have investment-grade quality.

Spalding emphasizes total return over current yield. All of the fund's bonds are rated single-A or better. The fund's average maturity is slightly over twenty years. There are over 165 different issues in this $1.3 billion portfolio.

CURRENT INCOME ★ ★ ★

Over the past three years, Nuveen Municipal has averaged an annual income stream of 6.9 percent, a little lower than its group average.

EXPENSES   ★ ★ ★ ★
The expense ratio for Nuveen has averaged 0.63 percent for the last three years. This is a little lower than its peers.

Turnover for the fund has averaged only 9.3 percent annually for the past three years. This turnover rate is impressively low, giving it the lowest number for any tax-free bond in the book.

SUMMARY
Nuveen Municipal Bond has consistently done well over the past three, five, and ten years. It has outperformed 90 percent of all other tax-free bond funds. The fund's strong suit is its risk management. It is highly recommended.

Putnam California Tax Exempt Income

Putnam Financial Services
1 Post Office Square
Boston, MA 02109
1/800-225-1581

total return	★ ★ ★ ★
risk	★ ★ ★
management	★ ★ ★
current income	★ ★ ★ ★
expenses	★ ★ ★ ★ ★
symbol PCTEX	19 points

TOTAL RETURN ★ ★ ★ ★

Over the past five years, Putnam California Tax Exempt Income has taken $10,000 and turned it into $14,700 ($13,000 over three years). This translates into an average annual return of 8 percent over five years and 9 percent over the past three years.

A $10,000 investment at the fund's inception in 1983 was worth over $19,000 by the beginning of 1990. This translates into a compound return of 10 percent per year.

RISK/VOLATILITY ★ ★ ★

Over the past five years, Putnam California has been safer than 85 percent of all mutual funds; within its category it ranks in the top 40 percent. Since its inception the fund has not had a negative year. It has underperformed the bond index in three of the past five years.

MANAGEMENT ★ ★ ★

William H. Reeves has been the fund's manager since 1986. Prior to joining Putnam, Reeves was a vice president at Crockett Bank. He has an MBA from Wharton and over sixteen years of investment experience.

Although the fund does not get the attention that some of its California peers do, it has done better than most. The fund is made up exclusively of investment-grade issues and has a total value of over $1.8 billion. There are close to 160 issues in the portfolio, which has an average maturity of twenty-five years.

CURRENT INCOME ★ ★ ★ ★

Over the past three years, Putnam California has averaged an annual income stream of over 7.3 percent, the second-highest in the book's tax-free group.

EXPENSES ★ ★ ★ ★ ★

The expense ratio for Putnam has averaged 0.52 percent for the last three years, making it the second-most frugally run fund in its group.

The average annual turnover rate for the fund has been a somewhat high 83 percent for the last three years. High turnover rates usually translate into lower total returns.

SUMMARY
Putnam California Tax Exempt Income is a good solid performer. It has a superior yield. It has performed better than 80 percent of all municipal bond funds. The fund is best suited for California residents, since its income is exempt from state as well as federal taxes. This is a top choice for the Californian.

Putnam Tax-Exempt Income

Putnam Financial Services
1 Post Office Square
Boston, MA 02109
1/800-225-1581

total return	★ ★ ★ ★	
risk	★	
management	★ ★ ★	
current income	★ ★ ★	
expenses	★ ★ ★ ★ ★	
symbol PTAEX	16 points	

TOTAL RETURN   ★ ★ ★ ★

Over the past five years, Putnam Tax-Exempt Income has taken $10,000 and turned it into $14,700 ($13,000 over three years and $34,000 over the last ten years). This translates into an average annual return of 8 percent over five years, 9 percent over the past three years, and 13 percent for the decade.

A $10,000 investment at the fund's 1976 inception was worth over $32,000 by the beginning of 1991. This translates into a compound return of 9 percent per year.

RISK/VOLATILITY   ★

Over the past five years, Putnam Tax-Exempt has been safer than 75 percent of all mutual funds; within its category it ranks in the bottom 15 percent. During the past five years the fund had one negative year (off 1 percent in 1987), and has underperformed the bond index twice.

MANAGEMENT   ★ ★ ★

Portfolio manager David J. Eurkus has been at the fund's helm since 1985. Before joining Putnam in 1983, Eurkus was a bond investment officer for Aetna Life. Prior to that he was in charge of the bond department for Colonial Bank for twelve years. Eurkus has a BS from Babson College and over twenty years of investment experience.

Management has been successful at short-term market movements. The fund has a total market value of $1.3 billion. 97 percent of the fund's holdings are in bonds, with the balance in cash. There are over 170 different issues in the portfolio, all of which are investment grade. Average bond maturity is over twenty-five years.

CURRENT INCOME   ★ ★ ★

Over the past three years, Putnam has averaged an annual income stream of 7.2 percent, an average tax-free yield.

EXPENSES   ★ ★ ★ ★ ★

The expense ratio for Putnam Tax-Exempt has averaged 0.51 percent for the last three years, the second-lowest for its group.

Over the past three years, the fund's average annual turnover rate has been a disappointing 128 percent. This turnover rate is over three times greater than other municipal bond funds.

SUMMARY

Putnam Tax-Exempt Income scores impressively in the area of total return, and its current yield is very good. Management and risk reduction are not impressive. This fund is best suited for the long-term investor. It has outperformed 90 percent of all tax-free funds over the past five and ten years.

SAFECO Municipal Bond

SAFECO Securities
P.O. Box 34890
Seattle, WA 98124
1/800-426-6730

total return	★ ★ ★ ★
risk	★ ★
management	★ ★ ★
current income	★ ★ ★
expenses	★ ★ ★ ★ ★
symbol SFCOX	17 points

TOTAL RETURN ★ ★ ★ ★
Over the past five years, SAFECO Municipal Bond has taken $10,000 and turned it into $14,700 ($13,300 over three years). This translates into an average annual return of 8 percent over five years and 10 percent over the past three years.

RISK/VOLATILITY ★ ★
Over the past five years, SAFECO Municipal has been safer than 80 percent of all mutual funds; within its category it is ranked in the bottom 40 percent. Since the fund's 1981 inception, it has not had a negative year. Over the past five years it has underperformed the bond index twice.

MANAGEMENT ★ ★ ★
Portfolio manager Stephen C. Bauer has been with the fund since its inception date. He first joined SAFECO in 1971 as a fixed-income analyst. Bauer has an MBA in finance from the University of Washington.

Although some portfolio managers use traders as their go-betweens with bond brokers, Bauer prefers to be in direct contact. "I want a direct feel for the market . . . I know what our analyses of market conditions tell us and what the economic forecasts are predicting, but I want to gauge the actual direction of the market as it unfolds, not several hours later when it's relayed to me by a person who's been on the phone with the brokers." He deals with seventy-five to a hundred brokers each day.

On the analysis side of municipal bonds, the focus is on rate comparisons and where those rates are likely to be headed. According to Bauer, the trends are always changing. Management has to look constantly at prices and trends, trying to anticipate changes in the economy that will benefit the fund.

On an annual basis, the fund has always ranked in the top half in performance. The fund is made up of over 120 different bonds with a total market capitalization of $300 million. Close to 95 percent of the portfolio is in investment-grade issues, with the balance in cash. The average maturity is twenty-two years.

CURRENT INCOME   ★ ★ ★
Over the past three years, SAFECO has averaged an annual income stream of 7.1 percent, somewhat higher than the average tax-exempt bond fund.

EXPENSES   ★ ★ ★ ★ ★
The expense ratio for the fund has averaged 0.59 percent for the last three years.

Over the past three years, the fund's average annual turnover rate has been 91.3 percent, 25 percent lower than the average municipal bond fund.

SUMMARY
SAFECO Municipal Bond ranks as either "very good" or "superior" in all major categories except one, risk. Thus, this fund is a very good choice for the investor who is not overly concerned with a certain amount of risk. It is particularly attractive for the diversified tax-free investor concerned with current income.

SteinRoe High Yield Municipals

Liberty Securities
P.O. Box 1143
Chicago, IL 60690
1/800-338-2550

total return	★ ★ ★ ★ ★	
risk	★ ★ ★	
management	★ ★ ★	
current income	★ ★ ★ ★	
expenses .	★ ★ ★	
symbol SRMFX	18 points	

TOTAL RETURN   ★ ★ ★ ★ ★
Over the past five years, SteinRoe High Yield Municipals has taken $10,000 and turned it into $15,400 ($13,300 over three years). This translates into an average annual return of 9 percent over five years and 10 percent over the past three years.

RISK/VOLATILITY   ★ ★ ★
Over the past five years, SteinRoe High Yield has been safer than 90 percent of all mutual funds; within its category it ranks in the top half. During the past five years the fund has had only one negative year (off 0.25 percent in 1987), but has under-performed the bond index three times.

MANAGEMENT   ★ ★ ★
Thomas J. Conlin has been the fund's portfolio manager since 1987. Conlin joined SteinRoe in 1978. He has an MBA from Indiana University and is also a Chartered Financial Analyst and Chartered Investment Counselor.

The quality of the bond's holdings in the fund varies depending upon Conlin's appraisal of macro economics. He does most of his own credit research. Research is especially important for unrated issues (NR). "Unrated" does not necessarily mean lower quality; the issue may simply be too small to rate. Such research requires extra steps, but the results can be high yields and good quality. Conlin likes to look at economic changes and trends. Right now he favors those industries involved with senior citizens, alcohol abuse, and garbage.

Conlin seeks issues currently out of favor. The fund concentrates more on total return than yield. Such a focus helps to reduce shareholder risk. Bonds are sold when an industry becomes over-researched; portfolio sales also occur when he sees the first signs of credit deterioration.

There are 140 different issues in this $320 million portfolio, which has an average maturity of about twenty years. Close to 96 percent of the fund's holdings are in bonds, with the balance in cash. Most of the bonds are investment-grade issues.

CURRENT INCOME   ★ ★ ★ ★
Over the past three years, SteinRoe has averaged an annual income stream of just over 7.5 percent, the second-highest for its peer group.

EXPENSES   ★ ★ ★
The expense ratio for SteinRoe has averaged 0.73 percent for the last three years. This is the most expensively run tax-free fund in the book, but it still ranks better than average among the universe of municipal bonds.

Over the past three years, the fund has had an average annual turnover rate of 174 percent annually. This rate is somewhat higher than its group's average.

SUMMARY
SteinRoe High Yield Municipals has a superior return and current yield. Its management and risk control are very good. There are only a modest number of high yielding tax-free bond funds, but this is an idea whose time has come. The safety factor of high-yield municipal bonds is much greater than the public would suspect. There is little relationship between these kinds of bonds and corporate junk issues.

Van Kampen Merritt Tax-Free High Income Trust

Van Kampen Merritt
1001 Warrenville Road
Lisle, IL 60532
1/800-225-2222

total return	★ ★ ★
risk	★ ★ ★ ★ ★
management	★ ★ ★ ★
current income	★ ★ ★ ★ ★
expenses	★ ★ ★
symbol VKMHX	20 points

TOTAL RETURN ★ ★ ★ ★
Over the past five years, Van Kampen Merritt Tax-Free High Income Trust has taken $10,000 and turned it into $15,600 ($12,600 over three years). This translates into an average annual return of 9.3 percent over five years and close to 8 percent over the past three years.

RISK/VOLATILITY ★ ★ ★ ★ ★
Over the past five years, Van Kampen Merritt has been safer than 95 percent of all mutual funds; within its category it ranks in the top 10 percent. Since its 1985 inception the fund has not had a negative year. It has underperformed the bond index twice.

MANAGEMENT ★ ★ ★ ★
David Johnson has been the fund's manager since 1987. Co-manager Mark Muller has shared fund decisions with Johnson since 1989. Management diversifies as much as possible to keep yield high.

There are 170 bonds in this $650 million portfolio. Close to 100 percent of the fund's holdings are in bonds. The maturity of the bonds in the portfolio averages 22 years. Approximately 50 percent of the portfolio is invested in BBB-rated bonds or better, the balance is in non-rated issues. The fund's average weighted price is 95 percent of par; this 5 percent discount gives the portfolio a nice little added profit potential.

CURRENT INCOME ★ ★ ★ ★ ★
Over the past three years, Van Kampen Tax-Free has had an average annual yield of 8.1%, higher than any other tax-free fund in this book.

EXPENSES ★ ★ ★
The expense ration for the fund has averaged 0.8 percent over the past three years, average for a tax-free bond fund.

The average annual turnover rate for the last three years has been 76 percent, a figure that is slightly higher than its group average.

SUMMARY

Van Kampen Merritt Tax-Free High Income Trust has the best five year total return track record of any municipal bond fund. Its ranking of four stars for return is due to its three year record. This fund also has the highest tax-free current income figures; it beats everything else in the book. Management is considered superior. This fund is the number one choice for the investor looking for the highest possible current income that is free from federal taxes.

XII.
Summary

AGGRESSIVE GROWTH (10)
1. Acorn
2. Alliance Quasar A
3. Founders Special
4. GIT Equity Special Growth Portfolio
5. Janus Venture
6. Nicholas II
7. Pennsylvania Mutual
8. Putnam OTC Emerging Growth
9. Putnam Voyager
10. Royce Value

BALANCED FUNDS (9)
11. American Balanced
12. Dodge & Cox Balanced
13. Franklin Income
14. IDS Mutual
15. Income Fund of America
16. Massachusetts Financial Total Return
17. National Total Income
18. Phoenix Balanced
19. Phoenix Convertible

CORPORATE BONDS (4)
20. Bond Fund of America
21. FPA New Income
22. Merrill Lynch Corporate High Quality A
23. United Bond

GOVERNMENT BONDS (10)
24. Alliance Mortgage Securities Income
25. Federated GNMA Trust

26. Federated Income Trust
27. Federated Intermediate Government Trust
28. Fund for U.S. Government Securities
29. Kemper U.S. Government Securities
30. Lord Abbett U.S. Government Securities
31. Merrill Lynch Federal Securities
32. Putnam U.S. Government Income
33. Vanguard Fixed-Income GNMA

GROWTH FUNDS (19)

34. AIM Weingarten
35. AMCAP
36. Franklin Growth
37. Growth Fund of America
38. Guardian Park Avenue
39. IAI Regional
40. IDEX
41. Janus
42. Mathers
43. Merrill Lynch Basic Value—Class A
44. Mutual Beacon
45. Mutual Benefit
46. New Economy
47. New York Venture
48. Phoenix Growth
49. Security Equity
50. Shearson Appreciation
51. Thomson Growth B
52. United Accumulative

GROWTH & INCOME (11)

53. AIM Charter
54. Colonial
55. Dean Witter Dividend Growth Securities
56. FPA Perennial
57. Fundamental Investors
58. Investment Co. of America
59. Merrill Lynch Capital A
60. Putnam Fund for Growth & Income
61. SBSF Growth

62. Selected American Shares
63. Washington Mutual

HIGH YIELD (4)
64. CIGNA High Yield
65. Merrill Lynch Corporate Bond High Income Portfolio
66. Oppenheimer High Yield
67. Phoenix High Yield Fund Series

INTERNATIONAL BONDS (2)
68. MFS Worldwide Governments Trust
69. Van Eck World Income

INTERNATIONAL EQUITIES (8)
70. EuroPacific Growth
71. G.T. Pacific Growth
72. New Perspective
73. Oppenheimer Global
74. SoGen International
75. Templeton Foreign
76. Templeton Growth
77. Templeton World

METALS FUNDS (2)
78. Franklin Gold
79. Oppenheimer Gold and Special Minerals

MONEY MARKET FUNDS (11)
80. Cash Equivalent: Government Securities Portfolio (gov.)
81. Federated Master Trust
82. Federated Money Market Trust
83. Federated Liquid Cash Trust
84. Kemper Government Money Market (gov.)
85. Kemper Money Market Portfolio
86. Nuveen Tax Exempt (*tax-free*)
87. Trust U.S. Treasury Obligations (gov.)
88. Vanguard Money Market Reserves: Federal Portfolio (gov.)
89. Vanguard Money Reserves: Prime Portfolio
90. Zweig Cash Fund: Government Securities (gov.)

(all 11 of these funds are at least five years old; five of them are 10+ years old)

MUNICIPAL BONDS (10)

91. Calvert Tax-Free Reserves Limited-Term Portfolio
92. Delaware Tax-Free Income—USA Series
93. Kemper California Tax-Free Income Fund
94. MFS Managed Municipal Bond Trust
95. Nuveen Municipal Bond
96. Putnam California Tax-Exempt Income
97. Putnam Tax-Exempt Income
98. SAFECO Municipal Bond
99. SteinRoe High-Yield Municipals
100. Van Kampen Merritt Tax-Free High Income Trust

Appendix A:
Glossary of Mutual Fund Terms

Adviser—The organization employed by a mutual fund to give professional advice on the fund's investments and asset management practices (also called the "investment adviser").

"Asked" or "Offering" Price—The price at which a mutual fund's shares can be purchased. The asked or offering price means the current net asset value per share plus sales charge, if any.

"Bid" or "Sell" Price—The price at which a mutual fund's shares are redeemed (bought back) by the fund. The bid or redemption price usually means the current net asset value per share.

Broker/Dealer—A firm that buys and sells mutual fund shares and other securities to the public.

Capital Gains Distributions—Payments to mutual fund shareholders of profits (long-term gains) realized on the sale of the fund's portfolio securities. These amounts are usually paid once a year.

Capital Growth—An increase in the market value of a mutual fund's securities, as reflected in the net asset value of fund shares. This is a specific long-term objective of many mutual funds.

Custodian—The organization (usually a bank) that keeps custody of securities and other assets of a mutual fund.

Diversification—The policy of all mutual funds to spread investments among a number of different securities to reduce the risk inherent in investing.

Dollar-cost Averaging—The practice of investing equal amounts of money at regular intervals regardless of whether securities markets are moving up or down. This procedure reduces average share costs to the investor who acquires more shares in the periods of lower securities prices and fewer shares in periods of higher prices.

Exchange Privilege—An option enabling mutual fund shareholders to transfer their investment from one fund to another within the same fund family as their needs or objectives change. Typically, funds allow investors to use the exchange privilege several times a year for a low fee—or no fee—per exchange.

Investment Company—A corporation, trust, or partnership that invests pooled funds of shareholders in securities appropriate to the fund's objective. Among the benefits of investment companies, compared to direct investments, are professional management and diversification. Mutual funds (also known as "open-end" investment companies) are the most popular kind of investment company.

Investment Objective—The goal—e.g., long-term capital growth, current income, etc.—that the investor and mutual fund pursue together.

Long-term Funds—An industry designation for funds that invest primarily in securities with remaining maturities of more than one year. In this book the term means fifteen years or more. Long-term funds are broadly divided into equity (stock), bond, and income funds.

Management Fee—The amount paid by a mutual fund to the investment adviser for its services. The average annual fee industry wide is about one-half of one percent of fund assets.

Mutual Fund—An investment company that pools money from shareholders and invests in a variety of securities, including stocks, bonds, and money market instruments. A mutual fund stands ready to buy back (redeem) its shares at their current net asset value; this value depends on the market value of the fund's portfolio securities at the time of redemption. Most mutual funds continuously offer new shares to investors.

Net Asset Value Per Share—The market worth of one share of a mutual fund. This figure is derived by taking a fund's total assets—securities, cash, and any accrued earnings—deducting liabilities, and dividing by the number of shares outstanding.

No-load Fund—A mutual fund selling its shares at net asset value without the addition of sales charges.

Portfolio—A collection of securities owned by an individual or an institution (such as a mutual fund). A fund's portfolio may include a combination of stocks, bonds, and money market securities.

Prospectus—The official booklet describing a mutual fund that must be furnished to all investors. It contains information required by the United States Securities and Exchange Commission on such subjects as the fund's investment objectives, services, and fees. A more detailed document, known as "Part B" of the prospectus or the "Statement of Additional Information," is available at no charge upon request.

Redemption Price—The amount per share (shown as the "bid" in newspaper tables) that mutual fund shareholders receive when they cash in the shares. The value of the shares depends on the market value of the fund's portfolio securities at the time. This value is the same as "net asset value per share."

Reinvestment Privilege—An option available to mutual fund shareholders in which fund dividends and capital gains distributions are automatically turned back into the fund to buy new shares and thereby increase holdings.

Sales Charge—An amount charged to purchase shares in many mutual funds sold by brokers or other sales agents. The maximum charge is 8.5 percent of the initial investment; the vast majority of funds now have a maximum charge of 4.75 percent or less. The charge is added to the net asset value per share when determining the offering price.

Short-term Funds—An industry designation for funds that invest primarily in securities with maturities of less than one year. In this book the term means five years or less. Short-term funds include money market funds and certain municipal bond funds.

Transfer Agent—The organization employed by a mutual fund to prepare and maintain records relating to the accounts of its shareholders. Some funds serve as their own transfer agents.

12b-1 Fee—The fee charged by some funds, named after a federal government rule. Such fees pay for distribution costs such as advertising and dealer compensation. The fund's prospectus outlines 12b-1 fees, if applicable.

Underwriter—The organization that acts as the distributor of a mutual fund's shares to broker/dealers and investors.

Withdrawal Plan—A program in which shareholders receive payments from their mutual fund investment at regular intervals. Typically, these payments are drawn first from the fund's dividends and capital gains distributions, if any, and then from principal, as needed.

★ ★ ★

The Securities Act of 1933 requires the fund's shares to be registered with the SEC prior to their sale. In essence, the Securities Act ensures that the fund provides potential investors with a current prospectus. This law also limits the kinds of advertisements that may be used by a mutual fund.

The Securities Exchange Act of 1934 regulates the purchase and sale of all kinds of securities, including mutual fund shares.

The Investment Advisors Act of 1940 is a body of law that regulates certain activities of the investment advisors to mutual funds.

The Investment Company Act of 1940 is a highly detailed regulatory statute applying to the fund itself. This act contains numerous provisions designed to prevent self-dealing and other conflicts of interest, provides for the safekeeping of fund assets, and prohibits the payment of excessive fees and charges by the fund and its shareholders.

Appendix B:
Who Regulates Mutual Funds?

Mutual funds are highly regulated businesses that must comply with some of the toughest rules in the financial services industry. All funds are regulated by the United States Securities and Exchange Commission (SEC). With its extensive rule-making and enforcement authority, the SEC oversees mutual fund compliance by chiefly relying on four major federal securities statutes.

Fund assets must generally be held by an independent custodian. There are strict requirements for fidelity bonding to ensure against the misappropriation of shareholder monies. In addition to federal statutes, almost every state has its own set of regulations governing mutual funds.

While federal and state laws cannot guarantee that a fund will be profitable, they are designed to ensure that all mutual funds are operated and managed in the interests of their shareholders. Here are some specific investor protections that every fund must follow.

● Regulations concerning what may be claimed or promised about a mutual fund and its potential.

● Requirements that vital information about a fund be made readily available (such as a prospectus, the "Statement of Additional Information," also known as "Part B" of the prospectus, and annual and semi-annual reports).

● Requirements that a fund operate in the interest of its shareholders rather than any special interests of its management.

● Rules dictating diversification of the fund's portfolio over a wide range of investments to avoid too much concentration in a particular security.

Appendix C:
Dollar Cost Averaging

Investors often feel that they are "the kiss of death" when it comes to investing. They strongly believe that the market will go down as soon as they get in. For these people, and anyone concerned with reducing risk, the solution is "dollar cost averaging."

Dollar cost averaging is a simple yet effective way to reduce risk, whether you are investing in stocks or bonds. The premise behind dollar cost averaging (DCA) is that if several purchases of a fund are made over an extended period of time, the unpredictable highs and lows will "average out." The investor ends up buying some shares at a comparatively low price, others at perhaps a much higher price.

DCA assumes that investors are willing to sacrifice the possibility of having bought all of their shares at the lowest price in return for knowing that they did not also buy every share at the highest price. In short, they are willing to accept a compromise—a sort of *risk-adjusted* decision.

DCA is based on investing a fixed amount of money in a given fund at specific intervals. Typically, an investor will add a few hundred dollars at the beginning of each month into the XYZ mutual fund. DCA works best if you invest and continue to invest on a pre-established schedule *regardless of price fluctuations*. You will be buying more shares when the price is down than when it is up. Most investors do not mind buying shares when prices are increasing since this means that their existing shares are also going up. When this program is followed, losses during market declines are limited, while the ability to participate in good markets is maintained.

Another advantage of DCA is that it increases the likelihood that you will follow an investment program. Like other aspects of our life, it is important to have goals and objectives.

Example of Dollar Cost Averaging
($1,000 invested per period)

Period (1)	Price of Security (2)	Number of shares bought with $1,000 (3)	Total shares owned (3) (4)	Total amount invested (5)	Current value of shares (2)×(4) (6)	Net gain or loss Percentage (6)/(5) (7)
1	$100	10.0	10.0	$1,000	$1,000	0
2	80	12.5	22.5	2,000	1,800	−10.0
3	70	14.2	36.8	3,000	2,576	−14.1
4	60	16.7	53.5	4,000	3,210	−19.7
5	50	20.0	73.5	5,000	3,675	−26.5
6	70	14.3	87.8	6,000	6,146	+2.4
7	80	12.5	100.3	7,000	8,024	+14.6
8	100	10.0	110.3	8,000	11,030	+37.9

Appendix D:
Systematic Withdrawal Plan

A systematic withdrawal plan (SWP) allows you to have a check for a specified amount sent monthly or quarterly to you or anyone you designate, from your mutual fund account. There is no charge for this program.

This method of getting monthly checks is ideal for the income-oriented investor. It is also a risk reduction technique; a kind of dollar cost averaging in *reverse*. A set amount is sent to you each month. In order to send you a check for a set amount, shares of one or more of your mutual funds must be sold.

During periods when the market is low, the number of mutual fund shares being liquidated will be higher than at the times when the market is high. If you need $500 a month and the fund's price is $25.00 per share, twenty shares must be liquidated; if the price per share is $20.00, twenty-five shares must be sold.

Shown below is an example of a SWP from the Investment Company of America, a conservative growth and income fund featured in the book. The example assumes an initial investment of $100,000 in the fund at its inception, the beginning of 1934. A greater or smaller amount could be used. The example shows what happens to the investor's principal over a fifty-seven-year period. It assumes that $10,000 is withdrawn from the fund during the first year. At the end of the first year, the $10,000 is *increased by 4 percent each year thereafter* to offset the effects of inflation, which averaged less than 3.5 percent during this fifty-seven-year period.

THE INVESTMENT COMPANY OF AMERICA
initial investment: $100,000
annual withdrawals of: $10,000 (10%)
the first check is sent: 12/31/34
annual withdrawals increased by: 4%

date	amount withdrawn	value of remaining shares
12/31/34	$10,000	$115,000
12/31/35	$10,400	$201,000
12/31/40	$12,700	$166,000
12/31/45	$15,400	$277,000
12/31/50	$18,700	$253,000
12/31/55	$22,800	$484,000

date	amount withdrawn	value of remaining shares
12/31/60	$27,700	$ 652,000
12/31/65	$33,700	$1,042,000
12/31/70	$41,000	$1,251,000
12/31/75	$50,000	$1,314,000
12/31/80	$60,700	$2,364,000
12/31/85	$73,900	$4,931,000
12/31/86	$76,800	$5,926,000
12/31/87	$79,900	$6,168,000
12/31/88	$83,100	$6,907,000
12/31/89	$86,500	$8,852,000
12/31/90	$89,900	$8,822,000

Compare this to what would have happened if the money had been placed in an average fixed-income account at a bank. A $100,000 depositor who took out $10,000 each year would be in a far different situation. Her original $100,000 would be fully depleted by the end of 1945. All the principal and interest payments could not keep up with an annual withdrawal of $10,000.

The difference between ICA and the savings account is over $8 million. This difference becomes even more disturbing when you consider that the bank depositor's withdrawals were not increasing each year to offset the effects of inflation. The interest rates used in this example came from the *U.S. Savings & Loan League Fact Book*.

Next time some broker or banker tells you that you should be buying bonds or CDs for current income, tell *them* about a systematic withdrawal plan; a program designed to maximize your income and offset something the CD, T-bill, and bond sellers never mention: inflation.

Appendix E:
Load vs. No-Load—
Which Is Right For You?

Ironically, the debate over the relative merits of load and no-load funds has intensified even as the differences between the two camps have grown more blurred. No longer is the fund industry divided along clear-cut lines with the full 8.5 percent load funds on one side and pure no-load funds on the other. In recent years, full-load groups like American, Putnam, and Kemper have cut back from their front end sales charges, while formerly no-load groups like Hartwell, Pasadena, and Strong have attached front end loads to their funds. In addition, the immense popularity of deferred sales charges and 12b-1 fees has further clouded the distinction between load and no-load funds.

Despite the difficulties of defining load and no-load funds, many fund industry commentators continue to make dogmatic proclamations that investors should only buy no-load funds. While we agree that no-load funds are better options for some investors, the conclusion that they are the proper medium for *all* investors is misguided. Such thinking eliminates a number of superb portfolio managers such as Templeton's John Templeton, SoGen International's Jean-Marie Eveillard, and Putnam Vista's Gerald Zukowski. True investment talent is a rare commodity. To start one's mutual fund search by eliminating many top managers is hardly a promising cause of action. A better way to proceed is to try to separate good funds from bad ones. After all, an investor is clearly far better off in a good load fund than in a bad no-load one.

Making load versus no-load the paramount selection criteria can be dangerous oversimplification. A sales charge is just one of many considerations an investor must evaluate in appraising a fund. Too great a weighting on this or any other single variable can cause investors to neglect other considerations, such as risk levels, managerial ability, and portfolio strategy. Successful investing requires a multi-dimensional approach. To look just at sales fees, or even to weight them too greatly, distorts the evaluation procedure and can lead to poor conclusions. Should investors have neglected Fidelity Magellan because of its 3 percent front-end load?

LOADS IN CONTEXT
A fund's sales charge must be placed in proper context for effective evaluation. If an investor is considering two funds whose performance parameters are relatively restricted, such as two short-term bond funds, then the sales charge should be given

a high priority. If however, the choice is between two stock funds with relatively unrestricted investment boundaries, then the load becomes a lesser consideration.

Similarly, if an investor's personal time horizon is relatively short, say two or three years, then load considerations should be given greater priority than would be the case if a five-to-ten-year holding period was anticipated. While no-load funds can argue that their approach gives investors greater flexibility—in that money can be moved between fund groups without penalty—the rising popularity of fund families give load fund buyers a growing number of switching options.

More important than considering the penalty of a sales charge, however, is to consider the gain an investor receives from paying such charges. If an investor receives good advice, these fees can be a tremendous bargain. As one financial planner puts it, if it's worth paying a waiter 15 percent to 20 percent to bring food to a table, is not it worth paying a 5 percent premium to get sound financial advice? The danger, of course, is that an investor may pay the same charge to an uninformed sales person as that paid to a dedicated financial planner. Moreover, while the quality of the meal is known immediately, the merits of an investment portfolio take considerably longer to show. Still, sales charges are money well spent for investors working with a good broker or financial planner.

It seems odd that the benefits of financial planning are questioned, when our society places similar professions like law and accountancy in such high regard. It is important to recognize that many of the vocal critics of load funds and their sellers are in direct competition with planners for an investor's dollars. Book writers, newsletter editors, and financial magazines are the most vocal critics of load funds and are in direct competition with planners for an investor's dollars. Book writers, newsletter editors, and financial magazines want individuals to spend money on their publications rather than pay it to a broker. Therefore, they argue that investors should take a more active role in their investments, thus generating greater demand for investment information sources. While the initial cost may indeed be substantially lower than a front-end load, the ongoing subscription cost plus the time and energy output required to master the material could easily outpace the sales charge savings.

It is also important to recognize that a financial magazine or a newsletter has a vested interest in continuing to sell subscriptions. Accordingly, their fund investment systems are frequently geared toward rapid trading strategies that heighten a reader's need for the publication. Because brokers receive no added fees for moving an investor within a fund family, there is less incentive to trade a load fund account rapidly. Not surprisingly, load funds typically report longer average shareholder holding periods than do no-loads. Any increase in trading adds to the potential whipsawing and the triggering of a tax event.

We are not suggesting that investors should consider only load funds. But with all the load fund bashing in recent years, we think it is important to recognize that these funds do offer substantial benefits and that no-load funds are not the perfect answer for all investors. To divide the industry across such simple barriers not only flies in the face of the growing reality of mid-load funds but generates a great deal of misleading advice and unfairly discredits the work of many fine financial planners and brokers.

Investors who have the temperament, time and expertise may wish to consider using a no-load fund.

The following is a list of the no-load funds in this book:

Aggressive Growth Funds
> Acorn
> Founders Special
> GIT Equity Special Growth Portfolio
> Janus Venture
> Nicholas II
> Pennsylvania Mutual

Balanced Funds
> Dodge & Cox Balanced

Government Bond Funds
> Federated GNMA Trust
> Vanguard Fixed-Income GNMA

Growth Funds
> IAI Regional
> Janus
> Mathers
> Mutual Beacon

Growth & Income Funds
> SBSF Growth
> Selected American Shares

Money Market Funds
> All money market funds

Municipal Bond Funds
> SAFECO Municipal Bond
> SteinRoe High-Yield Municipals

About the Author

Gordon K. Williamson, JD, MBA, CFP, CLU, ChFC, RP, is one of the most highly trained investment counselors in the United States. Williamson, a former tax attorney, is a Certified Financial Planner and branch manager of a national brokerage firm. He has been admitted to The Registry of Financial Planning Practitioners, the highest honor one can attain as a financial planner. He holds the two highest designations in the life insurance industry, Chartered Life Underwriter and Chartered Financial Consultant. He is also a real estate broker with an MBA in real estate syndication.

Gordon is the author of several books, including *The Longman Investment Companion, Investment Strategies, Survey of Financial Planning, Tax Shelters,* and *Advanced Investment Vehicles & Techniques.* He has been the financial editor of various magazines and newspapers and a stock market consultant for a television station.

Gordon K. Williamson & Associates is an investment advisory firm located in La Jolla, California. The firm specializes in financial planning for individuals and institutions. Additional information can be obtained by phoning 1/800-748-5552 or (619) 454-3938.